Manifesto of a Music Snob
The Top 50 Greatest R&B Albums of All Time

By

Barry BornSelf Ousley

Marvel At The Son Shine

By

Barry BornSelf Ousley

is also **available** on Amazon

Manifesto of a Music Snob
The Top 50 Greatest R&B Albums of All Time

By

Barry BornSelf Ousley

TABLE OF CONTENTS

INTRODUCTION

Music. It's the elixir to our woes and the soundtrack of our triumphs. What would the world be without music? WHAT WOULD THE WORLD BE WITHOUT MUSIC?! My love for music began at an extremely early age. I have very vivid memories of singing along to the plethora of music that was being played in our little 3-bedroom apartment in Germany. Albums and reel to reels were a plenty in all of my childhood homes. Like any black household, typically when the music is queued on Saturday morning, it meant, "get up and clean this house!" It began to mean much more to me though. It wasn't just the crooning of the Temptations or the force of Patti Labelle's voice that was holding my attention anymore. It was the feelings attached to the music. Did a 6-year-old Barry understand what Bobby Brown meant when he was asking "Mr. Telephone Man" about his line? Of course not. What I understood was there was something wrong and the young King of R&B needed some answers immediately. The feelings transcended the context for me, and there in lies the power of music.

Black music has had many lives. From negro spirituals and down home blues to Hip Hop and Afro-Punk. Black Music has been and always will be one of the many classes on the report card of "Black America". R&B is one of my favorites, as it typically speaks to one of the most important issues in the black community. Love. How we navigate our romantic relationships and plans of building a life with our loved ones. R&B is the oldest love child of Blues and Soul music. It's rumored that Rhythm & Blues was the name created to replace the phrase "Race music". Something of a catch all name for black music in its totality from gospel to scat.

Rhythm & Blues is a form of music that grew from the Blues in the early 1930's. This was a sound that was championed by heavy instrumentation, provided by artists such as Muddy Waters, John Lee Hooker, & B.B. King. Soul music came to prominence in the late 1940's to early 1950's. This was a much more diverse sonic landscape with everything from melodic to organized chaos being the backdrop for artists such as Al Green, Sam Cooke, James Brown, Otis Redding and the incomparable Temptations. The much more significant difference in Rhythm & Blues and Soul music, would be songwriting. Some of the most timeless songs of all time and across any genre were created in the era of Soul, by the likes of Berry Gordy, Otis Redding and last but not least Smokey Robinson. If we're to use the same rubric that gives William Shakespeare the title of greatest writer of all time, because he's created works that have maintained relevance over the landscape of time and politics, then surely Smokey Robinson is the greatest songwriter of all time by that same scope. Another book for another time, but I want that on record. Smokey Robinson is the greatest songwriter of all time and across any genre. The man wrote "My Girl", "Tears of a clown", and "The way you do the things you do" for god's sake.

My research tells me that the seeds of contemporary R&B were planted in the late 1960's and early 1970's. The music was a platform to forecast and report on the dynamics of romantic relationships and life in a post-Vietnam war United States of America. Turned out to be quite the cocktail of emotional and political drama. The artists of that era did a great job conveying the temperature of the country. The lines are so blurred between Soul and R&B that it's hard to give you an artist that universally sits on either side at the inception of R&B. Some people would say that Teddy Pendergrass is a Soul artist, and I'd say that he's undoubtedly an R&B artist. There are opinions that Sam Cooke was an R&B artist, and I couldn't disagree more. He was a Soul artist by every possible box that can be checked, but again that's subjective for the artist in range of the inception of R&B.

As R&B grew into the 80's and most certainly the 90's, the lines between Soul and R&B became much more defined. I don't think anyone would confuse Luther Vandross, Miki Howard or Keith Sweat as Soul artists. No. By the time we got into the 80's and before New Jack Swing hit, we were well aware of what contemporary R&B was. Again, I was only a child, but the music resonated so early for me that I don't remember NOT having it in my life. R&B has an incredible catalog of songs that span over decades. There have been many one hit wonders in R&B, but those that were able to give you complete bodies of work are far and very few. That's what I want to focus on. Not so much the great artist, because there are artist that were great vocalist/songwriters but they never put together a *great album*.

What we individually consider "Greatness" is skewed. I get that. Some people think that an artist greatness should be measured by album sales, popularity and/or, more recently, their appearance. Yes, I'm talking about you BeyHive. We're going to take a look at the top 50 greatest R&B albums thru a much more refined lens in this book. At times things like sales and popularity will matter, but it will never be the crux of my argument(s). Before we get started let's get a few TRIGGER WARNINGS out of the way. This will be my fairly assessed take on ALBUMS as a complete body of work. Not an assessment of the artist or their abilities as vocalist or songwriters. This will also not be an assessment of who these artists are as people. Whatever political or ethical ills you may think that these artists may have imprinted on the world will NOT go into account here. Just in case you missed what I'm subtly hinting at, let me be clear, R. Kelly IS ON THIS LIST. I know I know, and yeah I think he did it too, but we don't know for sure and I can separate the artistry from the artists in most cases. Another TRIGGER WARNING: Although I didn't purposely try not to repeat any artist, for the most part that's what happened. No matter who your favorite artist is, do NOT expect for their entire discography to be a part of this list. Again, I'm talking to you BeyHive. There are a few artists that will have more than 1 album on this list, but they are indeed the exceptions. I could've just as easily loaded this list up with Stevie Wonder albums and challenged anyone that disagreed to a duel, but that wouldn't be very tactful of me since he's my favorite artist of all time.

TRIGGER WARNING, this list will NOT be in order. I decided against putting this list in order. Certain albums will have more weight with specific people than others, and music is too important to minimalize its emotional value to anyone. I'll likely share a few rankings to explain the impact that certain albums had on the world, or myself personally, but there will not be a particular hierarchy. This will also be a list of albums made by solo artist and groups.

Whether you're a casual fan of R&B or a super fanatic of this music, my advice for using this book will be the same. Listen to the album as you're reading about it. Answer the questions at the end of each chapter truthfully and in the moment. One of the many beauties of music is not only can it serve as a time capsule for moments in our lives, but it also has the power to give us the calm we need for introspection. It's a busy, busy world these days with a million distractions. As you dive in this book, I challenge you to put your phone on do not disturb, ignore ALL of your social media, cut the TV off and just be still. Enjoy the album. Let the music move you in whatever direction your heart sways. There are albums that didn't make this list because, frankly, if you haven't already listened to New Edition's *Heart Break* or, more recently, Anthony Hamilton's *Comin' from Where I'm From* then you already know what your home work will be. Shame on you if that's true by the way. There's no wrong way to read this book. You can either go in order of the chapters, or randomly turn to a page, but either way you choose to read, I want you to put the album on and let it run in order. Let this book be a vehicle to return to deep listening with no distractions.

CHAPTER 1

MAKE IT LAST FOREVER

It was November 24th, 1987. My family and I were still living in Germany at the time. We'd been in Europe for some years and music was one of our only links to what was going on in the states at the time. There was a lot of noise about a new singer coming out of Harlem and his hit single "I Want Her". It was definitely a popular song around our little apartment. It was a dose of high energy in a New Jack Swing style curated by the incomparable Teddy Riley. This was a time that the average album was no more than 8 or 9 songs. This particular masterpiece is only 8 songs. The album served as 43 minutes and 15 seconds worth of introduction to one of the most renowned R&B artists of all time.

Of the 8 songs on the album, is Keith Sweat's interpretation of the 1972 hit "In the Rain" by the Dramatics. One of the greatest sad songs of all time. I personally like Keith Sweat's version better. Not sure if it's because of the familiarity from that period of my life or the more modern feel to the song, but Keith Sweat's version is my preference of the two. This is also the only song on the album that wasn't produced by Teddy Riley. Keith approached this song with a bit more desperation in his vocals. It's likely the reason that over time he came to be known as "Begging ass Keith". The gift of communicating heartbreak through song is definitely his calling card.

Once again the lead single was "I want Her". A popular song in the clubs at the time and honestly anywhere adults were gathered. Just a fun song. Not much in the neighborhood of vocal acrobatics on this song, but it's well delivered and meant to be a sing along type of song for the listener. Co-written by Keith and Teddy, and even though we as R&B fans collectively STILL don't know whether he actually saw her in the club or not, we can all agree that this is a jam. The numbers tell the same story. To this day "I want Her" is the highest charting song ever by Keith Sweat on the Billboard hot 100, landing at the #5 spot. That surprised the hell out of me considering the strength and the cultural magnitude of the title track for this album, "Make it Last Forever".

I don't care how many songs you have on your duets playlist, across any genre. If "Make it Last Forever" isn't on it, then your list is incomplete and fraudulent! No. Seriously. "Make it Last Forever" is one of those rare songs that lives comfortably in the multiverse of the black BBQ, the old school party and a house get together. In that respect, it's also important to note that whenever this song is queued and those first 5 notes drop, that you'll feel the same joy EVERY SINGLE TIME. There's something special about that type of magic in this song. "Make it Last Forever" is the statement piece of this album. The duet features vocals from Keith Sweat, of course, and the woman on the song is the singer Jacci McGhee.

During my review of this album, for the first time ever, I came to the realization that the biggest reason I LOVE this song is Jacci and what she adds to it. Don't get me wrong, Keith gets busy on it for certain, but Jacci just added a sprinkle of commanding charm to it. Any good DJ knows to shut the music off and let the ladies put in work from 1:26 to the 1:31 time stamp. Only 5 small seconds, but that moment speaks to the command of this song and one of the key reasons that this album cracks this list. That small 5 seconds conjures a universal sense of joy and maybe even hope. Just a dope song with relentless replay value and definitely the crown jewel of the album. Overtime the song's groove has been sampled in several rap and R&B songs, with the greatest success of it's usage coming from Mariah Carey and Joe in one of her many remixes ("Thank God I Found You"), but none as pure and powerful as the original.

As I said before, I'm not going to do much in the way of ranking these albums chronologically, but this album is definitely important. Keith Sweat is a legend and his career has spanned for over 30 years and counting. In conjunction to this being Keith Sweat's introduction to the world as a soloist, it's also widely known as one of the more important projects at the beginning of the "New Jack Swing" era. A must have for any true R&B fan and historian.

FUN FACT: Keith Sweat could've had the song "Just got paid" on this album as well, but he turned it down, days before Teddy Riley gave it to Johnny Kemp. That would've made the album stronger than it already is, and would've been fitting for Keith since he was once a floor supervisor at the New York Stock Exchange.

1) What is your favorite song on the album?
   Answer:

2) What is your least favorite song on the album?
   Answer:

3) Which lyrics mean the most to you and why?
   Answer:

4) How did this album make you feel while you were playing it?
   Answer:

CHAPTER 2

FUNKY DIVAS

Although this is definitely a conversation for another time, let me start by saying that En Vogue is by far the best female group of all time. They checked all the boxes. Beautiful? Check (especially Terry and Dawn. Maaaaaaaaan.) Wildly talented? Hell yes! Great videos/performances? Absolutely! Great songs? You better believe it. I'm usually never a fan of music groups that have been put together by empty suits in an A&R office. In fact I can only think of a few groups over the throng of music that I listen to. Either way En Vogue is one of the exceptions to the rule. They were put together by a production duo out of California, working for Atlantic Records. It was always their plan to recreate The Supremes, but they wanted their version of the iconic group to be made of 3 lead singers for the purposes of versatility. They held huge rounds of auditions seeing somewhere around 5000 women, before deciding on the 3 that they liked the most. The intended trio was Cindy Herron, Dawn Robinson (*brushes my hair* Sup Dawn), and Maxine Jones. Rumor has it that Terry Ellis (*brushes my hair* Sup Terry) arrived late for her audition due to a late arrival from her flight out of Houston. She auditioned and in that moment they decided that their trio HAD to be a foursome. Who could blame them? We all know that Terry is an incredible vocalist and, I mean, you've seen her right? Sheeeeeesh.

Boyhood crushes aside, it's hard as a fan of music in general to not appreciate this group. They were incredible. Although I'm speaking in past tense, the group En Vogue still performs as a trio, but only 2 of the original members are still active. Apparently Cindy and Terry (*brushes my hair* Sup Terry) won a rather contentious legal battle with Maxine and Dawn (*brushes my hair* Sup Dawn) over the use of the name En Vogue. I don't know the details, but like most groups, they broke up. Before they were chasing solo careers and joining fringe groups like Lucy Pearl, En Vogue did some amazing songs and bodies of work together.

The group's very first single was "Hold On" from the album *Born to Sing* in 1990. Considered a dance song by most at the time, but the song charted well on R&B/Hip Hop charts as well. No doubt due to the soulful vocals and airtight harmonies of the song, or the intro of the song with the group doing their own a cappella rendition of The Jackson 5's "Who's lovin you" with lead vocals by Terry (*brushes my hair* Sup Terry). With the overall accolades that this song received, I never really liked it. Loved the vocals. Loved the lyrics. Never really liked the production on it. The song did however do the justice of giving us a proper introduction to what would become this group's staple. Harmony. "Hold On" was lead by Cindy, and I wonder how much her recent California pageant success played into that. At the time she had recently been awarded Miss Black California, Miss San Francisco, and came in 2nd runner up for Miss California. Suffice to say that her public persona had a few more stems on it at the time from her counterparts.

The album that's widely considered their masterpiece is *Funky Divas*. This was their sophomore album, and it was released March 24th, 1992. What I love most about this album is the experimentation. Although this album was released only two years after their debut, they'd already proven to the world that they were incredible vocalists. *Funky Divas* was the group's declaration of versatility. The album has hints of Rock, Soul, Dance, New Jack Swing, Hip Hop, Blues and Doo Wop. A sonic stew made of 13 different ingredients.

The lead single was "My Lovin' (You're Never Gonna Get It)". It's an upbeat dance track with lead vocals by Maxine and the bridge by Dawn (*brushes my hair* Sup Dawn). Songs with a bridge. Remember those? It's a song about a man trying to walk back into the life of the woman that he dogged out, and the ladies were NOT having it. A good choice since this is the peak year of the infused product of R&B with Dance music. Everyone had at least one of these kinds of records in their repertoire. Songs like this were the runway to the biggest dance hit of that year "Keep on Walkin" by CeCe Penniston. The song did well, and served as a good reminder to the world that these beautiful women could still deliver any kind of song that they choose.

"My Lovin'(You're Never Gonna Get it)" is a great song and it hit the mark that I feel "Hold On" missed. It peaked at #2 on Billboard and the video won two MTV video music awards (*brushes my hair* Sup Terry. Sup Dawn). The second single and one of the three remakes on the album is Aretha Franklin's song from the Sparkle soundtrack "Giving Him Something He Can Feel". It was written and produced by the legendary Curtis Mayfield but the keys were played by the Queen of Soul, Aretha Franklin, herself. I've been thinking of how I can talk about this song, and more specifically the music video, in a way that wouldn't anger the psych...I mean wife. I meant WIFE. I've been thinking of how I can talk about this song, and more specifically the music video, in a way that wouldn't anger the maniac. I meant wife. Yeah. WIFE. There we go. Fixed ☺. "Giving Him Something He Can Feel" is a doo wop/soul song about forgetting the worries outside of your bedroom door

and...well. You know *wink wink*. The album version of this song was almost twice as long as the single version which makes total sense, in light of the groove. Lead vocals for the entire song, done by Dawn (*brushes my hair* Sup Dawn). She sung the hell out of this song, with the updated production, it paired perfectly with En Vogue's vocal styling. This song charted well at number one on the R&B charts, but the video...Maaaaaaaaaaaaaaaaan. The video was set in a 60's style gentleman's club, with En Vogue performing as the music act. An audience filled with only well-dressed men enjoying their libations and cigars, until they're interrupted by the start of En Vogue's performance. All four ladies wearing form fitting red dresses, looking like a million bucks, while doing a minimalistic doo wop style of choreography. If I had to categorize this video, I'd say
that it's appropriately sensuous. Appropriately sensuous for adults at least, but as a pre-pubescent boy IT WAS DOWN RIGHT SEXUAL! Even now as a fully-grown, HAPPILY MARRIED MAN (Hi Tiffany ☺), the video is still worth a trip to YouTube. One of the things I've always loved about En Vogue, is that they never had to sell sex/sex appeal because they were wildly talented. The sex appeal was simply the icing that they occasionally spread on the cake. "Giving Him Something He Can Feel" was their nod to the soul sound from the late 60's to early 70's.

The third single was "Free Your Mind". Another up-tempo single, but this was En Vogue dipping their perfectly pedicured toes in the pond of Rock. Probably better described as a more melodic stepchild version of Rock, but for all intents and purposes, still Rock. I love this song because all four of the ladies sing lead in a much more aggressive tone. The context of the song is about prejudice and how it can be misleading. Perceiving someone's social, economic or moral status by his or her appearance alone and the consequences of that action. The energy on this song is catching and even though the song is Rock based these sirens still blessed it with their trademark harmonies on the bridge and hook. I can get with the sentiment of this song, and the lyrics were well written, with the exception of the drivel that Maxine sung from 0:44 to 0:53. Ummm yeah. No. That's EXACTLY what that means ma'am. Argue with your mother about it, not me. Another book for another time I suppose.

A good barometer for whether an album was considered monetarily successful or not is the number of singles that are released. This is especially in a pre-internet music industry. This album had five of the thirteen songs released as a single. The fourth single from this album, is a pure R&B mid-tempo groove called "Give It Up, Turn It Loose". It's a beautiful song about getting past heartbreak, by simply moving forward. Letting the chips of life fall where they may and allowing yourself to be free of the pain that's been holding you back from happiness. Lead vocals by Maxine with the ladies doing a little more harmonic painting on the canvas of this song. I understand why Maxine would lead this song, because it's one woman giving wise advice to another woman on how to reclaim her happiness by letting go of a bad experience, and of the ladies in En Vogue, I've always felt like Maxine had the most mature, in tone, voice of them all. There was nothing even remotely young and girly about Maxine's voice. When she sung, you knew it was a grown ass woman singing.

Funky Divas was not only the chance for En Vogue to expand on their personal sound, it was also the chance for the Denzel Foster and Thomas McElroy to experiment with new sounds. When they envisioned putting this group together, they probably had no clue that they'd find women so dynamic that they'd be able to do an album as alive as this. Everything from the singles, the order that they were released, vocal mapping and the visuals/videos attached to this album made for a great rollout and an even better album. While the etymology of En Vogue is to be fashionable or in fashion, this album did it's job in making sure that Maxine, Terry (*brushes my hair* Sup Terry), Cindy and Dawn (*brushes my hair* Sup Dawn) legend was solidified as the *Funky Divas*.

FUN FACT: En Vogue was the inspiration of The Muses for Disney's "Hercules".

1) Who is your favorite singer in this group?
   Answer:

2) What is your favorite song on this album? Why?
   Answer:

3) Do you remember what you were doing in 1992 (If you were alive)?
   Answer:

4) What song from this album, would you most likely suggest to a friend as a statement of whom En Vogue is as a group?
   Answer:

CHAPTER 3

ONE IN A MILLION

Love me baby love me baby love me baby. Ms. Haughton. Your sweet, soft voice. The gentle way that you spoke in your interviews. Your quiet sensuality. The harshness of adulthood being thrust upon you in one of the most heinous way known to man. Babygirl, you will never be forgotten. You will never be unappreciated. You will never be duplicated. We truly miss you.

Aaliyah was born in Brooklyn, but she and her family moved to Detroit when she was 5 years old. She began performing shortly after the move in plays and musicals. That's where she fell in love with singing. Aaliyah's love for her brother, and family in general, has always been widely publicized. It's the family closeness that kept her within arms reach of her uncle, Barry Hankerson. Hankerson is a famed entertainment lawyer who was once married to Gladys Knight. As Aaliyah's interest and skill grew in singing and performing, Hankerson decided to take her under his wing on a professional level. From age 6 to age 12 Aaliyah auditioned for commercials, stage plays, TV (including Family Matters and Step by Step), before finally landing a national spotlight on the entertainment competition show Star Search. She even got the chance to perform with Gladys Knight, her aunt, for a few tour dates as a child.

After several years of operating as an entertainment lawyer, Hankerson, launched his own label called Blackground Enterprises in 1993. Eventually becoming Blackground Records and the proving grounds of many, many talented people. Aaliyah was signed to the label by age 13. Hankerson used his connections as R. Kelly's manager at the time (I know. I know, and YES, we'll get to that), with Jive Records to broker a deal for Aaliyah's first album to be distributed as a joint venture between Jive and Blackground. The first album was called *Age aint Nothing but a Number* and it was released on May 24th 1994. The lead single "Back and Forth" owned the summer, and every urban radio station. This entire album with the exception of her rendition of "At your best (You are love)" was written and produced by R. Kelly. It was a 14 song introduction to us all. Okay, now as we all know, that album title took on a whole new meaning as we learned that R. Kelly and Aaliyah, not only had an illegal and immoral romantic relationship, but that they had in fact got illegally married in upstate New York. At the time she was only 15 and R. Kelly was 26 years old. Disgusting. *Age aint Nothing but a Number* was a successful album on all fronts. Culturally it was a young sound, with a mature production style and it faired well on R&B/Hip Hop charts, peaking at 18 on the Billboard 200 and going triple platinum. The album sales and momentum were immediately affected by the news of R. Kelly and Aaliyah's marriage. News broke nationwide on every outlet from BET to PBS. People were shocked, baffled, and quite frankly appalled at the news. How could this GROWN ASS MAN, marry this child? It's just not in my nature to discuss things that there is no concrete evidence for, but it's safe to say that R. Kelly committed several felonies with the young Aaliyah. If anything, we do know that he married a child. As a man, a black man in particular, I'd love to whoop his entire ass over this. I have a 16 year old niece, 1 full year older than Aaliyah at the time, and I can't even fathom her dating, let alone getting married. The illegal marriage was annulled and Aaliyah took a partially self-imposed break from recording. She needed to live. She needed to be with her family to unpack the fact that she had been thru something bigger than heartbreak. She'd been the victim of a crime, and apparently the industry was putting a little blame on her too. A CHILD!! The scandal gave Aaliyah and her people leverage to negotiate a release from Jive records for a personal and professional separation from R. Kelly as well. After leaving Jive she signed with Atlantic Records and she began working on her new album. Started kind of slow because producers were weary to work with someone so close to a scandal as big as her marriage was. Her original team had connections with Puff Daddy and Jermaine Dupri, but her new team at Atlantic Records had a young production duo (Timbaland and Missy) on staff that they were eager to get working with Aaliyah.

One in a Million was recorded in August 1995 and released on August 27, 1996. The bulk of the production and songwriting was done by Timbaland and Missy. In fact Aaliyah had no writing credits on this album. That's one of the big factors that I weighed for the review of these albums, but *One in a Million* is exempt in this regard. The lead single was "If your Girl Only Knew". It's a mid tempo song with a heavy bass line and busy drums. It was another perfect single for the summer, doubling as Aaliyah's reinsertion to the mainstream. Timbaland and Missy put this song together for Aaliyah and make appearances in the video as well as a certain young FEMcee...in her original form at the time. SMH

The second single is the title track of the album. "One In A Million" is again a Timbaland and Missy created song. Timbaland's signature drum programming and audio collage, being serenaded by Aaliyah's smooth voice. Aaliyah always does well with ballads and this is no different. "One In A Million" is a slow, sexy song. Not sexy in the sense of the lyrics being on the nose of sexuality, but the context and energy of the song most certainly is. The signifance here is that this is the first time Aaliyah could present herself to the world as a sexy young woman. I use the word woman very loosely because at the time she was only 17. Even months later after the album and the music video was released to the world in November, she was only 17. I guess after the news of her and R. Kelly, there was no way to move forward and continue to do bubble gum kiddie music, and after all she'd been thru, I don't see how she wouldn't want to do more adult content anyway. "One in a Million" was a hit. The video and the radio play were massive and the song's infectious nature pierced the minds and hearts of us all. "One in a Million" topped at #2 on Billboard in 1997.

"4 Page Letter" was the third single on this album. This is a ballad about a woman's crush on a man, and how she planned to share that crush with him in a letter. I like this song being rolled out after "One in a Million", because it gave Aaliyah another chance to show her skills as a ballad songstress. This is also one of the main songs I point to when I talk about the brilliance of Aaliyah and Missy's talents when molded together. It's never really been Aaliyah's vocal style to scream all over her songs ala Fantasia or Jennifer Hudson. That works for some but she kept this song smooth as well. A melodic ballad over the type of sound forming that only Timbaland can provide. Vocally Aaliyah always took a minimalist approach, until you get towards the end of the album.

The 4th and final single, released over a year after the initial release of the album was " The One I Gave My Heart To". One of the few songs on the album that was neither written or produced by Timbaland and Missy. Strange because the song was written by Diane Warren. Diane Warren is one of the greatest songwriters of all time. Famed for songs across different genres that were huge hits like "I Don't wanna miss a thing" by Aerosmith, "For You I Will" by Monica, "Un-Break My Heart" by Toni Braxton and "Rhythm of the Night" by Debarge. "The One I Gave My Heart To" was also produced by Daryl Simmons. Excuse me, THE LEGEND, Daryl Simmons. Known for his work with LaFace Records. Simmons has production credits on monster hits like "Don't be Cruel" by Bobby Brown, "Can We Talk" by Tevin Campbell and the chart topping "End Of The Road" by Boyz II Men. So between Diane Warren on the pen and Daryl Simmons on the boards, can you imagine how much money Blackground Records spent on this damn song?! I commend Aaliyah and her team not letting the budget dictate the order that the singles were released, and going with the lesser known production duo of Timbaland and Missy. "The One I Gave My Heart To" is much more of a pop song than an R&B song. In my opinion, this is the one song on the album that Aaliyah travels outside of her vocal comfort zone and lets it rip a little bit. It's a perfect song about the disappointment and pain of a broken heart. There's nothing on record about this song being personal to Aaliyah, but there's definitely a little something intimate in how she delivered it. As a fan of N'SYNC (Yes you read that right), I always wanted there to be a remix, collaboration of this song. Not sure how it didn't happen with her connections to Jive Records other than just needing a complete and total separation from the company. It would've been magic though.

The album has features from a few legends in Treach from Naughty by Nature and Slick Rick. It's also rounded out with a few remakes in "Got to Give It Up" by Marvin Gaye, and an incredibly beautiful, and sensuous version of "Choosey Lover" by The Isley Brothers. "Heartbroken" is another good mid-tempo song on the album. This album ensured that Aaliyah's artistry didn't remain in stasis, and in fact evolved. Though still a young woman at the time of its release, her personal life and professionalism propelled her to be able to carry an incredible album. We miss you babygirl.

FUN FACT: This album was supposed to be executive produced by Diddy, but schedule conflicts got in the way of Diddy and Aaliyah finishing any of the songs that they began recording. This album could've sounded completely different if fate hadn't put Aaliyah with Timbaland and Missy.

1) What song most describes Aaliyah as an artist off of her "One in a Million"?
   Answer:

2) Where were you when you heard that Aaliyah had passed away?
   Answer:

3) Which single had the best video in your opinion and why?
   Answer:

4) Would the collaboration with a wider variety of production teams have made the album better or worse in your opinion?
   Answer:

CHAPTER 4

SOULSTAR

It's important for me to repeat, that this list is not in any chronological order. I'm plugging in the chapters from a pre-written list and mostly choosing randomly how to add them to the book. Why would I mention something so inconsequential to you as the casual reader? Simple. Because if I don't hurry up and mention Musiq Soulchild, my brother Derek Sewell is going to kill me. Don't get me wrong. I wasn't bullied into any artist having an album on this list, and Musiq most certainly has a discography that would've given him entrance to this party either way. I know that most people consider his song "LOVE" from his classic first album, *Aijuswanaseing*, the crown jewel of his career as a vocalist and songwriter, but the fact is he has several songs that could hold that title. And again, Derek will kill me if I don't hurry up and get to Musiq, so let's talk about *Soulstar*.

Soulstar is Musiq's third album. Released on December 9, 2003. I say it was Musiq's album because he'd briefly dropped SOULCHILD from his moniker in 2001. This was also his last album on Def Jam/Def Soul before he moved over to Atlantic Records. Maybe the name change had some legal implications in light of that transition too. Either way, at this point in Musiq's career, the general public had a pretty good understanding of who Musiq was from his debut in 2000 up to this stage of his career. He's a meticulous songwriter, and a powerful, versatile vocalist, capable of carrying both up-tempo songs and heavy ballads with an exact proportional delivery and quite possibly the greatest bridge vocalist of all time. Not many artist can where that badge of honor. Some are only good at what they do, and nothing more. No challenging themselves as an artist whatsoever. That's never been Musiq's issue and in fact, there are even industry stories of how his artistry has interfered with his business. Ahhh yes. Industry rule #4080.

The first song on the album is the title track "Soulstar". It was never released as a single, but I think it's important to mention for a few reasons. One, it's a DOPE song. DOPE. Two, I think the tone and the imagery in the lyrics best describes Musiq's greatest gift to the world. VIBE. This is a mid-tempo song over a mix of a sample from "I Found Love" by the Spinners and original production. It's an easily delivered song. Not much vocal flexing on it at all, which is good, since the song is perfect in it's nominal state. A short song at 3 minutes but it definitely serves as the amuse bouche of what's to come on the album.

The first single is "forthenight" featuring Aaries (twin singing duo). It's the quintessential radio hit. Up-tempo, light hearted and easy to sing along to. In fact it's down right hard not to sing along with it. It makes you feel good! It makes you feel like everything is fine in your life. The gist of the song is two people throwing all the caution and titles attached to the many levels of dating to the wind and simply enjoying their time together for one single night. Something that we all wish we had the courage to do when dating. Another thing I love about Musiq's discography is that so many of his songs are complimentary to one another. In that regard "forthenight" is the perfect sequel to his first national single "Just Friends (Sunny)". It speaks to the comfort that so many of us never get to feel, from just...being. The song did well, briefly, and peaked at #18 on Billboards Hot R&B charts.

The second single was "whoknows". Produced by Musiq's longtime and main production team Carvin Haggins & Ivan Barias. This is by far, one of my favorite songs in Musiq's entire catalog. It's a ballad, about two people spending their first night together * wink wink *. Journeying into the mystery of the positive impact that connecting on a physical level could have in their burgeoning relationship. Too wordy for you? Okay. It's a song about two people having a magical, mind-blowing sex filled night. There. Fixed it for you. A song that should easily be a fixture on any slow jam mix that you might have. Musiq wrote this song, this wildly sexual song, without being crude, direct or offensive. If you're not paying attention you'd think it was just a simple love song. I can't talk about this song without mentioning the brilliance of the music video as well. The video starts with Musiq in an empty white void, and slowly starts to be built into a home around him as the song progresses. The house is complete as Musiq finishes, yet another, legendary bridge punctuated by another note that nobody else on the planet could hit. Then he stands up and finally invites the leading lady into the house. It came across as a message for men to have their proverbial "shit together" before inviting a woman into their life. That was my interpretation of it at least. "whoknows" spent 4 months on the charts and peaked at 23 on the R&B charts and 65 on the Billboard hot 100.

Soulstar only had 2 official singles to hit airwaves, but the magic most certainly didn't stop there. "Babymother" is another song on this album that provides a unique moment. It's of course about the circumstances between a man and woman that spent a night together and made a child. But not your typical run of the mill, "I hate my baby momma", "all she does is make my life hard" rhetoric. It's more in the vein of "Let's figure out how we can make our lives work for the child.

Let's both be responsible." A heavy and dramatic song. Even the music sounds dramatic. Carvin and Ivan produced this song as well. It's a song that still holds relevance today, and it was needed for this project as non-traditional family structures have become more and more prevalent in society.

One of the few songs on this album that wasn't produced by Carvin & Ivan is a very important song for me. It's personal. Personal in the sense that it's one of the songs I play the most when everything in my world is going wrong. "momentinlife" was produced by Junius Bervine and it features Kindred The Family Soul and Ceelo. It's a song about taking the bad and frustrating moments in your day to day life and cherishing them, because you know those moments are building a bridge to a better future. I've never played this song and didn't immediately feel better afterwards. The music and the lyrics give the feeling of a trance. "momentinlife" even goes off, sounding the way music sounds on movies when the big problem has finally been resolved. It's just a beautiful song and a collaboration that we never knew we needed. In the end *Soulstar* wasn't a heavily lauded album and it really isn't even considered a cult classic. Most people just see this as a run of the mill good album. A closer look at the aforementioned songs in conjunction with other songs like "womanopoly", "infatueighties" and "Givemorelove/leaveamessage" can paint a clearer picture of the brilliance that is *Soulstar*.

FUN FACT: During the recording of SOULSTAR, Musiq was dating India Arie.

1) What is your favorite song off of this album?
   Answer:

2) The production on this album is incredible. What song has the best production?
   Answer:

3) Can you name the songstress that calls in on "givemorelove/leaveamessage"?
   Answer:

4) What could have made this album better for you?
   Answer:

CHAPTER 5

THE COLORED SECTION

One of the beauties of R&B has been its ability to evolve past its original purpose. Oh sure, there are love songs a plenty, but every now and then someone has the courage and intention of spreading the wings of their brilliance beyond the traditional boundaries and context of love. On the other hand, we could have a full and fluid conversation about how R&B has devolved too. Not the case here. One of the things I love about my style of music consumption is how I allow music to find me. I never go searching for it. I never listen to radio other than sports radio, but there's only so much I can stomach hearing about the flaming pile of mediocrity that my Atlanta Falcons have become (THEY OWE US A 2UPER8OWL. THAT WASN'T A TYPO). I'm not even sure if there are any more music video shows. I allow music to find me organically. Usually by the suggestive opinion of a fellow music snob or by it finding my ear randomly. With all that said, I have NO CLUE how I found Donnie. It could have been by the suggestion of my cousin Eugene who is also a proud music snob and knows Donnie personally or it could have been on a random R&B mix tape. I'm just not sure. All I can tell you is that I'm extremely happy it found me…or did I find it? Again. Not sure. What I am sure of is that *The Colored Section* is one of the greatest R&B albums of all time.

Donnie (born Donnie Johnson) was raised in Kentucky but his more known artistic roots are in Atlanta. As a vocalist and pianist Donnie worked the independent music scene in Atlanta for years. Like most vocal powerhouses Donnie started in the church. He was honing his talent, and mastering his craft in Atlanta, he was part of a music crew known as Groovement, which once consisted of a few great artist including India Arie, Anthony David and Jiva (an AMAZING band). Over time Donnie became pretty well known on the Atlanta music scene not only as a vocalist but also for his prowess as a live performer. The man is a beast of an artist and songwriter. His work got him a label deal and from there his debut album *The Colored Section* began to take flight.

The Colored Section was released in 2002. To be honest I'm not even sure if 2002 is when I first heard the album. One of the many gifts my parents gave me was the pride in being a black person and more specifically a black man. Many would call me "Pro Black", and I neither apologize or explain that stance. Come to your own conclusions on it. I only mention this because *The Colored Section*, in all its glory and versatility, speaks to the black experience in America. The romance, the confusion and the pain of that experience are presented in this audible account that came to be called *The Colored Section*. Bottom line is I LOVE every song on this album, but I'll focus on a few that I think are necessary listening outside of the fact that this whole album is cohesive and beautiful.

    The Colored Section has 14 songs on it. "Cloud 9" is the 3rd song on the album. Although I don't remember where or how I first any of the songs on this album, I do remember that the first song I heard was "Cloud 9". In the first 20 seconds I was mesmerized by the lyrics. The sentiment attached to it, and the imagery. "Cloud 9" is about the pride of being a black person and the stigmas of the physiology, history and sentiment attached to said blackness. In common jargon, to be on cloud 9 means to be in a state of happiness or total bliss. Donnie is referring to his hair (afro) as "Cloud 9" and the personification of his blackness on this song. It's an ode to his blackness and his love for the history and stigma attached to it. Donnie's way of saying, "I love this. I love being black. I'd choose to be black every chance I could." The song has heavy djembe drum and percussion, with a funky bass line to it. I'd be very surprised if it wasn't completely done with live instruments. It's an incredible song with Donnie painting the canvas with a powerful clutter of vocals. There's some serious slap going on here.

    "Big Black Buck" is the 5th song on the album. Appropriate since mathematically 5 is indicative of power. This particular song is a double entendre about the power of the black dollar in the US economy, the appropriate way to use that dollar, and the personification of that very dollar being a large black man or a "Big Black Buck" as it was termed in post-reconstruction America, and that same "Big Black Buck" being seen as dangerous because of the power he'd possess if he did what was best for him, instead of what he was told to do. That was a lot. I know. But I needed to point that out, and you needed to read it. This is a much more laid back song than "Cloud 9" and sonically has a vaudevillian/ragtime feel to it. I think it's a proper angle with Donnie's affinity for the history of black people and their impact on America as a whole. This is one of the most lyrically heavy songs on this album. DONNIE REALLY STUFFED A LOT OF JEWELS in this song in terms of perspective. I strongly suggest listening to it completely unencumbered or by reading along with the lyrics online. He even managed to squeeze some rather...graphic lyrics in there, but they're appropriate to what he's suggesting is happening with the help of black people and their spending decisions. Pointing to the fact that how a people spend their money, or in African American's case 3 trillion in buying power, is their politics.

"Do You Know" is the 7th song on this album. Of course there are traditional love songs on this album. What did you think was happening here?! "Do You Know" has a very casual and vibey feel to it. I blame the flutes and guitar for that, but it all blends perfectly with what I THINK, this song is about. As I said before, this book will highlight albums and artists that may offend your personal sensibilities, for whatever reason. Music is art though, so that's partly its job. Either way I guess we all still have a bit of growing up to do in this regard. So if the following sentences offend you, I don't apologize for it. I want you to seek help for caring so much about what a complete stranger does in their personal life. Although the overwhelming sentiment of "I like you, I know you like me, and there's a brief window of opportunity for us to capitalize off of this mutual like" is indeed brilliantly hidden in plain sight, I think it's deeper than that. Even on my very first listen, it sounded like Donnie telling someone (a man) that he should come out of the closet and be with him. It sounds like him telling this man "I won't wait around for you to be comfortable with who you are and love me back as openly as I'm loving you". As if he's saying "I won't continue to see you in private and be ignored publically." No matter what your personal preference is, I'd hope you could listen to this song and appreciate a man or woman's personal declaration of their value and the cost of their affection as being invaluable. We all need to love ourselves enough to have boundaries on how we can be handled in a romantic situation. Great song. Can't be skipped.

I JUST NOW, in this moment, decided to wrap this chapter up, because frankly there's only one song on here that I even deem remotely skippable, and I won't say which one. Again, music is subjective. Unfortunately that means I won't get to wax poetic about the triumph of "Heaven Sent" and the trance like state that "You Got A Friend", & "Rocketship" was constructed to put you in. We will however discuss the title track and the last song on the album "The Colored Section". It's the longest song on the album checking in at almost 6 minutes.

"The Colored Section" is equals parts inspirational, history lesson, and the embrace of the beauty and struggle of blackness. You know something is special in the first minute as the piano solo, harkens the times of visiting your Southern Baptist grandmother's house on a winter Sunday. Everything about this song says "You've been thru so much and you didn't let it break you". It's a reminder to black people that we're capable of so much more than where we are now. This is also the closest representation on this album of Donnie's gospel roots. There's organ, and a very choir like feel throughout the song. It's intentional. The song was built to be HEARD, not just listened to. Even the mastering of the vocals in their lower range were skewed to be crisper and clearer than most of the songs on the album. After attacking so many different subjects and energies on this album, choosing this song to be last makes perfect sense. Although art of any kind can be enjoyed by anyone, make no mistake about it, this album was very specifically made for black people. Everything isn't for everyone and that's fine. Doesn't make it personal or offensive, unless you're a person that doesn't understand their place in the world. All I can really suggest in regards to this album is to BUY IT. Don't just stream it, or YouTube it. BUY THIS ALBUM. BUY THIS ALBUM. BUY THIS ALBUM. BUY THIS ALBUM. BUY THIS ALBUM. BUY THIS ALBUM. BUY THIS ALBUM. BUY THIS ALBUM. BUY THIS ALBUM. BUY THIS ALBUM. BUY THIS ALBUM. One last note.

!!!!!!!BUY THIS ALBUM!!!!!!!

FUN FACT: Justin Ellington is one of the producers on this album and he's a direct descendant of Duke Ellington.

1) What do you think is the best song on this album?
   Answer:

2) With all the topics specifically concerning black life, what do you think is the most important song on this album?
   Answer:

3) Who are a few of the artist that Donnie sharpened himself as an artist with?
   Answer:

4) Did you buy this album yet? WHY NOT?!
   Answer:

CHAPTER 6

COMPLEX SIMPLICITY

I just learned this about Teedra Moses, and pardon me as I choke back my vomit to type this but, Teedra Moses was born and raised in...New Orleans. I hate that god-damned city because it hatched Saints Fans. They're quite honestly the lowest life form in the galaxy. WE DAT! But I digress. Teedra was born and raised in New Orleans and later escaped that toilet bowl called New Orleans and moved to Los Angeles with her mother and siblings at 13, after her parents split. She was raised by her mother who was a gospel singer and she was exposed to a wide variety of music.

As talented as Teedra is, she didn't always do music as a profession. She was originally an industry stylist, and a successful one at that. She worked with everyone in music and film from Will Smith to Ras Kass. It was quite the spectrum of professional interface. Teedra was never run off from the fashion industry either, her decision to try and commit to music came from an epiphany while healing from a broken leg that she sustained on set of a music video. Music was always a peripheral of her day-to-day life so it came to her pretty naturally. Teedra was involved with a musician at the time of the epiphany, and he helped to put feelers out for where she should begin her singing career. Teedra fancies herself a free spirit and puts a lot of faith in things that she's passionate about, so once she became passionate about the potential in her music career she had faith in wherever the wind would blow her. Eventually that gust led her to TVT records where she began nurturing her singing and songwriting skills. She wrote "Still in Love" for Nivea in 2003 and the monster hit "Dip it low" for Christina Milian in 2004. It's as if she has a penchant for working with Lil Wayne's baby momma brigade. The lioness eventually released her debut masterpiece *Complex Simplicity* in August of 2004.

The exact date that *Complex Simplicity* dropped was August 10th, 2004. A late birthday gift for me, but damn I loved it when this dropped. I'd already been playing her lead single for a month and some change and watched the video ad nauseam. I couldn't wait to find out who this beautiful siren was as an artist. People were still reading CD inserts at the time, and I was even more excited when I saw that she wrote on every song. I've always respected songwriters, so it's no surprise that I became one. When you actually had to go the store to buy your music I had a process. A process that I still use today, just slightly adjusted. I'd go to the store and buy the CD. In the car ride home from the purchase I would only listen to the single on repeat. Listening to the album as an actual body of work didn't happen until I got back to the house.

The 2nd single was "Be Your Girl" and also the first song on the album. This is a song that deserves to be on any and every Vibe playlist of the true R&B fan. I imagine that even Sade would be proud of how incredibly smooth this song is. Teedra wrote this song about the crush that she had on NAS. Yes. That NAS. She said that at the time of writing it she felt so in tune with him. At the time they were both mourning the death of their mother's. She was listening to a lot of his music at the time, trying to cope. When the track was introduced to her it also had the same piano sample that was used on Nas' song "One on One". In Teedra's mind it really was kismet. So she wrote this song, about her crush. The funny part is the juxtaposition of the first line in the song and the reality of his, at the time, very, very public relationship. HA! I see your shade Teedra! You knew. You f*cking knew! Teedra brings the listener into her mind. From the surface thoughts of how much she likes him to the intimacy of how she pretends to..."be with him" * wink wink *. You get it. Teedra keeps most of her vocal ability tucked in to stay on par with the vibe of the song. You're not going to find a lot of wailing on this song. It's unnecessary and would quite honestly just disturb the groove. The song charted into Billboard's top 100 at 87 and the video was directed by the legendary Hype Williams.

The second song on the album was actually the first single. "You'll Never Find (A Better Woman)" featuring Jadakiss, is a collaboration that made sense. Jadakiss had, at that point, already seen big success doing features with other female artists like Mariah Carey, Jennifer Lopez and Mary J Blige. It's an up-tempo song with a hard hitting sample and drums. I can see why this would be the first single chosen. It was built for radio success. Teedra is one of the very few female artist that can make songs about a woman having confidence and worth, devoid of demeaning men at the same time. Teedra opens the gates of her vocal ability a bit more on this song, while still letting it build up. Teedra talks about being underappreciated and how there's really no improvement from her love. Jadakiss sprinkled his raspy genius all over the track, making it as radio ready as possible. "You'll Never Find" came in at 87 on its Billboard peak.

Complex Simplicity never really hit its monetary stride, but being on a major independent like TVT, Teedra was able to put out a third single to promote the album. "You Better Tell Her" was released a full year and some change after the release of the album in December of 2005. The vinyl single featured the prince of crunk Lil Scrappy and Pitbull well before he found success selling pelvic thrusts and making club music. "You Better Tell Her" is another up-tempo song. Teedra is warning her man about a woman that confronted her. She's saying that she doesn't give a damn if the rumors are true or not. All she knows is he better handle it, before she does. Real grown ass woman style. Teedra is as frank as possible when explaining that she doesn't even give a damn what the woman's name is. Just get that woman in line before I do.

There's sensuousness to Teedra's writing style. She never really gets vulgar or hyper sexualized, but what's an R&B album without at least one song dedicated to activities of intimacy? I'll tell you what it is. It's an incomplete R&B album. Hell, I've never heard of Heavy Metal being referred to as baby making music. "Backstroke" is about wanting to take a moment away from a toxic relationship to enjoy that one part of the relationship that you always enjoy. Sex. I'm talking about sex people. Good old fashioned, passionate, stress relieving, mind blowing, orgasmic sex. "Backstroke" is Teedra doing her best Halle Berry ala "Monster's Ball" impression because she's telling her man she just wants him to make her feel good. As you listen to the song, if it crosses your mind that the song reminds you of "Dip it Low" by Christina Milian, it's because it should. Same writer & producer in Teedra and Paul Poli. Teedra doesn't over sexy the song, but you'd be a fool to not use it properly.

"Rescue Me" is the sixth song on the album and I'm not sure if the sentiment of the song is PC in today's easily offended world. Teedra is saying that she's tired of putting her all in relationships that go nowhere and that one day the right man will come along and save her from this loop of failed relationships. Now I'm sure that the thought of a woman needing to be saved is offensive, patriarchal and blah blah blah. Whatever ridiculous and hyperbolic terms you want to apply just remember this one small thing: Teedra wrote the song and I'm sure a gun wasn't pointed at her head when she did it. Relax and enjoy the damn song. It's romantic. It's human to get to a place in your romantic life where you want things to feel good and right for once. That's all she's saying.

Teedra went on to do a string of mix tapes after *Complex Simplicity* from 2004 to 2014. There was a lot to deal with. Her record label, TVT, folded from financial struggles in 2008 and, frankly, *Complex Simplicity* didn't do what it should have financially. *Complex Simplicity* is unfortunately one of those pieces of art that is beloved, but it became beloved at the wrong time. We love the music but the music business will always be a problem. Teedra didn't release her second project, an EP, until 2014. Technically the second album, *Cognac and Conversations*, didn't drop until 2014. Teedra never really lost any steam as a songwriter either, penning songs over several projects in her hiatus. *Complex Simplicity* is a sweet, pure and sincere artistic moment that the universe was lucky enough to capture. If you pay close enough attention, you'll hear the influence that this album had on another talented songstress. We didn't give Teedra the roses that she deserved at the time of *Complex Simplicity* and it's rollout, but it's become a cult(ure) classic since then and recently celebrated it's 15th anniversary by re-releasing the album as an extended release with 4 additional songs. I hope you find the time to enjoy the original and the re-release. I also hope, and I mean this with the utmost sincerity, that Miss Teedra the lioness, is **NOT** a Saints Fan.

FUN FACT: The bulk of the vocal production and arrangements on *Complex Simplicity* were done by Shaffer Smith, or more commonly known now as Ne-Yo. Although it should be noted that Moses did her own arrangements on "Caution". Teedra had never written or recorded a song before until she started working on *Complex Simplicity*.

1) What city was Teedra, unfortunately, born and partially raised in?
   Answer:

2) Who are some of the artist that Teedra has written for?
   Answer:

3) What is Teedra's most successful song on the charts?
   Answer:

4) How did this album make you feel from the beginning to the end?
   Answer:

CHAPTER 7

BROWN SUGAR

Born Michael Archer in the musical hotbed of Virginia. A state with a musical history that spans every genre from GWAR, a dark heavy metal band out of Richmond (A seriously disturbed group of people. Trust me, and Google their videos. WTF?!) to Wayne Newton and his big Vegas show tunes, out of Roanoke and everything in between. He was born in a totally Pentecostal family and in fact his father was a Pentecostal minister. A prodigy that began playing the family piano at age 3 and quickly added drums, guitar and bass to his repertoire. In 1991 at the tender age of 17 he'd already had a band that he was performing with locally in Richmond, and they decided to try their luck at the famed Apollo theater in Harlem, New York. After a 3-week stint of wins, Michael knew he wanted to do music for the rest of his life. He dropped out of school and moved to New York to continue work on his demo and work the music scene. His songwriting, producing and vocal abilities were self-groomed over the next few years and eventually, with the help of his manager, Michael was signed in 1993. Michael went on to become the artist that we all know as D'Angelo.

I started this book by saying that I won't be ranking these albums. I'm not going to stray from that either, but it's no coincidence that I chose D'angelo's debut album *Brown Sugar* as the 7th chapter of this book. In concern to everything from Supreme Mathematics to numerology, 7 is widely known as a very special number. It's the number of perfection and completion. There are seven oceans, seven physical chakras, seven layers of the atmosphere, biblically speaking God rested on the 7th day, after he was done, etc.; Everywhere you look in the world, you'll see a parallel of perfection, wonder, and completeness to the number 7. Let me be clear here. What I'm saying in my most humble opinion is that *Brown Sugar* is THE GREATEST R&B album of all time. It has always and continues to check all the boxes of the perfect R&B album. Nuance, lyricism, vocals, instrumentation, inspirational, stimulating and so on and so on. D'Angelo's personal life struggles have caused 1 or 2 extended hiatuses that have made it harder for the younger generations to fully grasp his brilliance and impact. It all started with *Brown Sugar* though.

Brown Sugar is commonly seen as the album that ushered in Neo-Soul, which is simply a style of R&B. Sometimes it's characterized as something outside of R&B. A couple of things to remember in this regard though: Neo-Soul is a phrase termed by D'angelo's manager at the time Kedar Massenburg in the early 90's, and he created the term to distinguish D'angelo's live instrumentation style of music from what was on the radio. Neo-Soul is NOT different than R&B. It's simply a style of R&B. *Brown Sugar* was released on July 3rd of 1995. After the title track slowly brewed on the radio and video shows for a few months, the album finally dropped that summer. This 10 song masterpiece clocks in at just under an hour. It made it really easy for me to play this tape (YES TAPE!), over and over again. I played this tape so much that I had to rebuy it 3 times. When CD's came about I bought it twice, because the first one started skipping from the wear and tear of playing it so much. *Brown Sugar* is and has always been a necessary purchase for me, and no matter what platform it lands on from holograms to braille, I will ALWAYS purchase it. I could do a brief summary of every song on this album because frankly, NO SONG IS SKIPPABLE. Be that for the reason of lyrics, vocals, production or the amalgam of the three. This is a perfect album in every way, but I'll do my best to only focus on a few songs. It will be hard to pick which songs I discuss because it's the equivalent of choosing which brushstrokes on the Mona Lisa are the favorite. You can't. It's a complete body of work.

Brown Sugar is the title track of the album, the first single and the first song on the album. I'll never forget when I first heard this song. It was on the radio, back when radio wasn't dog shit. I was walking from the commissary on base headed back home after a long day of playing basketball. Cutting thru the neighborhoods and there was a man washing his car in his front yard with all the doors open as he cleaned out the inside. Luckily I had one of my walkman (YES WALKMAN!) headphones off of my ear when I heard the song in the background. The crooning was loud and clear. It was smooth. It was chill. It was unlike all the other R&B on the radio at the time. I was playing Mobb Deep's *The Infamous* album pretty heavy at the time but I had to cut it off to listen to the music coming out of the car. I was immediately tapped into the frequency that the music was putting out. I actually stopped dribbling my ball in front of the house, and just listened to the song. That young soldier looked at me strange as hell. I know he was wondering what I wanted. I wanted to know what I was hearing and feeling at that moment. He said "You good? You like that song don't you?" I said "Yes sir. It sounds good!" He said "That's right. It's a jam." When I got home, I sat by the radio for the next 2 hours with my blank tape, waiting to record the song off of the radio and I FINALLY got it!!

"Brown Sugar" is brilliant in the sense that you don't know whether D'angelo is talking about how much he sexually enjoys a black woman (Black/Brown Skin), or how much he enjoys smoking a blunt (Brown wrapper). As far as I know, he's never confirmed either interpretation, but the brilliance of it is, either way you envision what he's saying, it fits. He worked the hell out of that double entendre! He weaves laid back crooning over a heavy leading bass line and the cadence sounds a lot like a conversation he's having with his lover. Taking his time to let her know that she takes him to ecstasy every time they...well, you know *wink wink*. D'angelo wrote and co-produced this song with the renowned Ali Shaheed Muhammad from A Tribe Called Quest. D'angelo also played EVERY INSTRUMENT on this song.

"Alright" is the second song on the album. It starts with heavy drums, reminiscent of the boom bap Hip Hop at the time. Not surprising since D'angelo's favorite Hip Hop producers (Premier, Marley Marl, and J-Dilla) are known for their drums. Somewhere between these heavy drums and baseline strolling on the track, D'angelo found a little space in the groove to casually serenade the music. Mid-tempo but the song just feels more laid back than that, even with the aggressive drumming. It's a song about knowing no matter what the disagreement thrown at a relationship is, if two people love each other, everything will work itself out and be "Alright" in the end. Not a very wordy song, but the lyrical value is still there. The song vamps on for a few minutes in the end. Probably less to do with the song being light in words and more about D'angelo just showing off as a musician, since he not only wrote this song, he also played EVERY INSTRUMENT on it.

D'angelo has never hidden his love of Hip Hop and it's influence over his art. A huge part of Hip Hop, is the ability to tell a story. Being able to recollect/create a story and paint it clearly with words. That was the approach he took when he created the fifth song on the album "Shit, Damn, Motherfucker". It's the most sonically eerie song on the album. A tale of D'angelo catching his best friend and his wife in bed together. I won't ruin the story for you. You'll enjoy the song. Narrated by Bob Power, the main collaborator, on the guitar and D'angelo playing every other instrument. The music sounds like it could've been the background for the upside down of *Stranger Things*. I won't spoil it for you. "Shit, Damn, Motherfucker" is a simple song in construction of vocal arrangement and instrumentation but it plays thicker than it actually is.

"Cruisin" is the 7th song on the album. Yes the rules still apply to the 7 here. Re-imaginings, remakes, or interpretations, however you'd like to label a song being recreated, the beauty of this practice is that the artist remaking the song, has the opportunity to breathe new life and lay claim to the creation. A chance to make a song your own, by doing it infinitely better than it was done the first time. Whitney Houston did it with "I Will Always Love You", Luther Vandross did it with "A House Is Not A Home" (and several others), and every single year some misguided asshole tries to redo Donny Hathaway's "This Christmas" on their Christmas album and FAIL MISERABLY. For the love of all things holy, PLEASE STOP TRYING TO REDO THAT SONG. "Cruisin" was originally written and performed by Smokey Robinson for Motown in 1979. Smokey is the greatest songwriter of all time, and one of the most influential artists of all time, but make no mistake about it, D'angelo OWNS this song now. He kept all the live, heavy orchestral elements of the song, but the pocket of the groove is fuller. Maybe that's a testament to the technology of audio equipment evolving. Maybe that's a biased opinion about the sonic ride from "Brown Sugar" up to "Cruisin", or maybe D'angelo just had a better understanding of the impact that his version could have. Respectfully, where Smokey missed the opportunity to be more dynamic vocally, is where D'angelo shines much brighter.

     "Lady" is the 9th song on the album and the only song that wasn't recorded in NYC. "Lady" was co-written and co-produced by Raphael Saadiq and recorded in his home studio called Pookie Lab in Sacramento, California. "Lady" was the third single off of the album and one of the more successful songs on the album as well. It came out in early 1996, well after the album had been released. The song charted well, and even got D'angelo a Grammy nomination (for those that care about that type of thing). It's a good old fashion song about the admiration that D'angelo has for the woman in his life. He talks about his worry of other people not knowing that they are together and for those that do know, not respecting that relationship. The guitar and the bass line of this song are so utterly infectious. We can thank Raphael Saadiq for that. D'angelo played some additional guitar as well, but the core of the groove is thanks to Raphael. This is one of those songs that you absolutely have to play as loud as possible. By this time, the album had a little more budget being thrown at it and the famed Hype Williams directed the video for "Lady". There was an additional remix to "Lady" featuring AZ with Cameos by a young Erykah Badu and Faith Evans as well. It was a completely different delivery on the remix. I prefer the original. Not as a slight to the remix, I just think the song is better served in the musical context of the original.

     Brown Sugar was a very special moment for me in my life as a fan of music and as a creator of music as well. It was something that I'd never heard before. The marriage of music and lyrics in a refreshing yet reminiscent way. I truly think that *Brown Sugar* could've been a successful album in any decade. It was assembled with real instruments, written from a pure place, and deals with feelings that span over time. The same reason that Shakespeare is renowned as the greatest writer of all time. D'angelo wrote, produced and demoed *Brown Sugar* in his bedroom. The very foundation of this album was poured and solidified in an intimate setting and bloomed to influence the entire world. There will never be a time that I don't play this album. There are certain pieces of media (books, music, movies, etc.;) that I will always have on me. If you see me with my phone, ipad, or a laptop I will always have this album on me, because it's that important and that timeless.

FUN FACT: At the tender age of 20, and well before his *Brown Sugar* acclaim, D'angelo wrote and co-produced with Brian McKnight "U Will Know" for the *Jason's Lyric* soundtrack with a collection of some of the most talented male vocalist of that time. Although he's not particularly featured on the video you can see a pre-cornrowed D'angelo playing the piano at the 3:50 mark on the video, and you can hear Brian McKnight introduce him at the 3:26 mark when he says "Come on D and sing the song now..."

In addition, it should be pointed out that Anthony Hamilton went on to be one of D'angelo's backup singers as well as Angie Stone, with whom he shares a son with.

1) What is the one song on this album that D'angelo didn't write?
   Answer:

2) What is the one song on the album that wasn't recorded in NYC?
   Answer:

3) Which song was the first single off of this album?
   Answer:

4) What is your favorite song off of this album?
   Answer:

CHAPTER 8

WHITNEY HOUSTON

Let's get this out of the way. Whitney Houston is, unequivocally the greatest vocalist of all time. That's not up for debate. That's not up for discussion. That's not up for conversation. She is, to this day, even posthumously, the greatest vocalist of all time. The average human being could take voice lessons for 20 years and still not be able to accomplish, vocally, what Whitney did to the soundscape of music while being a chain smoker. For f*cks sake, look what she did to the Star Spangled Banner! Incredible. Whitney is also one of the very few artists on this list that was never renowned as a musician (playing actual instruments) or songwriter, although she does have writing credits. A gift as precise and powerful as her voice can't be denied and I'm glad I got to live thru the experience of her sprinkling her gift on the world.

Whitney Houston was born in Newark, New Jersey and raised in East Orange (I LOVE me a Jersey Girl!). Her father, like mine, was in the army and her mother was a gospel singer. She was a first cousin to Dionne and Dee Dee Warwick on her mother's side and her "God Aunt" was Aretha Franklin. She met Aretha at a very young age as she was beginning to sing in the church circuits of New Jersey. Did you read that? She basically had no choice but to be great, with all of that greatness that she was associated with early on. By 10 Whitney was already performing on the professional Gospel circuit as a soloist. By 14 she'd already begun singing backup for a few bands and solo artist, including Chaka Khan. She continued to perform with her mother in clubs and churches up until she graduated from catholic school. After passing on several other opportunities to sign a record deal, Whitney finally signed with Arista records, with an offer coming in person from the head of the company at the time, Clive Davis. He was blown away by her live performance and offered her a deal on the spot.

In 1983, only 2 years after graduating high school, Whitney began recording her debut album *Whitney Houston*. The album was released in February of 1985. She'd already recorded a duet with Teddy Pendergrass, shortly after signing with Arista, and it charted as a top 5 song on the R&B charts. That was her very first sip from the chalice of global success. Clive and the team at Arista were very strategic in how they rolled the album out. He knew there was something special about to happen, and they were very particular about who, their budding star worked with on the album. Initially there were 3 first singles for the album. The album didn't chart very well at first, considering the budget was double of what was originally meant to be. The album's acclaim and success began to turn as the U.S. single "You Give Good Love" began to heat up the charts with the help of the music video. Nobody can resist the lure of a beautiful woman with an incredible voice. It's a winning formula.

"You Give Good Love" came out in February of 1985 and is the first song on the 10-song album. The song was produced by the legendary producer Kashif. Although it was the lead single, the collaboration came together well after initial production of the album had begun. It was almost as if he was doing a favor for Whitney's A&R at the time. They put a few songs together on the album, but "You Give Good Love" was the most important of their works. "You Give Good Love" was an easy choice as the first single, because it gets right to the root of what would become Whitney's legacy, which is simply that, this woman can sang!! Not sing. **SANG**! It's a calm love ballad with the trademark minimal instrumentation that Kashif became known for. Whitney sings about finally finding what she's wanted in a man. The song builds as she voices her enthusiasm for trusting him with her heart and totally submitting to their love. I'm a fan for a sappy love song, which is exactly what this song is. The song did well on the urban charts, but from her very signing, the urban charts were always a peripheral target by Whitney's brass.

"Saving All My Love" was the second official single of the album. Most people don't know this, but this song is actually not an original for Whitney. This song was originally recorded and featured on an album called "Marilyn & Billy" in 1978. Another commonly unknown fact is, that the song in itself may very well be the most romantic side chick song of all time. Not sure how I could've heard this song a million times and why it took so long to come to that conclusion, but it is the truth! In the first 4 lines of the song it's made rather plain that the narrator, Whitney in this case, is a woman on the side that feels trapped by her love for a married/family man. I know I'm not the only one that was shocked at this revelation of the songs' context. No way I'm the only one that missed that at first or hundredth listen…right? It's easy to get caught up in the delight of Whitney's voice and completely miss the message in the magic. This is another ballad, but it's a much more immersed ballad than "You Give Good Love". Not just in tempo or milieu, but in the very texture of Whitney's voice and her control over it. This song is an emotional performance and it came across as very personal to Whitney because it was. Whitney admitted that at the time she was indeed in the middle of a love affair and she was the side chick. She could relate to the song. Whitney's mother didn't want her to record this song originally. She thought it would reflect poorly on the "good Christian girl" that she raised. That's right. We almost missed out on one of the greatest songs in Whitney's catalog thanks to good old fashioned, traditional Christianity rearing its judgmental little head. Thank goodness Whitney went ahead and recorded the song because it blew up to be her first official hit. "Saving All My Love" did very well on the charts. It quickly went to number 1 on the Billboard 100 internationally. It was also a great hit in the UK, so it made sense to shoot the video there. "Saving All My Love" became the first of seven consecutive number 1 hits on the Billboard top 100 for Whitney. A record that, I think, she still holds. "Saving All My Love" really catapulted her into a stratosphere of stardom that she didn't come down from until her more public and troubled times later in life. The first version of this song was turned down by Arista. The brass, including Clive Davis, thought the first version that she turned in was "too black". As I've said before, with Whitney's beauty and talent, it was always Clive's intention of having Whitney run the pop charts, and any success on the R&B charts would be by happenstance. They liked the song but thought it needed to be softened up a bit. So the song was re-worked to sound a bit more jazz like, and they even called in one of the founding members of The Blues Brothers band, Tom Scott, to do an epic saxophone solo on the song. Michael Masser wrote this song, along with others for many artists, and he eventually worked with Whitney directly when he wrote "Didn't We Almost Have It All", which was a song inspired by a story Whitney shared with him about the breakup between herself and NFL Legend Randall Cunningham. In 1986 she won a Grammy for the single, and even had it awarded to her by her first cousin and an early influence, Dionne Warwick.

"How Will I Know" was the third single and the first up-tempo song to be released by Whitney. It was released with the very intention of introducing Whitney to a younger crowd. After all she was only 19 herself at the time, but due to the seriousness of her first two singles, her fan base was rooted in adults. Up to the point of "How Will I Know", teenagers really didn't know who she was. She hadn't made anything for them. "How Will I Know" is all the sappy, confusing and irrational thinking that young people typically have when they're crushing on someone. We've all been there, so it's no surprise that the song did well. So well that it found it's way into the MTV market, which at the time, was tough for a black artist to do. It was well done for the purpose of the song. The song was sufficient, but not overwhelming, on the lyrical content and very easy to sing along with. The video was bright and vibrant, full of happy, dancing young people and top of the line graphics for that era.

"The Greatest Love Of All" is the fourth and final single from this album. The 9th song on the album and another remake as well. It was originally done by George Benson, and it turned out to be the biggest hit, chart wise, for this album. The song spent almost a month at number one on Billboard. This is the closest semblance of Whitney's church roots that Arista was comfortable in allowing her to share. "The Greatest Love Of All" is a song that still holds plenty of weight, especially in our modern times of people seeking validation via social media, social status and gravitas. The song even ends with the feel of Whitney being backed by a choir. Masser wrote this song as well, and even re-produced it for Whitney. She was able to perform this song on all the regularly scheduled stops and it helped to solidify her album as number 1 on billboard as well as "The Greatest Love Of All" as the number 1 single. This album was our introduction to an artist that would entertain and inspire the some of the same people that would revel in her ultimate demise. She shared her gift, and I'm happy that I had the chance to watch her flourish into an actress and her ultimate title of mother. She will be missed.

FUN FACT: "Saving All My Love" was a classic remake and as I stated before, Whitney admitted that at the time she was indeed having a torrid love affair with a married man. What most people don't know is that it was widely **RUMORED** (can't sue me!) thru the industry that the married man she was involved with was none other than Jermaine Jackson. After all the two had worked very closely together during the course of creating the album, to the tune of 2 duets and 3 songs produced by Jermaine himself. That's a lot of time to be spent together. Also, whether by design or coincidence, the leading man in the music video for "Saving All My Love" looks a LOT like Jermaine did then. The video chronicles how their working relationship grew to be romantic, but he wouldn't leave his wife for Whitney. At the time of them working together, Jermaine was married with two kids to the outstanding Berry Gordy's daughter Hazel, and they were fully divorced by 1988. This was just a few years after the release of *Whitney Houston*. There were never any true confirmations, but it sure seems like a lot of things add up. After all, art imitates life imitates art...or maybe it's just a rumor. What do you think?

1) What song do you think shows the best vocal range for Whitney on this album?
   Answer:

2) Do you have a favorite video from this album's roll out?
   Answer:

3) Where were you the first time that you heard Whitney Houston's voice?
   Answer:

4) Which song is the most memorable for you?
   Answer:

CHAPTER 9

FOREVER, FOR ALWAYS, FOR LOVE

Let's just get to the root of it. Shall we? If you've ever been to a black wedding, or you're headed to one in the near future, you will undoubtedly be hearing some Luther Vandross played there. It's really impossible not to. Outside of being the greatest balladeer of all time (Argue with your mother. This isn't up for debate.) Luther had a penchant for making some of the most timeless music of all time. Love songs in particular. Luther became the hub that love and romance met. As a vocalist, songwriter and pianist Luther definitely had the opportunity to put his stamp on the world. Luther was born and raised in the diverse landscape of New York City. Luther was raised on the lower east side until his father passed from diabetes when Luther was 8, and his family relocated to the Bronx. Luther fell in love with music around 4 years old, when he started teaching himself to play the piano. Music was always a safe place for Luther. After his father passed he became more interested in music as a profession. Luther spent his high school years doing everything from theater productions, to mastering his craft of songwriting and performing. Oddly enough he also established the very first ever Patti Labelle fan club in America. After graduating high school in 1969, he spent 1 year in college at Western Michigan University before deciding to leave and return to New York and fully pursue his dream.

Luther quickly became a fixture on the New York Circuit as a backup singer. Luther performed with a wide range of singers. Luther sung background with everyone from Bette Midler to Chaka Khan and wrote songs for artist such as David Bowie and The Brecker Brothers Band in the early 70's. He had a couple of group efforts that he attempted to gain traction with, but inevitably found himself as more of a solo artist than a group member. In 1976 Luther released his debut album *Luther* on a subsidiary of Atlantic records. He did the follow up to *Luther*, *This Close To You*, with Atlantic records as well. His first official solo album debut came in 1981 when Luther left Atlantic and joined Epic records. It was there that he released *Never Too Much* and the general public got a true primer into Luther as an artist. In 1982 Luther released, what would become his referential opus and the very sentiment that will always be attached to his name, *Forever, for always, for Love*.

Forever, for always, for Love was released on September 21st in 1982. It's an 8 song (44 minutes) collection of Luther's brilliance. At this point in Luther's career he had a pretty strong understanding of what he wanted his music to be. Vocally, Luther was clear and intentional. Luther could sing AND sang. It was apparent that Luther had mastered the art of his vocals, but still had the free range of artistry to do some good old-fashioned SANGING. I always considered Luther to be where Pavarotti meets Donny Hathaway. He was a true vocal technician, efficient in everything from crooning to power housing. Hell, he even had great non-regional diction. Luther could've used that voice to do anything from TED talks to being a news anchor, but instead he chose to bless us with his music. All of that is on display in this masterpiece.

"Bad Boy/Having a Party" is the first song on the album. It's a mid-tempo song. Growing up, I can't think of one BBQ or house party that this song didn't infiltrate. For a while, it seemed like the only way to alert people that the party had indeed begun. It's either a recollection or a story of a young teenage boy sneaking out of his mother's house to go to a house party. The party that nobody else wanted to miss, but the problem was he was still in trouble from the last party that he went to, because he came home so late. He went out and had the time of his life nonetheless. I see why this was the song used on *House Party*. "Bad Boy/Having a Party" is a fun song. It's a song that doesn't come with any guilt or bad memories.

"Since I Lost My Baby" is the third song on the album and one of the best examples of the gift and curse of a Luther ballad. A Luther ballad can either leave you high on the purity of blissful love, or wallowing in the darkest pit of heartbreak and misery. Really just depends on the songs context. Always listen to a Luther ballad with caution, because "Since I Lost My Baby" can put you in the memories of a sad place. We've all been there. The song is a remake. Most people don't know that. It was originally recorded by The Temptations in the 60's, and it was written by none other than Smokey Robinson. Damn, he really is the greatest songwriter of all time isn't he? "Since I Lost My Baby" is a song that explains the universal and hopeless feeling of heartbreak. I won the lottery, I'm on vacation, lost 5LBS and my credit score is in the 800's, but life is STILL horrible because I've lost my love. That's what the song is about. That's what any heartbreak is about. Heartbreak being such a delicate and common topic, Luther took his time with it. Luther's version is damn near 6 minutes long, while the original version by The Temptations was less than 3 minutes long. Everything about this song screams to the intent of creating a safe space for people to wallow and feel the pain of heartache. Luther let's the song build and vamp, as if he were cooking a lobster risotto. Slow and attentive.

"Forever, for Always, for Love" is the title song and the 4th song on the album. It's a song about the redemption in re-committing and re-finding love. We've all messed up in some capacity relationship wise. "Forever, for Always, for Love" talks about what that 2nd chance should look like. It starts off with an intro of sorts and Luther walking us into the memories of the beginning of the relationship. It sounds and feels conversational, up until the point that he gets into the beginning of the actual verse. One of the things I love about this song is the instrumentation. The actual music. I'd listen to this song and have the same feels if it were an instrumental. The music has a very symphonic feel to it. Strings, piano, and light percussion. The balladeer himself choosing his spots in the song. Luther didn't over sing on this song. He filled the holes of the music with the right moments and created a masterpiece that's found it's way into the hearts of us all.

"Promise Me" is the shortest song on the album at 4:43. I was having trouble deciding if I should feature "Promise Me" or "Better Love". Both songs are incredible and have a place on this album that makes sense. The sentiment of "Promise Me" and "Forever, for Always, for Love" are so akin that I almost stayed away from it, but in the end it won. "Promise Me" is catching. It's a piano lead song, and even though it's somewhere between slow and mid in tempo, the piano hits feel aggressive. Where "Forever, for Always, for Love" is more of a discussion of can we get back together, "Promise Me" is more in the vein of, can we promise to always work it out. Can we promise to always find our way thru the tough times and stay together?

What never gets talked about is Luther's pen game. With the exception of "Since I Lost My Baby", Luther wrote every word on this album as well as others. I would've loved to know what his process as a writer was. What we did know about Luther was his dedication to creating moments via song and that's all we deserved to know. I hope you didn't assume we were going to talk about his health issues or…that other rumored thing. We're not. He has a right to all the privacy that all of us do, and we won't sully that. Just know that in his time on this physical plane, he blessed us with some of the most iconic songs of all time and we should thank him for this particular collection of songs. *Forever, for Always, for Love* went platinum and held the #1 position on the R&B charts and #20 on the Billboard top 200. Rest in peace Luther.

FUN FACT: Well. Maybe not so fun, but "Forever, for Always, for Love" got Luther a Grammy nomination, but he lost to Marvin Gaye and "Sexual Healing".

1) Do you prefer Luther singing sad or happy love songs?
   Answer:

2) What's your favorite song on this album?
   Answer:

3) Which one of Luther's remakes is your favorite?
   Answer:

4) Have you ever listened to Lalah Hathaway's version of "Forever, for Always, for Love"? NO?!! GO LISTEN TO IT IMMEDIATELY!!

CHAPTER 10

TRUE TO MYSELF

Eric Benet is one of my favorite vocalists of all time. After a short stint in a group effort with his sister, Eric Benet burst forward with his solo album *True To Myself* in 1996 with Warner Bros. Records. It took a lot for Eric to get to *True To Myself*. Between 1993 and 1995 Eric lost his father to colon cancer and his longtime girlfriend (and mother to his first child) to an automobile accident, leaving him to be a single father. He signed with Warner Bros. in 1994. *True To Myself* is 13 songs and clocks in at just over an hour long. It's a full length by today's standards for sure.

"True To Myself" is the title track and the first song on the album as well. I have a lot of mantras for life and many of them come from music, but this is one of my favorites. "True To Myself" was the second single on this album. "True To Myself" speaks to the power of doing what's right for you. It's a mid-tempo song and he wrote and produced it with his longtime collaborator and first cousin, George Nash Jr. It's a pretty mature song for a man in his late 20's to have written. Eric touches on the happiness one can create for themselves in innately knowing what is and isn't right for themselves and their lives. Considering his vocal prowess, Eric didn't really press the gas on the singing. He just delivered the song and set the tone of the albums underlying theme. Perspective.

"Femininity" was the third and largest selling single on the album. It peaked at 24 on the Billboard top 100. A slow smooth ballad and a stealthily hidden song about the pleasure that only a woman can give a man in the bedroom. It's not crass, but it's pretty indicative of what Eric is saying. The song is seductive in context and tone. The piano and bass are heavy but subtle in their appearance on the song. All the elements of a good old-fashioned baby making song are here, and it wouldn't be an R&B album if there weren't at least one song like this on the project.

"While You Were Here" is one of the more haunting songs in R&B lore. It speaks to the gift and curse of hindsight. As we all know hindsight is 20/20 and here, Eric shares with us his personal clarity on the tragedy attached to the untimely death of his longtime girlfriend. This is one of the saddest songs of all time, because it's based in regret. What's worse is, it's based in a regret that can never be fixed. It can only be accepted. This is a song he wrote to basically apologize for not being a better man to her while she was still alive. No, not like that. There are no real specifics, other than the general sentiment of, "I should've been nicer and more attentive to you while you were here". He talks about the regret of becoming the man that she deserved after she'd already passed and not being able to share that with her. Even if you've never personally, had the same circumstances that he did, regret is a pretty universal emotion. Even if your regret for not treating someone better isn't based in romance, or family, the regret of not being a better person towards someone is common, and usually that clarity comes at the cost of a catastrophic event or some other form of grief. This is one hell of a song and I honestly don't think it could've been any better. Hearing it is a reminder to cherish each day with your loved ones. You may not get a chance to share good news with them tomorrow.

"Chains" is the 9th song on the album. It starts off with an acoustic guitar lead and is an up-tempo song. This is a song about getting past the things that hold you down in life. Everyone has their struggles, and Eric gives several different examples of how a terrible situation has the power to destroy people, but the choice is yours to reclaim your freedom from the things that are holding you back. It's written in a way of reminding the listener that their circumstances could be much worse, and that they could be free of it all if they choose to be. The music only drops in full during the hook, and Eric really gets to let his vocals fly here. There's everything from crooning to whaling, and even his signature falsetto. Heavy energy on this song.

It was really hard not to discuss more songs on this album, because I love "I'll Be There", "Spiritual Thang", and "All In The Game", but my hope is for anyone that hasn't heard this album to discover all of the elements for their self. It's so close to a perfect album, and I've personally had it in constant rotation since 1996. This album is entrenched with all the right elements of a great R&B album. Eric and his main collaborator Gary Nash JR, wrote all but one song on the album, the funky remake of "If You Want Me To Stay". Sorry I couldn't paint any pictures for you about his alleged philandering, but I didn't think it mattered in the context of this great album and honestly we just don't know. Here's a hint to an ironic chuckle tucked away in the album. Check out the first 2 lines on "I'll Be There". Ha!

FUN FACT: Eric Benet's first single as a solo artist "Let's Stay Together" was featured on the soundtrack for Martin Lawrence's *A Thin Line Between Love and Hate*. The song picked up a little steam on mainstream radio and the brass over at Warner thought it would be a good idea to do an additional version (remix) of the song. I love both versions, but I personally think the remix is the better of the two.

1) Do you think Eric Benet is a better singer of slow or up-tempo songs?
   Answer:

2) How old was Eric Benet when he broke out as a solo artist?
   Answer:

3) What is your favorite song on this album?
   Answer:

4) What would have made this a better album in your opinion?
   Answer:

CHAPTER 11

RAPTURE

Anita Baker is one of my favorite heroines in music in general, not just R&B. Her talent is so boundless that she can't truly even be classified to just R&B. She does jazz, soul and R&B. I won't discuss any music from Bluegrass to 70's Soul with anyone that ISN'T a fan of Anita Baker. She's that important to me. I know that music is subjective and everyone has a right to their opinions and blah blah blah. Yeah. That's great. F*ck all of that. If you don't like Anita Baker, then your opinion on all music is invalid. Okay? There, I said it. That's out of the way, and we need to talk about one of the masterpieces that she blessed us with before she broke our hearts and retired.

Most people don't know that Anita began her career as a member of a funk band in late 1975 and performed with the group on a small record label until 1982. The label was bought out by the music giant Arista records and they promptly dropped the band that Anita was playing with. She spent a few years back in her hometown of Detroit, honing her skills as musician and singer, until she got a chance at a solo career with an old associate from her time with the band. It wasn't until 1983 that her solo album *The Songstress* was released. The album was a success, both monetarily and impact wise, but like most young artist her contract was very one sided. Baker was basically not being paid royalties despite her success, and she had to spend two years in litigation getting out of the contract and that's when she signed with Elektra records. Artist move on from labels all the time, and often it's over money, or creative control. In this particular case, it was both. Part of the deal with Elektra was Anita having more control over her work. That's why *Rapture* is so important. In a way, this was the first time Anita got to use her voice. She had her fingerprint on the production and songwriting. She even, much to the dismay of her new label, tapped her old band mate Michael Powell, to assist in writing and producing.

Rapture is the second solo effort from Auntie Anita. No? Alright, fine. I won't do that again. It was released March of 1986. It's an 8-song album. The playtime is about 40 minutes, which at the time, was considered a fairly long album. Anita really got to spread her jazz influenced wings on *Rapture*. Even with the album getting it's fair share of play on the radio, there were music critics that didn't really appreciate the album or, Anita Baker as an artist for that matter. The unmitigated gall of those philistines! Despite the white noise Anita moved forward and let the album unfold with the same mastery that she composed it under.

"Sweet Love" is the first song on the album and the lead single. It starts with an attention grabbing piano solo and leads into a seamless transition of the Queen singing. "Sweet Love" is a song with full instrumentation. Every part of it moves from calm to cascading. The songstress sings about the joy of the love she's sharing, the overall belief in that love, and how she'll do anything to protect it. The structure of the song differs from the norm of an R&B song. There are 3 verses and one of them comes after the bridge. "Sweet Love" is a long song, checking in at 4:26. This was Baker's first big chart topping hit, coming in at number two on the Billboard top 100 R&B, and number 8 overall on the Billboard top 100. "Sweet Love" won a Grammy for best R&B song in 1987. For Baker that meant that she was winning as the performer and a writer. It was one of her first international shining moments.

"You Bring Me Joy" is the second song on the album. Even though it's not the title track on the album, to me it's always been the most important song on the album. Nobody else on the planet could've made that song. No one. The way she takes her time building the song, and the passion that she puts into it are unmatched. My favorite moment on the entire album is on "You Bring Me Joy" from 00:31 to 00:50. Just as Anita starts singing the song, she eases into that song with the precision of a seasoned surgeon. It's beautiful in it's quiet power and, truthfully it's impossible to not listen to the song from there. The song was written by David Lasley, who's written for many artists including Luther Vandross, Whitney Houston, Patti Labelle and Bonnie Raitt. Baker didn't have any writing or production credits on this song, but make no mistake about it, she owns every second of it. It's a ballad by every imaginable standard. "You Bring Me Joy" comes across as more of a poem than a song, and not just in how it was written. There's no true structure in the song. It really feels like a conversation. Baker is talking about how the joy of knowing someone, as a friend and a companion, can be confusing. Are you my friend? Are you my man? Is this serendipitous? At it's center, the song is about having the courage to be in the moment of your romantic, happiness. The background vocals on this song feel like a full choir is behind her, and maybe one was brought in for her. I love this song so much.

"Caught Up in the Rapture" is the 3rd song on the album. It's also the longest song on the album. Only the brilliance of an artist like Anita Baker can pack so many wildly sappy love songs into one project and make them all feel completely different. With that said, "Caught Up in the Rapture" is that indeed, a sappy love song. I love it, because it vamps on. The song itself is a rather short one, but it get's to 5:17 because the hook and the music go on well after the meat of the song is done. "Caught Up in the Rapture" was written by the writing duo of Gary Glenn and Dianne Quander and produced by Baker's hand picked/main collaborator Micheal J. Powell. It's about being hopelessly in love. It's a very well done song. Always the tactician, Baker decided to keep the vocals calm. This is one of her more popular songs because it's easy to sing along to. No hard notes to hit or hold. It's one her more vocally friendly songs. That's probably why it's also one of her few songs that's ever been covered by other artists. Lots of artists have taken a swing at re-interpreting "Caught Up in the Rapture".

"No One in the World" is the 6th song on the album and the 5th and final single to be released for the album. Fifth? This album was so successful that they released 5 of the 8 songs on the album as a f*cking single?! Yes. That's how absurdly beautiful that this album is. "No One in the World" was another hit single, as Baker continued her campaign of greatness to all of her protractors from Arista records. "No One in the World" is about trying to fix the mistake of leaving a relationship and wanting it back. Hindsight is 20/20. Looking for greener pastures in your relationship is a common topic in traditional R&B, because as far as relationships go, mistakes are unfortunately the best teacher. Not for nothing, she's begging. Begging for the love that she let go to come back and make her life whole again. Even the sad song on this album is a beautiful ballad. "No One in the World" peaked at 44 on Billboard's top 100.

Rapture went on to bring Baker two Grammys and sold over 6 million copies. It's the album that propelled her into legendary and iconic status. Baker has writing and production credits from this album. *Rapture* was released in 1986 and there were singles being rolled out until 1987. That's a lot of life on an 8-song album, and I didn't even talk about "Same Ole Love", or "Been So Long". I was lucky enough to grow up in a house full of albums and music, and *Rapture* was definitely in my parents GET UP AND CLEAN THIS HOUSE, mix.

FUN FACT: Tributes are all the rage on award shows nowadays. It's a way to convince legends to show up and be engaged in the proceedings. They prop them on the front row and get as much b-roll of them as humanly possible. Some of these tributes have been great, and others have been an ABSOLUTE DISASTER (yes, I'm looking at you VH1 and Rich Homie Quan). The best of all the tributes was Anita Baker's on The Soul Train Music Award show. There were a slew of performers and all of them were incredible, but my personal standouts were, Faith singing "No One in the World", Goapale and Dionne Farris singing "Same Ole Love", Lalah Hathaway KILLED "Angel" (such a beautiful rendition) and last but not least Tamia singing "Giving You The Best That I Got" (SHE SUNG THE HELL OUT OF THIS SONG BY THE WAY). Here's the fun fact. "Giving You The Best That I Got" is a song about loving your companion to the best of your abilities. Tamia was introduced to her husband of, then, 19 years by none other than Anita Baker in the mid 90's. Tamia even nods to the history of her union during the performance by showing her wedding ring in step with the lyrics of the song. THIS TRIBUTE IS WORTH GOING TO YOUTUBE TO WATCH.

1) What's your favorite song on the album?
   Answer:

2) Do you know which songs Anita Baker played piano on for this album?
   Answer:

3) What city did Baker record 2 of her videos for "Rapture" in?
   Answer:

4) Did you notice how I made this chapter 11? Ya know, like the number 11? As in the "angel number"? As in angel? As in the 1st song ("Angel") on Anita's first album? Ya get it? No? Alright fine...
   Answer:

CHAPTER 12

12 PLAY

If discussing R. Kelly and his prowess as a singer and brilliant artist offends your sensibilities, **I TOTALLY UNDERSTAND**. As I wrote this book, and even at it's completion, I questioned several times whether I should or shouldn't completely strike this chapter all together. Besides the last thing I want is for anyone to assume that I support the things that R. Kelly is being accused of, and for that matter all the things that we **KNOW** he did. I'm just as disgusted as anyone with good sense would be at the stories we've been hearing about R. Kelly. I included this chapter for two reasons. One, in the pantheon of R&B and all the things that have transpired in the genre over the years there is NO WAY to exclude R. Kelly and his contributions. If you erase his influence over music, far too many people will lose memories, lessons, or moments from their lives. Myself included. Two, artist are difficult people. Sometimes that difficulty comes from them being deeply troubled and/or deeply demonic people. Some of the greatest works across many mediums were created by bad people. In order to appreciate these works, you have to separate the artist from the art. If you are one that can't do that, understandably, you should skip this chapter. Again, this is **NOT** a praise of the man R. Kelly, only of his artistry. If you can't do that, then skip this chapter, and I truly hope you enjoy the rest of the book.

Okay. So...I get it. I really do. My parents gave me the gift of common sense. Good old fashioned, country, down home common sense. They left Albany, Georgia and traveled the world armed with it as kids. I'm well aware that, 9 times out of 10 where there's smoke, there's a fire. If you look in the window of your favorite coffee shop and see smoke, then one of the machines may very well be on fire, but sometimes, SOMETIMES, it's just some asshole walking around the building with a vape pen (I hate all of you by the way). **I want to be perfectly clear, I 100% believe most of the accusations against R. Kelly. 100%!** Fact of the matter is, we really don't know, and in a world where black men are notoriously considered guilty until proven innocent, I have to at least partially, even if it's only based in legalese, fathom that he's innocent until proven guilty. Not for nothing, we do know that he snuck off and married a child Aaliyah, which is sick as f*ck too. It begs the dilemma of separating art from the artist. Is there a space where we can morally consume the art of unethical/evil people that happen to produce art that we can't live without? Woody Allen molested and married his adopted stepdaughter and now you can see him at playoff games on TV hand in hand. It never even slowed his career down and people still willfully work with him. With all that the world has learned in life lessons from The Cosby Show, should we all take an oath to never watch another episode? The real question is, if we support the art of an artist, does that mean that we support the artist? The answer is probably as subjective as art in itself. This past week, a banana duct taped to a canvas sold for $120K because a couple thought it was worth that much, and I'm just thinking "WTF?!" to myself. All I'm really saying is that, usually, I can separate the art from the artist, and R. Kelly and all the ethical/legal woes associated with him UNTIL HE'S PROVEN GUILTY, are one of those cases. **Just to be clear and to repeat it plainly though, let me reiterate, I do not support R. Kelly. I do NOT support R Kelly. I do NOT support R.Kelly. I. DO. NOT. SUPPORT. R. KELLY.** Are we clear? Can I talk about the album now? Yeah? Good.

R. Kelly burst into the public eye as the lead singer in a group effort. I use the word group very loosely. Apparently Kellz was writing, producing, leading, arranging and even choreographing everything for the group. After the success of their debut album *Born into the 90's*, Kellz renegotiated his deal with Jive records. Pretty easy to do when the lead of the group that just charted #3 on the Top R&B chart and #42 on the Billboard top 200 comes to you and says he's unhappy. Kellz had leverage and he used it. That leverage turned into Kelly's debut solo album *12 Play*.

12 Play was released November 9, 1993. The album is a mixture of hip-hop and heavy, sensual ballads. After re-listening to the album a few times, it comes across as an album that is a mixture of newly recorded ballads by Kellz and throwaways from the *Born into the 90's* album. You can even hear The Public Announcement singing background on most of the hip-hop songs, including the skit at the end of "I Like the Crotch on You". We all know what makes this album great though. It's the ballads and all of their baby-making prowess that make this album standout. *12 Play* is one of the more prominent albums to take crass and sexually, sometimes overt, lyrics and make them melodious. That's the core of this album, the ballads. I know. I know, but let's just try and focus on the art and not what that art may have been based in, since we don't fully know.

The first single on the album was "Sex Me". A very, VERY, risky call for 1993. Radio wasn't as explicit friendly as it is nowadays. He even shot a steamy video for the song. Truthfully though, this HAD to be done. There's no better song to lead this album, and frankly his solo career, with other than "Sex Me". "Sex Me" is a graphic detailing of a night with a sexy woman. "Sex Me" was broken into 2 parts on the album and spans for 11 minutes and 28 seconds. Kellz released part 1 as his lead single. It's the lighter of the two versions. What I love about this song is that it gets straight to the action. There is no warming up to the sentiment of sex throughout the course of the song. There is no hinting at what Kellz wants to get into. The title is the very definition of indicative and the first line of the first verse doesn't stray from that either. The song is kind of light on the lyricism, but that's not the point of this song either way. The frequency of this song is sex and nothing short of it. "Sex Me" did its job. It introduced the world to a modern, semi-raunchy, hip-hop infused brand of ballads, and Kelly's signature solo sound. The single charted well and reached #2 on the R&B charts and in the top 40 on the Billboard Hot 100.

The second single was "Bump n' Grind". This was the first single released after the actual album release. "Bump n' Grind" gave *12 Play* the national attention that it needed. "Sex Me" was a strong single, but not exactly the type of song you could go and perform on Arsenio and Leno. Again, this was 1993/1994. The Simpsons were considered edgy at this time in history. There was no way in hell that the powers that be were going to let a black man get on national TV and sing something as explicit as "Sex Me" to their 50 million live viewers. "Bump n' Grind" was different in context and delivery. It had a much more radio friendly vibe to it and was a little faster in tempo. The video really helped sell it too. Upon the release of the single, it shot to #1 on the Billboard Hot 100 and spent over 10 weeks at #1 on the R&B charts. Kelly was already a respected vocalist (yes VOCALIST. Hi Jason and Ty), but he really didn't get to do much in the way of tapping into that power on "Sex Me". It would've changed the mood of the song. On "Bump n' Grind" he let his powerful voice fly.

"It Seems Like You're Ready" was never officially released as a single, although there were plenty of radio stations playing it in their quiet storm mix. For the confused millennial' tuning in, let me explain. The "quiet storm" was a nightly show that all urban radio stations had, where the programming would very specifically only be ballads and love songs. "It Seems Like You're Ready" is the 4th song on the album. Sultry and much more reserved than "Your Body's Callin'", and "Bump n' Grind". Appropriately "It Seems Like You're Ready" cooks the overpowering theme of, you guessed it, sex with more couth and patience. The song borderlines on romantic, but still very much a sexual song. Kellz has a gift of storytelling, and I'm not talking about the "Trapped in The Closet" series. I'm more so referring to his gift of imagery thru lyrics. When he chooses to, he can illustrate what he's saying and that was the stance he took on this song. It's one of the longest songs on the album for this particular reason. "It Seems Like You're Ready" is one of the songs I point to for Kellz when I'm discussing how he has full control of his vocal abilities. He has the vocal power to pelt thru all of his songs, but he chose to pull that back for the sake of letting the song maintain the tone of patience.

"Sadie" is the 10th song on the album. It's a cover of the 1975 hit by The Spinners, and more importantly the ONLY song on the album that strays from the overwhelming theme of sex. "Sadie" is about the love one has of their mother. It speaks to how a mother can be a beacon of light in even the darkest of times. Kelly had a very close relationship with his mother. Although I know that she died the same year that *12 Play* was released, there's no evidence that he covered this song after her death. It may very well have just been a nod of admiration and respect to his mother's love and resilience while raising him and his 3 siblings in such a troubled and impoverished time. Again, there's no proof that he covered this song posthumous to her death, but I really can't see why anyone would choose such a somber song that expresses missing your mother if they hadn't already transitioned. Safe to say that she had already passed and that's what pushed him to add this song to the project. Even though this song diverts from the albums' content it holds it's own within the structure of the album. There's a very human element to "Sadie" and "For You" that helps *12 Play* spread it's wings as an album.

"12 Play" is the last play, if you will, on the album. Over time we as the general public have come to know this song as "12 Play", but on the original artwork the title of the song is actually "...............". Don't believe me? Look it up. The song is an untitled song. Why he wouldn't go with the obvious "12 Play" as the actual name, instead of this extended ellipsis, we may never know, but that's why artists are artists. Sometimes things make sense in their minds, and nowhere else. This is the last song on the album, and it delivers as such. This is the main song that R. Kelly freely runs on. The song, in structure, is actually pretty short. There's only one real verse and no bridge in sight. The bulk of the song is Kellz simply going apeshit with his vocal power and vocal runs. One of my favorite moments on the album happens between the 3:15 and 3:33 time mark. Your average vocalist can't do that. That's special. The song was created on stage while Kellz was opening for Gerald Levert & Glenn Jones. He wanted to add something to his show that would build excitement and talk about his set, because he was tired of performing for half empty crowds, as most opening acts do. So he started telling people that he had a dream about making love to none other than Miss Mary J. Blige. The piano player would begin to play and Kellz would begin the countdown. This is how "12 Play" the song came about. This song would get the ladies so excited that Kelly got switched to second billing, pushing Glenn to be the opening act. That had to be a humbling experience for Jones, but the people had spoken. Kelly made this song highly requested while on tour before he even recorded it, and his star was on the rise.

12 Play was a success by every possible measure. It became an instant cult classic and R. Kelly ushered in a new wave of R&B. A more modern, street, direct, and sexually charged form of R&B. In the end *12 Play* went on to go 6X platinum. The album was number one on the top R&B/Hip Hop list for nine weeks straight, and peaked at number 2 on the Billboard top 200. People couldn't get their hands on the album fast enough. R. Kelly is one of the greatest R&B artists of all time. There's no denying that. No matter what measure you use, in the end, R. Kelly will be in the mix of the greatest. We can't ignore, what seems to be the obvious though right? R. Kelly had problems. As of now, we can't prove some of the things that have been rumored or talked about with R. Kelly. Some. We do know that Kelly married Aaliyah, who at the time was only 15 and he was 26. Sick. Disgusting. Horrible. With that being a truth, it's really not a far stretch at all to believe that the other things are true. I do believe it. Hell, all of it. Then why discuss someone that's been aligned with some of the most heinous acts on the planet? That begs the question of whether one should or shouldn't separate art from the artist. There's no wrong answer here. I'm one of those people that can at times. Picasso was a raging misogynist that enjoyed destroying women on an emotional and mental level and used that as a huge part of his creative process. He wasn't shy about it either. It wasn't some quiet little dark secret. He's even on record calling women "Machines of Suffering". He pushed two women to commit suicide and two to insanity and being committed to mental hospitals, but he's still renowned as one of the greatest artists of all time. Caravaggio the famous renaissance artist was a known murderer and pimp since his teenage years, and still played a huge role in pushing the envelope with his gory imagery. Paul Gauguin wasn't only a famous artist; he's also famed for slicing off Van Gogh's ear, abandoning his wife and 5 kids to live in Tahiti, then taking 3 child brides once he got to Tahiti and giving all 3 of them syphilis. I mean…Shit. Dude was a monster. The list of artist and their offenses to humanity in general span as far and wide as the ocean. Whether it's Percy Grainger and his white supremacist views and practices or Eric Gill and his penchant for incest and bestiality (yep you read that right), artist can be some of the most deeply disturbed people on the planet. I'm not sure how we separate who they are from their work though. Their works have some of our best memories attached to them. If/when R. Kelly is proven to be guilty of these acts, I hope he's convicted to the very fullest extent of the law. We already know he married, and presumably, raped a child Aaliyah so karma will most certainly check in eventually. No matter what other things come out about Kelly and his addiction to young women, we can't discuss the greatest R&B albums without discussing *12 Play*. It is a masterpiece. No questions, but I will give you a fun fact about the album.

FUN FACT: R.Kelly wrote or produced, every single song on the album. With the exception of 3 songs of 12, which he still co-produced. Over the years R. Kelly became a very sought after writer and producer, eventually creating for everyone in the industry including Michael Jackson, Celine Dion, Britney Spears and Tamia.

CHAPTER 13

SONGS IN THE KEY OF LIFE

I'm just happy that I've lived in a time that was touched by Stevie Wonder and his genius. Stevie has been performing as a professional artist since the tender age of 11. He scored his first number one hit ("Fingertips") on the Billboard top 100 when he was only 13 years old. Stevie Wonder was labeled a child prodigy and began painting a lifelong masterwork of love and musicality from the early 60's to today in 2020. Over that time he's done things as an artist, musician, songwriter and philanthropist that others have only aspired to do. He's recorded 26 albums over the span of his career. Of those 26, I could very easily put 10 of them on this list. Easily. It's important for me to shine the light on the one that I consider his masterpiece. His pieta. His Rachmaninoff's third and his Eiffel Tower. *Songs in the Key of Life* was released in September of 1976. This album almost didn't happen, because just a year before Stevie was seriously considering quitting the music business and moving to Ghana to work with handicapped children. It took a little coercion, but the brass at Motown was able to change his mind with a little begging. I'm sure offering him total artistic control and the largest, most lucrative music contract of that time helped push the negotiations thru as well.

Songs in the Key of Life was considered to be a very ambitious work for its time. It was a double LP before it was all the rage in the music business. It takes a lot of work and extreme focus to do such a thing. The great bulk of the album was recorded in Hollywood, California at the famed Crystal Sounds studios. Stevie's work ethic during this period is famed. He's said to have often chosen creating, over all of the life essentials including eating and sleeping. Totally locked in to his creativity and the integrity of his process. It's impressive to hear that kind of dedication from someone that had already tapped into success. The outcome was a timeless piece that, even today in 2020, holds a lot of contextual and sonic value. The very life force of this album is of course from the veins of Stevie Wonder but, it was touched by well over 100 other artists, including the legendary Herbie Hancock and Minnie Ripperton.

"Love's in Need of Love Today" is the very first song on the album. It makes sense to me. Stevie was pretty upset with how the country was being run and the general negativity that the world was in. It's his love song to the world. Stevie said that he remembered writing this song in his hotel room in New York and looking at his pregnant partner at the time. He had the realization that love is something that has to be fed and nurtured. Replenished even. He thought that it was the only way that love could be effective. The song, in lyric, is actually pretty short. The tone of the song is what stays with you for the entire 7 minutes. Stevie starts the song as if it's a PSA. He even refers to himself as the "friendly announcer". His message is that there's a drought on love, and that the world is in desperate need of more of it. A shame that this song was written and released in the mid 70's and still rings true to this day in 2020. It speaks to his brilliance. To be able to write something as ageless as "Love's in Need of Love Today" and have it's relevance span over the course of decades is Shakespearean. With the exception of the Kalimba drums, Stevie played every instrument on this song.

"Isn't She Lovely" is one of the more popular songs on the album. It was never released as an actual single. Due to good old-fashioned radio programming and airplay the song still reached the top 20 on the Billboard 200. I guess there's no holding a great song back. I'd argue that it's also the most important song on the album. Stevie wrote this song for a life changing moment in his life. He was becoming a father for the first time, and he made this song to commemorate the love and beauty of his daughter Aisha. As a parent myself, I can relate to that overwhelming feeling of your first child being born. It's an emotional high that is unmatched, and a day that none of us ever forget. There were two different versions of this song. The extended version of the song has a long intro with the actual audio of a baby's first cry at birth, and the outro is audio of Stevie giving his daughter Aisha a bath. The shorter version cuts the intro and outro, to give the song a more radio friendly length. He even managed to squeeze in a shout out to Aisha's mother Yolonda (Londie), in the song.

"I Wish" was the very first single on the album to be released. It's a strong, funky full instrumentation song with a serious groove to it. Stevie wrote this song as a means of reliving his childhood thru song. Like most of us, it was just a happier time in our lives. Before we busied ourselves with careers, investment portfolios, the dangers of gluten and the importance of spinach in our diet. Before we complicated our lives with things that we've been told are important. He goes on about the mischief he used to get into as a child, and the fun he had getting into that mischief. That's how the song sounded to me growing up. As a grown man now, the song sounds more like missing the times in your life where learning a lesson and making mistakes was a lot less costly than it is as a responsible adult. The single hit number one on Billboards' top 100 and R&B. I guess he wasn't alone in his wishing for lighter days.

"Knocks Me Off My Feet" is a ballad. It's the type of ballad that only Stevie Wonder could conjure. Stevie brushes a picture of spending the day with the person he's madly in love with. If you've ever had the fortune, or misfortune, of being so in love with someone that you're happy to just be in his or her presence then this song will speak to you. It's a slow tempo song with a minimalist approach to the instruments used. Stevie is saying that he's so weak for his woman's love that it could knock him off of his feet. Not just figuratively, but emotionally. Her love could make him lose control of his faculties and sensibilities and bend to whatever was required to keep her love. After all, isn't that what love does? Make you stupid. Stevie not only wrote the song, he also played every instrument on it. This song was never released as a single by Stevie, but it's an extremely popular song. Stevie is one of the artists that should never be covered. He has very few songs that any other artist can do justice to. It hasn't kept people from trying though. There are only 3 Stevie Wonder songs that have been successfully covered by other artists in my opinion, and this is one of them. In 1996 Donell Jones covered "Knocks Me off My Feet" and released it as his second single. It's the best cover of this song. Tevin Campbell did an acceptable version for the soundtrack of *A Thin Line Between Love and Hate*, but it doesn't compare to Donell's version. The other two covers that were successfully done by artist are "Ribbon In the Sky" by INTRO and "Lately" by Jodeci.

"As" is the last single to be released from the album. It was released in October of 1977. A full year after the release of the album. "As" is a song that says the impossible will have to happen before the love for his woman fades. Oceans will have to be mountain high, dolphins will have to fly, Donald Trump would have to respect women, etc.; You know. The impossibilities of life would have to become realities. With the way the song riffs on, about the things that would have to happen before his love fades, you would assume that the title should be "Until". For whatever reason he chose the first word of the song as the title. This song signaled the end of *Songs in the Key of Life* and the marketing campaign for it. "As" did well on the charts too. It peaked at 36 on the Billboard Hot 100.

Songs in the Key of Life is widely considered to be people's favorite Stevie Wonder album. It's a good argument. The album went on to sell 5 million copies during it's campaign. It was certified at diamond (10 million copies) in 2005. It broke sonic ground, making use of electric equipment over conventional live instruments and the gamble that Stevie Wonder took artistically doing a double LP and Motown took offering the deal paid off. *Songs in the Key of Life* is proof that everyone can win, if the business gets out of the way of the artistry. I play this album in its entirety once a month, and every time I do, I walk away with an appreciation for a different nuance within it. Stevie says that of all his works, that *Songs in the Key of Life* is the one he's happiest with. It's a time capsule of when every part of his life was changing, as a new father, as a life partner, a philanthropist, a businessman and an artist. *Songs in the Key of Life* spent 13 weeks at number 1 on the Billboard Hot 100. It's an album full of easy listening for any day that ends in Y.

FUN FACT: During the almost two years of recording that went into the creating of *Songs in the Key of Life*, Stevie Wonder was heralded for his work ethic. He was known to do 48 hour recording sessions, and only taking breaks to rotate out his personnel of engineers and musicians. He was a machine. Stevie was so tapped into his process that he had to be coerced to sleep and take a break.

1) What medium did you first hear this album on? CD? Vinyl? Stream? Cassette?
   Answer:

2) What is your favorite song on the album?
   Answer:

3) Which song do you think was the best lyrically?
   Answer:

4) Has your current favorite R&B artist ever referenced "Songs in the Key of Life" as a favorite of theirs?
   Answer:

CHAPTER 14

TONI BRAXTON

Born in Maryland and raised in a very religious household, Toni Braxton originally planned on being a teacher. Music was always a big part of her life with her mother being a former opera singer and her father being a vocal leader in the church. Toni and her sisters performed as a group in many local talent shows and showcases and eventually got signed to a record deal with the giant Arista records. It was the early 90's and they released a single, with little to no fanfare. Luckily there was a new subsidiary imprint on Arista called LaFace being ran by a couple of geniuses and they caught wind of the group. In an impromptu performance/audition with Babyface and LA Reid, the duo decided to take creative control for Arista, but they weren't interested in the whole group. All they wanted was Toni. It took a little coercion by Babyface and a little soul searching by Toni, but she eventually signed a solo deal and joined the LaFace roster.

The first time I heard Toni Braxton was when the video for "Give U My Heart" debuted on B.E.T. MTV still had a bit of trepidation showcasing black artist at this time. It's a duet with Babyface from the *Boomerang* soundtrack (UNEQUIVOCALLY THE GREATEST SOUNDTRACK OF ALL TIME). Even though I was only a child at the time I remember thinking to myself "WHO IS SHE?!". That voice. That haircut. That...hell, everything. I LOVE her. I love the richness of Toni's lower register, and yes she's always been easy on the eyes. Black women weren't being held to European standards of beauty at the time, so Toni and all of her black girl magic were flowing freely and I couldn't get enough of it. Babyface and Toni performed all over the country. Makes sense to break your new artist by keeping them at your side as much as possible. While traveling, promoting the single and learning the ropes of stardom Toni was recording her debut album.

Toni Braxton was released in July of 1993. Toni was still riding high off the success of her first national single "Love Shoulda Brought You Home". The song was released in December of 1992 and was a single off of the *Boomerang* soundtrack, not necessarily her debut album. Most of its noise was being made on the urban charts, but it was still significant noise. It would be ridiculous to not put this on the album, so of course it made the cut. "Love Shoulda Brought You Home" was written and produced by Babyface and Daryl Simmons. The melody, the key and the power necessary to pull this song off, made Toni an easy recipient of the song. The song and the title are a play on one of the more famous lines in the movie. It's a song that reminds people that their words and actions have to match. You can't say you love something and not do what's necessary to take care of it. If you love a plant, you water it. If you love your car, you keep the oil changed. If you love your woman/man… you take your ass home to them instead of spending the night with someone else. Marcus really screwed that up. The song did well on the radio and video shows. The song peaked at 33 on Billboard's top 100 and set Toni up for the release of her album debut single.

"Another Sad Love Song" was Toni's actual album debut single. It was released in June of 1993. This is a ballad, once again, written and produced by Babyface and Daryl Simmons, but also with LA Reid in tow on production. I love this song, and there's just something about Toni Braxton playing the heartbroken girl next door that plays well with my sensibilities. It's a song about dealing with heartbreak, while being reminded of said heartbreak by every song on the radio. I know I've definitely been there before. A time when everything you hear, see or smell reminds you of the person that you poured so much of yourself into, or vice versa, is no longer a part of your life. The song played well and people seemed to really like it. This was Toni's first top 10 song on Billboard's Hot 100. It peaked at 7 and remained in the top 10 for several consecutive weeks.

The second single on the album was "Breathe Again". A ballad written and produced by, you guessed it, Babyface , Daryl Simmons and LA Reid. Is her biopic and the LaFace litigation storyline in it starting to make more sense to you yet? "Breathe Again" helped to build the broken hearted sweetheart storyline for Toni. It's a song about the nostalgia of a relationship and that overwhelming feeling of never being able to let go. It's also about the hopelessness of the void that a broken heart can create. They really kept beating the drum of heartbreak for Toni, but all the songs felt different. They all genuinely have their own context and tone. The song says that Toni wouldn't be able to go on if she and her man were to part. I'm not sure how that sentiment would play today in the face of modern day "feminism", but it was timely for the 90's when people still believed in love. "Breathe Again" is the most successful single on the album. The song peaked at 3 on the Billboard hot 100 and was her 3rd consecutive gold single.

"You Mean the World to Me" was the 4th single off the album. It feels like more of a summer song, but it was released in April of 1994. It had the right feel for the radio. Written and produced by…well. C'mon. You know who it was. After a string of singles based in heartbreak, I think we were all ready to hear this beautiful little woman, sing about being happy, and that's the direction this song leads to. It's on the happier end of the spectrum of emotions that come with a relationship. "You Mean the World to Me" is an upbeat song and it did well on the radio. It peaked at number 7 on the Billboard hot 100 and up to 3 on the R&B charts.

"How Many Ways" was the 5th and final single on the album. Straying away from the much successful, and much maligned formula of singles, written and produced by the trio of Babyface, Reid and Simmons, this song was written by Vassal Benford and Ronald Spearman and produced by Benford himself. If you followed the rollout of *Toni Braxton* you could even tell there was a difference. The difference was less in the sound of the music, but definitely in the pitch. This felt like a different artist. Toni sings in her higher register, there's a little more spunk in her delivery and she just sounds like she's having more fun on this song than the rest of them. Taking a peak at the production notes, maybe she was happy to get in the studio with someone other than Babyface and LA Reid. When an artist starts out, they usually want to work with as many other creatives as possible. It's usually not until later in their career that artist, want to narrow down who they work with. Toni also recorded this song in New Jersey. I'm sure it felt good to get out of Atlanta and record in a fresh environment. It's an upbeat song that reeks of love and happiness. After 4 singles, the cute girl next door finally found the love that she'd been pining over and we loved it. The video for "How Many Ways" was even brighter than the other videos. She'd come full circle in her insinuated story of finding love that LaFace had brilliantly rolled out. The song was released in June of 1994. A full year after the release of the album. The song didn't fair as well as some of the other singles on the album, but it still did very well peaking at 28 on the Billboard Hot 100. The video did far better by comparison, co-starring a young Shemar Moore as her paramour. In the spirit of Nino Brown, I never really liked the video (bless your heart if you don't get the totality of that reference). To be fair the video did it's job and so did the song. It put a bookend on the story of the girl next door finally finding love and being happy after heartbreak.

Toni Braxton was a successful album. LaFace had its first lady and personal in-house diva with Toni. The album went on to sell 8 million copies, Toni won 3 Grammys and 2 American Music Awards. A star had been successfully planted, nurtured and grown. On a broader scale, Toni helped to break down some of the barriers that were holding back other black women that weren't being given the chance to shine, because they didn't look like LA Reid's wife (Pebbles). Colorism has always been an issue in the black community, and even in 2020 it continues, but here we were in the mid 90's and this brown skinned black woman with her broad nose and short haircut was the most talented and beloved woman on the charts. I loved it and I wasn't alone. *Toni Braxton* set the stage for us to watch Toni grow as a woman and an artist. Starting out as a flirty, talented girl next-door type, to the full-blown siren, sex-pot and icon that she is today.

FUN FACT: "Love Shoulda Brought You Home" was originally written and produced by Babyface and Daryl Simmons for none other than the amazing Anita Baker. Toni Braxton was just supposed to demo it for her. They thought that Toni's lower register would play well in helping Baker see herself singing it and bringing her own brand of genius to the song. Also her star power would only boost the already brilliant compilation that was the *Boomerang* Soundtrack. Baker being the visionary that she is, decided that Braxton should keep the song for herself, since she'd done such a great job with it. Baker was also pregnant at the time, and couldn't devote the necessary energy to one up Toni on the song. We're all the beneficiaries of timing and circumstance, because Toni delivered a certified classic.

1) What's the best song on the album?
   Answer:

2) Do you prefer Toni doing ballads or up-tempo songs?
   Answer:

3) Which song gives you the strongest memories of your own personal life?
   Answer:

4) Do you have a favorite music video attached to this album?
   Answer:

CHAPTER 15

SONS OF SOUL

Tony! Toni! Toné! is a band out of Oakland, California. Originally, the band was comprised of brothers Dwayne and Charles (later known as Raphael Saadiq) Wiggins as well as Timothy Riley. The band began making noise in the late 80's and had a string of hits from their first and second albums including "Little Walter", "Lovestruck", "Whatever You Want" and "It Never Rains(In Southern California). There are some people that consider their 4th album *House of Music* to be the masterpiece, but I personally think that *Sons of Soul* is the album that they hit the bullseye of excellence on. It was their third album and it was released on Mercury records in 1993. By this time the band had accomplished a modicum of success and they were ready to have more control of their creative process. They produced the entire album, and did the bulk of the recording in Trinidad, to get away from the noise of Los Angeles. *Sons of Soul* was released in June of 1993.

"If I Had No Loot" was chosen as the lead single. The song was released just weeks before the album, at the top of June. A fast paced, 90's club banger, with heavy New Jack Swing influence. A style popularized and created by Teddy Riley. "If I Had No Loot" was made with a mixture of original production by the band and two samples (The Wrong Nigga to Fuck Wit" by Ice Cube and "Remix for P Is Free" by Boogie Down Productions). It's a song about fake friends, and fake relationships in general. It begs the question of whether or not someone would be in your life without any personal benefit to themselves. Would you be my friend if I were broke? Would you be my friend if I wasn't famous? Would you be my friend if you didn't need me in general? Fair questions I suppose. Especially for the nou·veau riche and those with a newly acquired fame. The song was partially written by Raphael Saadiq. It has a nontraditional 3 verse format. The song peaked at 7 on the Billboard Hot 100.

The second single and the crown jewel of the album was released that summer in September. "Anniversary" has been a vibe from the first time I heard it to the 1000th time. This a classic song in the style of slow jam, and a must have on any slow jam mix. The song is laid back, and full of strings to paint the mood. The album version of the song is just over 9 minutes long. The longest on the album and the second to last song on the album. They knew exactly what they were doing. Well played gentlemen. Well played. The song is about celebrating your love. Getting to a place in your relationship that you feel comfortable enough to create a moment that commemorates the time that you've spent together. What I like most about the song is that it doesn't specify what type of anniversary is being celebrated. It was written open ended. Whether you're celebrating your casual romantic relationship, a newly formed dating situationship (whatever the hell those are), or 10 years of marriage like me in a few months, this is a song for you. It fits all relationship circumstances when there's something to celebrate. The song did well on the charts peaking at 10 on the Billboard Hot 100 and up to 2 on the R&B charts. Isn't it strange how love songs by... "urban" artist always do better on R&B charts as opposed to broader scoped charts like Billboard? Peculiar right? No way in hell is "If I Had No Loot" a better song in any way, than "Anniversary", but it did better on the charts. The radio edit of the song was cut by roughly 1/2 down to 3:57, and your local quiet storm mix was all the better for it.

Tony! Toni! Toné! rode the wave of "Anniversary" from September to the start of the next year until they followed up with their 3rd single "(Lay Your Head on My) Pillow". The perfect follow up to "Anniversary". "(Lay Your Head on My) Pillow" is a ballad, that at first listen may only sound like a song about hanging with your lady. A deeper listen lets you know that this song is only about a night of pleasure with said lady. Discreetly hidden lyrics of certain sexual acts and a narration of how the night will go are the heart of the song. It's really hard to not love this song. The band paired the song with a controversial nudity laden video. The country just wasn't ready for a music video with a dozen people in the nude. This was pre BET-uncut and it still has a far more artistic use of nudity than the comparative content out there at the time, but in the end they had to dull down the use of the bare bodies before BET or MTV would play it. My how we've risen or descended a long way since then. The song peaked at 31 on the Billboard Hot 100 and all the way up to 4 on the R&B charts.

The time spent in Trinidad had an effect on the band. One of the reasons they decided to leave Los Angeles was to experience new things and isolate themselves from the personal and professional things that were swaying their focus. It's this time away that allowed the band to create "Slow Wine". "Slow Wine" was the 5th and final single off of the album. With all the success Tony! Toni! Toné! built on the quiet storm circuit with their steamy singles, it was an easy decision to return to that formula. "Slow Wine" is sultry, and intentional. They make no qualms about what that song is meant for, and I'm sure it was used well...and repeatedly. Dwayne Wiggins was one of the writers for the song, and he also sung lead. The song is a fusion of their signature vintage Cali sound and the influence of the carribean. Very laid back and sexy. "Slow Wine" never cracked the Billboard Hot 100, but it performed decently on the R&B charts, peaking at 21. It spent a couple of weeks on the chart before it disapeared, but it kind of became a cult classic amongst R&B tastemakers like myself.

Sons of Soul went on to sell 2 million copies along the span of their 5 single run and a world tour as the opening act for Janet Jackson. It's not the album that the so called purists like the most from Tony! Toni! Toné!, but it is their most successful album overall. Troubles from touring and wandering interest broke the group up, briefly before they came together for the final album. *Sons of Soul* had a very diverse cast and crew on the production side, with hip hop influences and programming being guided by Ali Shaheed Muhammad, and mastering done by Herb Powers in New York. For such a monetarily successful album, I don't know too many R&B lovers that have listened to *Sons of Soul*, but it's definitely worth an introduction. You're welcome ☺.

FUN FACT: The video for "Slow Wine" was shot while the group was back in California. Raphael actually didn't appear in the video though. There was a lookalike used in his place. The back story of why he didn't make the video has been mired in confusion over the years. Everything from a group rift, to personal choice has been reported over the years as to why he wasn't in the video, but noone really knows.

1) What Tony! Toni! Toné! album is your personal favorite?
   Answer:

2) When the group broke up and pursued solo careers, did you continue to be a fan?
   Answer:

3) What is your favorite song on the album?
   Answer:

4) Do you prefer the ballads or the up-tempo songs from Tony! Toni! Toné!?
   Answer:

CHAPTER 16

MAXWELL'S URBAN HANG SUITE

Wait wait WAIT!! Maxwell was only 23 when he made *Maxwell's Urban Hang Suite*? Whatthehowthehell?! How in the hell is it fair, that someone can create something so perfect, and timeless at such a young age? Apparently it's true though. Maxwell grew up being raised by his mother after the untimely death of his father and music was his escape. He taught himself how to play several instruments, and even though he was a shy kid he began performing as a vocalist around 12 years old. Over time Maxwell continued to craft his art and image and by 18 he was working the NYC club circuit. The young Brooklynite, wrote, produced and co-produced over 100 songs before he and his team whittled down what would become the classic that is *Maxwell's Urban Hang Suite*.

Maxwell's Urban Hang Suite was released in 1996 after Maxwell spent a year recording it between NYC and Chicago. Maxwell had recorded the album between early 1994 and 1995, but do to label politics and general disbelief in the success & probability of the album, he was shelved for nearly a year. If he weren't then *Maxwell's Urban Hang Suite* would've dropped the same year as D'angelo's *Brown Sugar*. Like D'angelo, Maxwell is one of the artists that got pinned with that neo-soul label, and people tried to pigeonhole him into this pretend sub-genre. The album had a slow rollout, in the sense that, it wasn't a success out of the gate. Although Maxwell was an artist for the multi-media giant Columbia Records, there didn't seem to be a lot of steam behind his promotion. That's been an unfortunate truth to the demise of many artists, but again after nearly a year his album was released as well as the first single.

"...Til the Cops Come Knockin'" was the first single off of the album. Not quite a ballad and not an up-tempo song either. It was released in May of 1996. Definitely closer to a ballad, but the energy of the song is so damn deliberate. I remember the first time I heard this song, and even as a horny little teen I was thinking, "Damn. Whoever he's talking about is going to have a long night". With all the vibe on this album, I wonder how this was chosen as the lead single. That's not to slight the song at all, because it's an incredible offering. My confusion is based in the range of Maxwell's voice. He has one of the more pronounced falsettos of all time, and can still bobble with the best of them in his normal tenor. At the time of the single, men singing in their falsetto wasn't even that popular. Maxwell starts the song off, in falsetto, asking his woman about a previous "performance" *wink wink*. It's as if he's asking her if the night went the way she wanted it to. He's asking her if she liked some of the things that he tried on her and, frankly, if he could try them again and again. That's the core of this song. The uncontrollable urge to relentlessly want to sleep with your lover, over and over. Until the day escapes you and you've been tucked away so long in your private moments that your loved ones send the police to make sure that you're okay. That's heavy. The song peaked at 98 on the Billboard Hot 100 and spent 3 weeks on the charts.

"Ascension (Don't Ever Wonder)" is the second single from the album. It was released in July of 1996 after "...Til the Cops Come Knockin'" came to a slow boil on the R&B charts. It's one of the longer songs on the album, and falls right in line with Maxwell's signature style of long instrumental preludes, prior to his vocals starting. My favorite piece of this song is the infectious bass line, being walked up and down the ambiance of the song. It's a mid-tempo song that deals with the more spiritual side of love. So much that Maxwell is comparing the feeling of love from that person as the parallel to being closer to GOD. Damn. I mean, damn. Putting the theism aside that's a very deep sentiment. Again, keep in mind that Maxwell was only 23 and probably 22 when he wrote it. Still being introduced to Maxwell as an artist at the time, I loved this song being picked for the second single. Maxwell sings the bulk of this song in his full tenor, but you don't hear his voice at all until :42 seconds into the song. Just a nice falsetto run to let you know the vibe of your next 5 minutes. "Ascension (Don't Ever Wonder)" is a song that could be played at a family get together, a lounge, a party on the beach or while cleaning your house on a Saturday morning. It is completely impossible to be anything other than happy when this song is on for me. This was Maxwell's first taste of commercial success. The song peaked at 36 on the Billboard Hot 100 and 8 on the R&B charts. The song spent 18 weeks in the Billboard Hot 100 and the video for the single faired even better, with it's performance style storyline. This single gave people a chance to sample Maxwell's live performance style, as well as his normal tenor register.

"Sumthin' Sumthin'" was the third single off the album released in December of 1996. It's another mid-tempo song off the album. I imagine this is the type of song that soundtracks a newly dating couple. The song is simply about taking a chance on getting to know someone. It's about stepping outside of your comfort zone and trying a new experience with a stranger that's caught your attention. The single charted middle of the road and peaked at 23 on the R&B charts. Every great album needs a song to frolic to. There was an additional mix of "Sumthin' Sumthin'" made for the *Love Jones* Soundtrack, known as "Mellosmoothe", but make no mistake, that song is not to frolic to. No, no, no. The objective here is far more racy than the brunch in the spring vibe of the original song. If you've never heard "Mellosmoothe", I highly suggest you search and experience it with that special person in your life. Sheeeeeiiiiiiiitttt.

"Whenever Wherever Whatever" is the 7th song on the album and the final single from the project. It's a song made from the vein of desperation. The production is minimal, and Maxwell's vocals serve as an additional instrument on the song. This song is a coffee house performers' dream. It's a very slow, intimate and melancholic song, because it's rooted in that place. There's a hopelessness that comes thru from the very beginning. The desperation is based in not having any direction. Maxwell is saying that he doesn't even care if his woman is in his life just to use him, just please be in his life. Ever felt like that? Have you ever been so attached to someone that you couldn't function without them, even that function was a malfunction? It sucks. The emptiness and pain of being emotionally immobilized, sucks. The very definition of "Can't get right". The album is built as a song cycle. In the story of a romance, and like all romances this song captures the bad times of a relationship. When there are no answers to fix what's ailing and no routes to reunion. "Whenever Wherever Whatever" is one of the shorter songs on the album. It serves as a bridge to the next song on the album "Lonely's the Only Company (I & II). Each song on the album is symbiotic to the next, but these two are some of the more important.

While the rest of the world was focusing on coining artist like Maxwell as a neo-soul artist, he was being a student of the greats. Perfecting his craft, and curating this masterwork. By the end of the year, the album barely cracked the Billboard Hot 100 coming in at 94, but Rolling Stone dubbed it as one of the 10 best albums of 1996. Maxwell received a Grammy nomination and 4 Soul Train music awards for the album as well, but more than anything it garnered him the undying respect of R&B artist all over the globe. At 23 Maxwell's debut performed and felt like the 3rd album of most artists. He was a little ahead of his time and *Maxwell's Urban Hang Suite* belongs on this list.

FUN FACT: The album is built in the form of a song cycle, which means a narrative. It's a story. Maxwell took a very particular love affair that he'd experienced, and from that he wrote/co-wrote, produced/co-produced the entire project. In the liner notes he even thanked her and mentioned that he couldn't have done the album without the experience of knowing her. He never mentioned her by name, but it was well before he dated the perpetually beautiful Ananda Lewis. Lucky mutherfu...never mind. To whoever that mystery lady is, we all thank you as well.

1) What was the first single you heard off of *Maxwell's Urban Hang Suite*?
   Answer:

2) Were you introduced to Maxwell via radio or a video show?
   Answer:

3) What's your favorite performance from Maxwell's MTV Unplugged session?
   Answer:

4) Does *Maxwell's Urban Hang Suite* sound different to you as an adult, if you first heard it as a kid?
   Answer:

CHAPTER 17

ALL THAT I AM

Joe Thomas, professionally known only as Joe was born in Columbus, Georgia and raised in Opelika, Alabama. Apparently my auntie used to babysit him. Pretty cool. Like most great singers, Joe began in the church at a young age playing instruments and singing. After high school Joe moved to New Jersey and continued working on his craft. He wanted to be closer to New York to improve his chances of being discovered. Growing up Joe learned how to play the piano, drums, and guitar. He produced and recorded a 5-song demo and eventually signed to Polygram records by 1992. His debut album *Everything* was a decent introduction to Joe as an artist. Not a bad album at all, but the only thing we walked away from that album knowing is, THIS DUDE CAN SING! *Everything* was a youthful album in context and sentiment. Joe did a great job with the album. It wasn't until his sophomore album that we started seeing Joe as the artist that he is today, which is one of the unsung heroes of R&B.

All That I Am was a re-introduction to Joe of sorts. It was released 4 years after his debut, in 1997. The album came via a new record label (Jive), and a new sound. Joe executive produced the album, with a mild influence from a few heavy hitters of that time including the amazing Gerald Levert. In a rather random act, the lead single "All the Things (Your Man Won't Do)" ended up on the soundtrack of *Don't Be a Menace to South Central While Drinking Your Juice in the Hood*. How the hell does a song that sexy end up as a lead single on a movie that is a spoof comedy? It didn't make sense then and it doesn't make sense now. I'll be damned if it didn't work out for us all though.

"All the Things (Your Man Won't Do)" was released on January 30th of 1996. To this day it's one of my favorite songs of all time. Every element of that song is intimate. All 6 minutes and 21 seconds of it. Joe is a singer's singer, and he could easily sing a song from beginning to end in 3rd gear, but he's patient on "All the Things (Your Man Won't Do). He allows the song to build up in its proper time. I hate nothing more than a singer that over-sings a song. The great ones can just deliver a song. Joe is asking a woman how she could deal with the things that she's dealt with from her man. Challenging her to see him as the better option between himself and her current man. The song is Joe's promise to put her on the pedestal that he thinks she deserves to be on. The song would've done well by itself, and did, but the music video was perfectly executed too. Joe was everywhere, when this song was released. Name a show and he was there performing it. I can remember one particular performance of "All the Things (Your Man Won't Do)", on one of BET's smaller video shows and he began by saying that he's a little horse in the intro. HE STILL KILLED THAT SHIT. The song shot to the top of the charts. It was number 1 on the Billboard Adult R&B charts, and peaked at 11 on the Billboard Hot 100. "All the Things (Your Man Won't Do)" is a crash course on how to properly make a slow jam.

The second single from the album is another song that was originally on a soundtrack. "Don't Wanna Be a Player". It was on the *Booty Call* soundtrack and originally released in April of '97 while "All the Things (Your Man Won't Do)" was still tearing up the charts. It's a mid-tempo song with a more electronic feel to the production style, similar to that of his music from his debut album. I love this song. Joe and a handful of writers were able to conjure a song that spoke to the blues of a raging lothario that was tired of living that life. That's right. Jon Mayer was not the first to do this. Not even close. It was a radio hit, because of its friendly approach to explaining a casual lifestyle in the mid 90's. It wasn't crude or malicious by the standards of then. Who in the hell knows how the song would fair on the moral landscape of 2020. Everything is offensive to someone nowadays. His sentiment should be lauded though. Joe is saying in the song that he's ready for a deeper and more intimate connection than the ones that he'd been sharing with a bevy of women that he'd been filling his time with. Saying that he just needs one woman that really likes him for him, and not for the glitz and glamour that comes with his fame and lifestyle. He'd had his fun and now he feels imprisoned by that lifestyle. The song did well on the charts peaking at 21 on the Billboard Hot 100 and up to 5 on the Billboard R&B/HIP HOP charts.

"Love Scene" was the first official single off of *All That I Am*. It was released in June of 1997 and was the perfect follow up to the previous two singles. Joe and his team were establishing him as the new power balladeer, because every slow song he dropped was an inferno. The song starts with a powerful and brooding bass line, and Joe showing off his top 5 falsettos. "Love Scene" is the third longest song on the album and a concept song. It's written and performed as if Joe is directing the storyboard of a movie scene or a night of passion. Narrating the song in takes. You can visualize each take as Joe sings the song. This is another song that Joe could've shown off his powerful voice and vocal acrobatics, and instead he wisely took his time and brought the song to a slow boil. A huge part of this album's rollout were the music videos that accompanied them. The "Love Scene" video, depicts Joe as a movie director. He and his not so hidden beautiful assistant are directing a love scene and become annoyed with how it's coming out. Joe leaves a note inviting his assistant to the wine cellar and she shows up wearing the dress that the lead actress was wearing in the scene that Joe was trying to capture. Joe and the assistant do a little caressing and pick a bottle of wine from the year '69 * ahem * to…share. Shut up. You get it. The bridge on "Love Scene" is one of my favorites from Joe. It takes on a different energy than the rest of the song. In this particular instance the bridge strays away from the insinuated and flat out says what Joe wants.

The 4th single from the album, "Good Girls", was released in November of 1997. Funny, I can remember when a woman I used to date text me around 2008 and asked me if I'd heard Joe's new song "Good Girls". I just knew that she couldn't be talking about this particular song from his second album in 1997. No way, right? She was. Not a surprise that a song called "Good Girls" could escape her, since she was the furthest thing from one. I said what I said. Back to the music. Joe just kept building that persona of a power balladeer. "Good Girls" is a ballad that, Joe, the same player that was tired of playing the field on "Don't Wanna Be a Player" uses to question why all the good women are always taken. Why are they always unavailable? This song has 3 verses to it. It's Joe venting about his frustrations of meeting the perfect woman only to find out that she is already involved with another man. Joe wrote and produced on this song just as he did the bulk of the album. By this point the album was moderately cooling down on the charts, but "Good Girls" still served as a viable single, following the title track of the album "All That I Am".

"No One Else Comes Close" was the 5th and final single from the album. It was Jive's, famed company for their success on the pop charts (N'Sync/Backstreet Boys/Britney Spears), attempt to throw some points on the board for the pop charts. It was an attempt at a crossover hit, because Joe was an all out, unapologetic urban artist. The song is an acoustic guitar lead song. Lyrically, it's the exact level of sappy necessary for a pop hit. The lighthearted melody is easy to sing along to and easy to remember. When the song was presented to industry titan Clive Davis who was running Jive, he said that he'd love for Joe to do the song, but that he also wanted it on the upcoming album, *Millenium*, of Joe's label mates and pop goliaths Backstreet Boys. I'm sure Joe didn't have a problem with the publishing implications of sharing a song with such a successful act.

By the end of 1997, *All That I Am* ranked at 40 on the Billboard R&B albums and went platinum. Joe was nominated for 4 Soul Train Music awards including Best

R&B single (Male), and Best R&B album (Male). He lost in the Best R&B single (Male) category in 1997 with "All The Things (Your Man Won't Do) to Maxwell's "Ascension (Don't Ever Wonder)". Both incredible songs, but there's no way in hell that "Ascension (Don't Ever Wonder)" is a better song than "All The Things (Your Man Won't Do). Joe wrote, produced or both for every song on the album. His personal fingerprint was all over the project, and most people consider this Joe's breakthrough album. Who he would come to be as a fully encompassed artist was carved out by *All That I Am*, but it wasn't Joe's most successful album. Joe's most monetarily successful album was *My Name Is Joe*, the album that followed *All That I Am*. Another great album, and it almost cracked this list too.

FUN FACT: There were many successful artists on Jive Records while Joe was there. Among that roster was R Kelly. How fortunate of Jive records, right? Over time it was alleged that R Kelly was sabotaging Joe's career. The story is that R Kelly would personally call program directors in staple markets and make demands for them to stop playing Joe's records. Well, less of a demand and more of a threat. He'd threaten to not show up for certain events, or to shadow ban certain markets if they wouldn't oblige. Joe was never able to prove it, but from what we've been unpacking about Kelly over the years this isn't hard to believe.

1) What's your favorite song on the album?
   Answer:

2) Which song was written by Gerald Levert on this album?
   Answer:

3) What is your favorite music video associated with this album?
   Answer:

4) What city is Joe from?
   Answer:

CHAPTER 18

MY LIFE

Okay, so I have a little confession. Maybe it's a big confession. Nonetheless, we're family right? I can be transparent with you…right? Here we go. I am NOT, a Mary J Blige fan. I'm just not. Never really have been honestly. I can remember the first time I heard her on the radio. It was her first single "You Remind Me", and by the end of the song I was thinking "Nope. That's not going to work". That was in 1992. It's 2020. Suffice to say that I was wrong about Auntie Mary. She's grown to be a titan in the industry over the years, with a string of hits that span over 2 decades. That's to be commended. Most people can't even make 2 albums, and Mary is on her 14th. With all that said, I'm just not a fan. Mary's vocal styling and song content has never agreed with me. I don't think it's the music snob in me either, but I could be totally wrong about that. Mary isn't the only much-loved artist that I feel that way about though. Hell, I feel the same way about Tupac. I know. I know, but hell, I said what I said. Another book for another time I supposed. With that said, I'd be some of the haterration that Mary was shrieking about if I denied the greatness of her second album *My Life*.

My Life was released in November of 1994. It's Mary's second album and one of her most popular as well. After the success of her debut *What's the 411?*, Mary wasted no time getting back in the studio after the tour ended. The glaring difference between *What's the 411?* and *My Life* is tone. *My Life* is not an album rooted in happiness. During the album's creation and release Mary had been diagnosed with clinical depression, and she was struggling with both alcohol and drug use. She had a lot of personal things happening in her life and she wanted the album to reflect that. *My Life* was recorded between 1993 and 1994. It was all Mary was focusing on. She wasn't touring or performing at this time. Mary was locked in to her work. So much so that Mary has a writing credit on 14 of the 17 songs. *My Life* is a very personal offering from Mary J Blige. Just as her debut, *My Life* was executive produced by Diddy. I say produced loosely because we all know that Diddy doesn't play any instruments, but he damn sure has the gift of knowing what sounds good. Under Diddy's orchestration the album, feels like the soundtrack to a 70's Blaxploitation film. Fitting since those films focused on some of the more painful moments of the black experience. This was Mary's experience. This was Mary's pain.

"Be Happy" was the lead single off the album. It was released in late October of 1994. The song was a hit. Mary had a very short hiatus from the limelight, but people were certainly ready to hear from her again. "Be Happy" is the building block of the album. It was Mary's rallying cry. It's an up-tempo song made with two different samples, Curtis Mayfield and Marvin Gaye. In fact Curtis Mayfield's influence pops up more than a few times on the album. "Be Happy" is a song Mary wrote about wanting to be happy despite her doubts of the future, and the uncertainty of her relationship. Mary is saying that above all else she just wants to be happy and doesn't really care how she gets there. Fed up with circumstances and happenstance. She just wants to be happy. Mary co-wrote the song with a few other people, including Diddy. Coincidentally "Be Happy" is the last song on the album at 17. The sentiment, the context and the strength of the production, gives you a visual of "Be Happy" holding up the rest of the album. The song did well on the charts too. It peaked at 29 on the Billboard Hot 100 and got all the way up to 6 on the R&B charts. There was a strong push on the album with Mary performing "Be Happy" everywhere that had a mic. After the success of her first album, it wasn't hard to push for a bigger budget, so they spent a few dollars on the music video, with Hype Williams being tapped to coordinate the visuals. To this day, it's one of Mary's more popular songs. A serious bop for sure.

"I'm Going Down" was the second single off the album. It's a cover that was originally recorded by Rose Royce in 1976. Mary's version was released in January of 1995. The song has heavy instrumentation with strings, busy percussion and guitar. Mary floated on this shit. The song is about the heartbreak of being dumped. How everything gets worse day by day with that heartbreak. Another anthem for those that just can't get right. This song has to be on any sad song playlist you make. No exceptions. The video followed the zeitgeist of its predecessor, being a white and black video, with a performance scene. Mary's attire and the narrative of the story fit the 70's roots of the song. Well... most of it at least. Tuh huh. The airplay on Mary's version was heavy in rotation and the song landed her an additional top 40 hit. "I'm Going Down" peaked at 22 on the Billboard Hot 100 and 13 on the R&B charts. The song burned hot for a short month before her next single dropped.

"Mary Jane (All Night Long) was the third single off of the album released in February of 1995. It's a mid-tempo song that feels good. It has a sample of Rick James' "Mary Jane", The Mary Jane Girls "All Night Long" and Teddy Pendergrass's "Close The Door". Unbelievable how 3 certified bangers were welded together to create a new one. This is one of the lighter songs on the album, but the replay value is optimal. It's one of those songs that you put on when it's time to relax on your patio. It puts you in a good mood. Good thing it's the second song on the album, because shit get's dark in places on the album for sure. I love everything about this song. Mary kept her vocals simple, and lighthearted. She let the music do most of the talking. The song peaked at 37 on the Billboard Hot 100 and got a little extra steam with a remix featuring none other than Uncle L (LL Cool J).

"My Life" was never an official single, but of course radio programmers found a way to squeeze in a little rotation. Title tracks aren't always released as singles. In my opinion, this is Mary's most important song. Long before mental health and talking about mental health was all the rage, Mary did this song. "My Life" contains a sample of Roy Ayers "Everybody Loves the Sunshine". It's a slow, personal song. It's intimate. Feels like Mary is sharing a secret with you. The song is about having the strength to move past depression and become a stronger person. Theism aside, I love this song. It's without a doubt my favorite Mary J Blige song ever. She put her foot in this one. Mary talks about doing that which will free you up from the things that are holding you back from being happy. It's a fairly short song at just over 4 minutes. I would've loved for the song to be a little longer. Even if it were only for the purposes of letting the music vamp.

My Life the album debuted at 9 on the Billboard Hot 100 and peaked at 7. However on the R&B charts it debuted at number 1 and stayed there for 8 consecutive weeks. People were not expecting such a dramatic album from the round the way girl that they fell in love with, just a year before. *My Life* was certified at triple platinum by the end of 1995. Mary shared her pain, confusion and story over the course of a 17-song storyline. The bulk of the production is credited to, of course, Diddy and Chucky Thompson. *My Life* had its monetary success for sure and has been raved about by critics over many different platforms, including being ranked at 17 on Rolling Stones Top 50 Female Albums and 57 on Blender's The 100 Greatest American albums of all time. Mary made a time capsule of one of the darkest and troubled times of her life and sprinkled her story all over the world. It allowed her to see that she wasn't alone, and for people to see a different side of her. Not her artist side, but the real Mary. This shtick became her calling card for the next 20 years. As I said before, I'm not a Mary fan, but there is no denying the weight that *My Life* carries.

FUN FACT: At the time of the recording for *My Life*, Uptown Records was falling apart. Diddy (still Puff at the time), had been fired and the label was trying to figure out where the money should go as the label transitioned. Mary was one of the staple artists on the label, and they weren't going to let her suffer. She was a guaranteed meal ticket. The brass allowed Diddy, even after his dismissal, to continue working with Mary as he was working on his own little project called Bad Boy Records. With the leverage to try new things, Diddy used one of his new artists The Notorious B.I.G (Biggie Smalls) on an interlude for the album. What Biggie recorded was so hardcore that they decided to pull the vocals and go another direction. Keith Murray was called in to do a simpler, certainly friendlier, set of vocals for the album that came to be known as the "K. Murray Interlude". Biggies version? Well that went on to be known as the infamous "Who Shot Ya". Recorded somewhere between late 1993 and early 1994, well before Tupac was robbed and shot outside of Quad City Studios. So again...that song was NOT written and recorded as a diss to Tupac. Enough of that please.

1) What is the reason you first heard this album?
   Answer:

2) When you play this album, do you play it in its entirety or only by certain songs?
   Answer:

3) What is your favorite song off of "My Life"?
   Answer:

4) Mary had writing credits on every song but 1 of the 17. Which do you think had the best penmanship?
   Answer:

CHAPTER 19

DON'T BE CRUEL

K-I-N-G. Bobby Brown is and always will be the one and only true king of R&B. Bobby lead in a brand of R&B that has been replicated and mimicked since he broke through as a solo artist. Everything from Bobby's performing style, song content and machismo has been copied by other artists on this list that went on to be great in their own right as well. Bobby was at the forefront of New Jack Swing with Teddy Riley and helped to push the new sound forward. As we all know, Bobby began his career with the famed and legendary group New Edition, and eventually broke out solo after being kicked out of the group. Bobby has been in most of our lives, for all of our lives. He's been active in the music business since 1981 and we're lucky enough to still have him around to share his stories. Bobby's first album was *King of Stage* in 1986, but his most important album is none other than the 1988 classic *Don't Be Cruel*.

Don't Be Cruel was released in June of 1988. It was Bobby's first adult album. I say that because *King of Stage* still had a bubblegum, teenager feel to it. Bobby had grown up though. He'd become a man, on and off stage, and it was time for his music to reflect that. This is a perfect album. Perfect! *Don't Be Cruel* was perfect by every standard from monetary to artistic. The 11-song offering shades all the textures of a relationship and they were all painted in a way that only the King could've done. The jams, the ballads, the energy. Time and documentaries have slowly revealed more and more about that time period for Bobby. Some of it is disturbing and some of it is inspiring, but nevertheless, *Don't Be Cruel* has proven itself to be unfading. I have the same level of joy every time I play this album. It reminds me of the time that my family and I were moving back to the United States.

"Don't Be Cruel" was the lead single and title track of the album. It was released in May of 1988. "Don't Be Cruel" is one of the many songs written and produced by the famed duo (really a trio) of Babyface, La Reid, and Daryl Simmons. All they gave Bobby was heat for this album. This is an up-tempo song with hints of New Jack Swing and traditional R&B. A hint of the old and new is the vibe of the song. "Don't Be Cruel" is about a man (Bobby in this case) doing everything he can to make his woman happy. Over the course of the almost 7 minute, 4 verse song, Bobby gives more and more examples of how he's being taken for granted. Bobby raps 3 of the 4 verses on the song. I love that this song makes it clear that Bobby is fed up. He's tried to wine and dine her. He's tried to give her all of his love. He's tried just about everything and now he sees his own worth. Bobby is giving her one last time to get herself together and appreciate him. KNOW YOUR WORTH KING! "Don't Be Cruel" peaked at number 8 on the Billboard Hot 100 and number 1 on the R&B charts.

"My Prerogative" is the second single from the album, released in October of 1988. It's one the few songs on the album that wasn't produced by the holy trinity of R&B production (Babyface/LA Reid/Daryl Simmons). Teddy Riley produced the song. Riley did the initial production on the song. The song was co-written by Brown, Aaron Hall and Teddy Riley. "My Prerogative" was one of the last songs to be made on the album. Some of the production and recording took place in Los Angeles (R.I.P. KOBE), but Bobby wasn't satisfied with the album. He felt the album was missing the high energy song that he needed for his brand of live performance. It was Brown's idea to travel to New York and meet with producers. Teddy Riley was one of them. "My Prerogative" was as a response to the media about his bad boy image that as it turns out, was NOT just an image. Bobby Brown was the bad boy of R&B before Jodeci, Kellz, and any other macho induced R&B act. They all got it from Bobby. It's an up-tempo song with heavy electronic instruments, aggressive drum patterns and an infectious bass line. Around this time, Bobby had minimal success with his first album and was still trying to make headway as a solo artist. People doubted him, and were questioning why he would want to do anything other than be a member of his already successful group New Edition. "My Prerogative" was Bobby's way of saying that he has the right to do whatever makes him happy and that he isn't going anywhere. Riley did initiate the song, and to be sure that it had the sonic uniform of New Jack Swing, Riley mixed the song too. So Riley definitely had his fingerprint on it. "My Prerogative" was a monster hit. It debuted at 61 on the Billboard Hot 100, but in a few short weeks shot all the way to the top. It was simultaneous number 1 on Billboard's Hot 100 and R&B charts. In addition to its domestic success, "My Prerogative" also charted high internationally. It did well on dance charts everywhere from Sweden to New Zealand. The song has been covered by a few artists over the years, with Britney Spears being the most famous of them all. Britney's version is absolute trash by the way and she had the unmitigated gall to release it as a single and do a video for it. Just...uggggggghhhh.

"Roni" was the 3rd single off of the album. It was released in December of 1988. "Roni" was the first ballad to be released from the album. Damn I love this song. Every moment of this song is epic, from the drums dropping at the beginning to Bobby wailing as the song vamps. "Roni" was written by Babyface and his old

112

group member from The Deele, Darnell Bristol. "Roni" is the second longest song on the album at just under 6 minutes. The production was also handled by Babyface with the assist from his partner LA Reid. This is another 3 verse song, as Bobby raps the last verse on it. I don't think that Bobby could've pulled this song off without Babyface on the background vocals. This song needed a vocal subtlety that only Babyface, Shawn Stockman and Q from 112 could've given it. "Roni" is a song about being smitten. It's a good crush song. It's the type of song that you'd play in the background when you were on the phone with a girl as a teenager in the 90's. Yeah…We did corny shit like that, but we also believed in love and all that it could do for us, unlike the kids of nowadays. Damn I sound old. Let me get back on track. "Roni" is a song about liking a woman so sweet that it would make even the toughest guy drop his guard and take a chance at love. This was a good single to show Bobby's versatility and to break the high energy of the previous two singles. "Roni" scored Bobby another top 10 Billboard Hot 100 single, peaking at number 3 and number 2 on the R&B charts.

"Every Little Step" was the 4th single off of the album. It was released in January of 1989, and the perfect way to start the new year. One of the most iconic songs of the genre. "Every Little Step" was written and produced by, you guessed it, Babyface and LA Reid. It's and up-tempo song that feels mid tempo because of how it was sung. There are lots of subplots to this song that eventually became the title to Bobby's autobiography. LA Reid was dating the singer Pebbles at the time, and wanted to tell her how he felt, so he began writing "Every Little Step "with Babyface. The song was demoed for another act. Bobby heard it and fought to keep it off of his album. He hated it. He was convinced to do the song, and the rest was history. The video for "Every Little Step" is one of the most spoofed, because it's one of the most iconic videos ever. Strange how something so simple could be so timeless. Bobby and his dancers performed on an all white set, with two simple wardrobe changes and a few models strolling, and made a damn classic. The song is so damn good that the average person didn't even realize that the second verse was the exact same thing as the first verse. The album gives you the variant second verse though. "Every Little Step" peaked at number 3 on the Billboard Hot 100 and shot to number 1 on the R&B charts. It also scored Bobby a Grammy for Best Male R&B performance in 1990. A jammington by every measure.

"Rock Witcha" ended the run for "Don't Be Cruel" over a year after it's release. It's another ballad off the album written and produced by…Well. Yeah. You guessed it. Another hit. Bobby was finally being celebrated as the artist he always saw himself as. He was performing at any place that had a stage, and destroying every performance. It was rightfully rated the number 1 album of 1989 and Bobby picked up a Grammy for his troubles, in route to selling 7 million albums. *Don't Be Cruel* solidified Bobby as a solo artist and the blueprint to what modern day male R&B would evolve to from 1989 all the way up to around 2014. Bobby didn't handle this stardom in the healthiest of ways, but you can read his book or watch his story on B.E.T. for that storyline. *Don't Be Cruel* is a time capsule for me, and lots of others.

FUN FACT: I hate to use this as a fact, but apparently, there were some ghost vocals by none other than Ralph Tresvant. As the story goes, Bobby was off on a bender, and nowhere to be found during an important session for "Every Little Step". Like most projects, there was a strict schedule that needed to be adhered to. Working in a pinch Rizzo was called in to do some vocals on the song and fill in for Bobby. I've heard this song fiftyleven times, and I promise you that I've never heard a difference in the tone on the song. It all sounded like Bobby. Sounded. As in past tense. After some research into this story, I'm about 95% sure that the second verse is Ralph Tresvant. Not the second bridge, only the second verse. Take a listen to the song yourself, and see if you can hear a difference in the first and the second verse.

1) What's the best music video from "Don't Be Cruel"?
   Answer:

2) Which song NOT produced by the LaFace brass is your favorite on the album?
   Answer:

3) Can you name 3 artist whose music/style was directly influenced by Bobby Brown and "Don't Be Cruel"?
   Answer:

4) "Don't Be Cruel" is an incredible album full of hits. What's the name of the song that Bobby dropped for a soundtrack around the same time that also charted as a top 5 hit on the Billboard Hot 100?
   Answer:

CHAPTER 20

GHETTO HYMNS

We all have a go to album/song when things are going bad in our relationship or our lives. Well, as far as relationships, I have a few of these albums and songs. I've even got a playlist dedicated to sad songs. I call it "Broken Noses, Broken Hearts". I haven't had to play these songs very much in the last decade or so, but they still hold a place in my heart, because they're just good songs. Every once in a while, I find myself listening again. Not because of you Tiffany. ←----- I have to mention that because my wife has a penchant for withholding home cooked meals when she's mad at me, and I'm skinny enough as it is. Love you dear ☺. Getting back on track, Dave Hollister has a lot to do with a few of my playlists. He's an incredible singer. Dave came to fame as the tacit lead singer of the R&B group Blackstreet. "Before I Let You Go" was the biggest hit Blackstreet had while Dave was still with the group and Dave sung the ever-loving f*ck out of that song. Due to creative and personal differences, Dave left the group and embarked on a solo career. Dave Hollister played the background of the industry for years waiting for his break as a solo artist, and finally got to come forward as a solo star with his cult classic album *Ghetto Hymns*. This album checks a lot of boxes.

Ghetto Hymns was released in May of 1999. By this time we'd all been familiarized with Dave's vocal ability from his work with Tupac, Blackstreet and background vocals for a slew of artist, including Mary J Blige. This is the same year that the top singles for R&B were by TLC with "No Scrubs" and Destiny's Child with "Bills, Bills, Bills" (I see you getting those checks Kandi!!). That's not to say that there wasn't any room for the men, but I'm not sure the world was ready for Dave and this particular scotch. There was something reminiscent of the soul in Dave's voice, while simultaneously sounding fresh and new with the production. There were some heavy hitters called in to create the album too, but we'll get into that later.

"My Favorite Girl" was the lead single from the album. It dropped in March of 1999. Dave co-wrote the song, and well before he became a toxic reality show stalwart and jester, Stevie J produced this banger. "My Favorite Girl" sounds eerie and scary. It's a song about how an affair can turn into an angry and dangerous obsession. Dave gets straight to the point, in the first line of the song, begging the question, of what the hell is wrong with his side chick. He's trying to understand, what part of "I'm never leaving my woman", she can't get thru her thick head. This is a time before having or being a side chick was lauded, and there was still a bit of shame attached to it. Whether it was one encounter or several, Dave is telling his side chick that it's over, he's happy where he is and that she has to leave him alone. It's the second song on the album and the longest as well. "My Favorite Girl" has a heavy funk element to it, with Stevie J's guitar solo and heavy electric guitar presence throughout the song. No matter what the song is about, Dave Hollister will always find a way to sprinkle some of his gospel roots on a song. This was no different, because he took us to chuuuuuch (not church) on this song. "My Favorite Girl" is Hollister's only song to crack the Billboard Hot 100, peaking at 39 and up to 10 on the R&B charts. As much as I love this song, I think people were a little uncomfortable with how dark this song was for that time, and the creepy stalkeresque, black and white video starring Roy Jones Jr and the impeccably beautiful N'Bushe Wright didn't help, but I think it was great storytelling. Dave played the narrator role in the video.

"Baby Mama Drama/It's Alright" are technically the 5th song(s) on the album. "Baby Mama Drama" while melodic, is an aggressive song. It's a mid-tempo song with oratory energy to it. With Dave's skill as a vocalist, I can't help but think that it was a purposeful decision to make this song sound like a monologue ala Sidney Poitier. Dave is in the middle of an argument with his ex and the mother of his child. Things have come to a boil in their relationship. Dave's tired of her using his child to punish him, and her argument is that Dave still owes her. This song was a little before it's time. It's very common nowadays for people to be co-parents before they have conventional parent ties, and not all of those relationships are healthy. This is another story in that likeness. I have friends that listen to this song, and see themselves in it, from both perspectives. In the end there's no resolve. There's just anger, from both sides. The music video was another black and white video, starring Allen Payne with Hollister playing the role of narrator once again. The video starts with Payne on the front lawn of his ex, arguing with her and saying that he hates acting that way in front of his child. They berate each other until the police show up and arrest Payne. Throughout the video it shows Payne's ex being a bad mother and just a general nuisance in Payne's life. Maybe this video is a little one sided, because I know some men that 100% deserve their "Baby Mama Drama". I love this song, but it wasn't considered a success. It spent one week on Billboard peaking at 39, and then made its run on the R&B charts for a few weeks.

"It's Alright" is arguably my favorite song on the album. It's a hidden song. This song has elements of R&B, soul and, of course, gospel. "It's Alright" was written by Dave Hollister & Eugene Peoples and produced by Eugene Peoples and Spanky Williams from the R&B group Men Of Vizion. As I'm writing this, I'm trying to decide whether I should share a personal story with you all or not...Back to the song. "It's Alright" is a mid-tempo song with a heavy bass line, and lots of electronic instruments. I refuse to play this song quietly. If this song were named "Giving it to God", then it would still be apropos. Being at your wits end with a bad situation, and knowing that you've tried everything in your power to make things work is a terrible feeling. This song is about making peace with that feeling. Hollister goes on about how his woman's been doing everything to ruin the family. He accuses her of being selfish and destructive. My favorite part of the song is Dave, trying to explain to her that she's just pushing him away, as she tries to hurt him. There are several points of the song where Dave goes full choir director. Dave's calling card as a vocalist has always been the power and fluidity of his voice, but he throws his falsetto around a bit on this one. If you've ever heard a Dave Hollister led song, you've likely said, "That boy sang the hell out of that song!" So yeah, Dave got super busy on this song. This song was released as a single with a video and it didn't even chart, but it's a monster of a song, with unlimited replay value.

"Can't Stay" was released as a single in early 2000. It's a ballad. "Can't Stay" comes on directly after the "Cheaterlude" on the album. It's a last straw type of song. Hollister wrote the song and it was co-produced with Eugene Peoples. The song is about watching your relationship deteriorate. Often relationships start off the way that Dave describes in the song. Passionate with good intention and promise. Overtime you see things getting worse in the relationship and even though you condition yourself to take more and more of what you dislike in the name of love, we all have a breaking point. This is the soundtrack to a breaking point. My favorite part of the song is the bridge. The bridge is filled with production and a choir style vocal arrangement. Of course. You didn't think that Dave was going to let this song get away without sprinkling just a smidge of chuuuuuuch on it did you? In the words of the infamous Clay Davis "Sheeeeeiiiiiiiiiit"

"Keep Forgettin'" is the 11th song on the album. Made from a slowed down sample from Michael McDonald and The Doobie Brothers fame. "Keep Forgettin'" is funky. It's a mid-tempo song with a lot of attitude. The construction of the song is short, when you consider lyric and song composition, but the track is just over 5 minutes long. The darkness is the lifeline of the song. On the first verse Dave politely sets the stage, but he goes full throttle on the second verse with the vocals. A short but appropriate transition for the song and Dave delivered it masterfully. The song is about reminding yourself that the fumes of what you liked/loved about someone are just that. Fumes. Memories. Moments that may never be captured again, and you can't let that make you forget the things that they've taken you through. You can't "Keep Forgettin'" that you're not in love anymore and the person you used to love is no more. I'm not sure how the decision to not release this song as a single was made, but I think that was a mistake. This song would have done well on the radio.

"My Feelin's" is the longest song on the album. This is entirely too sad a song to be called a ballad just because it's slow. This is something different. Lenny Williams would be proud of the song and sentiment. Dave co-wrote this song about falling short as the man in a relationship and losing his lover over his misstep. What's an R&B album without some good old-fashioned begging on it right? Well you can check that box. The song is very sad. If regret had a sound, it would be this song. It's one of the songs on the album that has some clear self-reflection to it. It can be a hard listen for someone in the midst of his or her own self caused storm. I think the song being on this album is appropriate. A recurring theme of the album is love going astray, and like it or not, sometimes it's your fault and yours alone.

Ghetto Hymns was eventually certified gold by the end of 2000, but it wasn't Hollister's most successful album by the rubric of charts and awards. The album was executive produced by Erick Sermon of EPMD fame and Dave Hollister. *Ghetto Hymns* is just over an hour long, and Dave didn't receive any nominations for this work. It was going to be tough sledding for him either way with some of the songs that dominated the charts that year. By the end of the year, *Ghetto Hymns* finished at 5 on the R&B charts. The empty suits in the front office of DreamWorks Records deemed the album a nominal success, but it's certainly lasted the test of time. This is one of the unfortunate incidents where the impact didn't match the money involved. Nothing is killing music faster than the music business. This album was painted with production by Jazze Pha, Redman, Erick Sermon and Dave himself. This is one of the albums that I prescribe to anyone going thru relationship problems. You can almost put the album on shuffle and land on something that speaks to your situation. A must have in any R&B lovers' collection.

FUN FACT: Dave Hollister is a first cousin to K-Ci and JoJo Hailey of Jodeci. Yeah. You just read that. He's also a first cousin with Calvin Richardson and, by marriage, Fantasia Barrino. Something is definitely working in that family's gene pool in terms of talent. When Jodeci moved to New York to work on their first album, not only did Dave live with them, he also did background vocals on quite a few of the songs for the album. Also, "Gotta Love" and "I'm Still Waiting" were specifically written by Dalvin Degrate for Dave, but it was decided to be put on Jodeci's debut album. I'd say it worked out for everyone either way.

1) Did you own this CD when it came out?
Answer:

2) What one word would you use to describe this album?
Answer:

3) What one song would you say best captures the context of this album?
Answer:

4) What is your favorite music video from this album?
Answer:

CHAPTER 21

112

Listen, there aren't many albums that can be called perfect, but I'll be damned if 112's debut album isn't one of them. I could argue that their first 3 albums are classics. People have short memories, but I have to remind you that there was a time that an R&B album was considered incomplete until Diddy gave it his blessing. When he got ahold of these 4 wildly talented young men from Atlanta, you just knew that great things were on the horizon. Originally known as Forte, the group changed their name to 112 after a successful impromptu audition with Diddy outside of club 112 in Atlanta. Seemed fitting, and shortly afterwards the group was living in New York and working with great young producers including Tim & Bob, Stevie J and the legendary R&B producer Chucky Thompson. I always wondered how they ended up on Frankie's album *My Heart Belongs To You* but I see the connection now. They were still teenagers at this time, but there was precisely nothing kiddie about what they were in the studio creating. *112* was recorded between 1995-1996, and finally released in August of 1996. The final product was a 19-song jewel, compounded with ballads and bangers. The album starts with what would become one of the staples of a 112 album, an incredible intro, but after that...man!! It's going to be extremely hard to try and do a quick cover of this album, because I think every song is important.

"Now That We're Done" is the first song, but the second track for the album. It was originally written and produced by the well-known writing/producing duo of Tim & Bob with the assist from Wanya Morris for Boyz II Men's eagerly awaited album *II*. The empty suits in the front office of Motown, foiled those plan and 112 became the recipients of a few classic records. I remember the first time that I heard this song and thinking to myself, "Is that Wanya in the background vocals?" It was. I guess I've always listened to songs in their elemental stage before their totality. Yeah. I was a strange kid in that regard, but it's allowed me to appreciate music on a deeper level as the years have gone by. The song was recorded in the Hit Factory in New York City. "Now That We're Done" is a sexy ass song. The song buds slowly as Slim tiptoes into the first verse. The second verse is split between a vocally relaxed Mike (112's resident choir boy a la The Five Heartbeats) and Daron (the Wanya of the group). Q doesn't have a lead on this song, but his smooth vocals are the most prevalent on the hook. What I love about this song is that it does a great job of captivating and story lining the moment and the thoughts attached to the first 5 minutes right after you've made love to someone. The songwriter in me also likes that a couple of lewd sexual acts were so brilliantly hidden in plain sight on the first verse. HA!! Go read the lyrics. I'll get sued if I put them in this book. Over the years Slim was always the group member to sing these kinds of lyrics, just like he did on the first verse of "You Already Know" and the first verse of "Peaches & Cream". I SEE YOU SLIM! "Now That We're Done" is one of the longest songs on the album, which makes sense from a context stance. What the song is replicating is a moment that should be savored as long as possible.

Should we talk about "Pleasure & Pain"? YES. However for the sake of moving this along, I'll just say that it too is an incredible song and this is an album that you can simply press play and relax. There's no need to skip even one song on this album, and that's what makes it perfect. We will however skip forward to "Cupid" for the review though. "Cupid" was released as a single. It's an important single because it was partly produced by group member Daron. It's Daron's first big production credit. Like any R&B artist of that time, 112 wanted to work with Babyface. The man was still churning out timeless hits, and they wanted some of that magic sprinkled on their album. Unfortunately their budget had champagne taste and kool aid money. Babyface was too busy and cost too damn much, so Daron and Arnold Hennings decided to take a jab at a LaFace type of record and "Cupid" is what grew from that void. "Cupid" was recorded in Diddy's personal studio Daddy's House Recording Studios. "Cupid" is a piece of minimalism. Although the group is beyond capable of a richer brand of harmony, they kept it very simple. There's a sing along feel to the record. "Cupid" is a ballad, totally led by Slim. "Cupid" is saying that love is true. It will feel real, sound real, and be real. It's written as if Slim is begging for his girl's trust. The song is a smash to this day. As a single it performed well on radio and on the video shows. "Cupid" peaked at 13 on the Billboard Hot 100 and got all the way up to 2 on the R&B charts becoming a platinum single and their third consecutive top 40 hit.

"Why Does" is one of the better ballads that 112 has in their catalog. It comes towards the end of the album as the 16th track. Produced by none other than Stevie J, as the resident hit man on this project, with Diddy in tow. "Why Does" is a slow, sensual, brooding song that couldn't have been built better. Q sings the first verse and it's as smooth as a hot knife on butter. The only person that could've delivered that first verse even closely to what Q did, would have been Shawn Stockman. Mike sings the second verse and takes the intensity of the song up a notch. Powerful and appropriate is probably the best way to describe his delivery. Mike has an old soul. Every time he sings it reminds me of all the soul singers with gospel backgrounds. Mike has always had the most adult voice of the group, so him bringing up the rear of the song makes sense. The climate of the song takes a turn with the Slim led bridge. The song moves from hopelessly in love, to "What went wrong?" The sentiment is weaved in seamlessly, but it's still there as Slim wonders how a love so sweet, could leave him alone, when he thought everything was going so great. "Why Does" isn't a very long song at just over 4 minutes, and could have easily been used as another single. It ended up being just one of the stronger songs on the album in the end.

"This Is Your Day" is the 17th song on the album. It was written and produced by none other than Al B Sure. This song has a lot of personal value to me because, for a while, it was the song I would sing at auditions, if I didn't sing one of my own. "This Is Your Day" is a lighthearted mid-tempo song, with an acoustic guitar lead. The song is made in vocals more than music. Not many artists can carry a song like "This Is Your Day" because they'd need to hide their shortcomings as vocalists within the plain sight of the production. It's easy to like this song. "This Is Your Day" is about being of service to the person you love, and doing whatever they want or need to be happy. Daron sings the first verse, and Q sings the second, which is interesting, because Daron is usually brought in later on songs to heighten the intensity, and Q usually starts the song because he's just a smoother vocalist. Shaking things up on the songs' delivery makes it a little more interesting than some of the other songs on the album, and shows the versatility of 112, even at such a young stage of their careers.

112 was a strong debut album. By the end of the year, the album sold over 2 million copies, finished at 37 on the Billboard Hot 100 and got all the way up to 5 on the R&B charts. *112* only generated 3 singles (4 if you want to count the remix of "Only You" featuring the Notorious B.I.G. and the newly signed Mase' debut), but it was a great rollout and it allowed the introduction to 112 to unfold slowly. There were no #1 singles from the album but it would be hard to consider *112* as anything other than a #1 album. No need to discuss the other key songs on this album like "Call My Name", "Can I Touch You", or "I Can't Believe" (featuring Faith Evans). If you know R&B, this is an album that left an imprint on your psyche. If you weren't aware of this album and it's greatness... you're welcome ☺.

FUN FACT: 112 being vocalists and songwriters, were naturally fans of Babyface. They really wanted to work with Babyface on their project. That's how "Cupid" came about. That's the part that everyone knows. What most people don't know is that 112 even did a private audition for Babyface in an attempt to convince him to come under budget and work with them. Budget was the main problem in the dealing. They were a new act on a growing label, and quite frankly, just couldn't afford Babyface. At that time, working with Babyface on a song pretty much guaranteed a "hit", so of course the tax was appropriate. Babyface decided to not come under budget and work with 112, forcing Daron Jones and Arnold Hennings to take a D.I.Y. approach towards a Babyface song. If it weren't for Babyface and his refusal to bend, we would've never been gifted "Cupid". There's a lesson in there somewhere.

1) What is your favorite song on the album?
   Answer:

2) Who is your favorite vocalist in the group?
   Answer:

3) Do you prefer 112 doing ballads or up-tempo songs?
   Answer:

4) Which group is better between 112 and Jagged Edge? (Ridiculous. I agree, but some people think this is an actual question.)
   Answer:

CHAPTER 22

ACOUSTIC SOUL

India Arie was a much-needed, and very necessary breath of fresh air at a time that the women of the music scene were being overtly sexualized in song and video. The women were becoming more and more naked in the videos, and offered up as nothing more than props for a male driven industry. India helped to change the winds of that stigma. India was unique, as a vocalist, performer and talent for that time, but her success bred a lot of "earthy" female performers. I hate using that term, but it's the only one I know that everyone can grasp. India was partially raised between Denver and Atlanta and her music is reflective of that. Her mother was once signed to Motown, so music has always been an important part of India's life. India began playing instruments at an early age, but the acoustic guitar really caught her attention and she stuck with it. Her personal interest took her to SCAD in Savannah, Georgia where she discovered that her songwriting connected her to people in a way that allowed her to understand the world better, and she crafted her performance skills. As a songwriter, I can understand that. Writing a song is a person's way of reaching out to the universe for connection. Returning to Atlanta and performing led India to being discovered by legendary executive Kedar Massenburg. Kedar had already seen massive success in his career as an executive with D'Angelo and Erykah Badu, so he was comfortable with the idea of breaking such a fresh, new artist. By 1999 India signed with Motown Records and began recording her debut album *Acoustic Soul*. *Acoustic Soul* was released in March of 2001. Arie was one of the main producers on the album.

"Video" was the first single from the album, and unfortunately, it made perfect sense. India, this chocolate woman with natural hair, homemade clothing, draped in crystals and flowers while holding a guitar was being presented to a world that had become used to their divas being light skinned with long hair and decorated with way more glitz and glamour than she was offering. "Video" is a proclamation of India's identity. What I love about the song is that, she gets this message across in the most polite and unapologetic way. She was saying, I'm me and I'm happy with being me. That kind of confidence is an act of bravery in a world full of people hell bent on being carbon copies of what they're told to admire. "Video" was released as a single in February of 2001, a month prior to the album release. The song was produced by India Arie and Carlos Broady, who was one of the original Hitmen from BadBoy Records. "Video" is about women doing what they feel is right while determining their own identity as a woman. For India, this means not needing to synthesize her image with plastic surgery, fake hair, fake eyelashes, expensive clothes, etc.; and to love who she is and see her own beauty as unique. On the music video for "Video" there's a scene where India gets dragged upstairs by a few "video girl" types to an audition. They're all on the auditioning stage and India looks so uncomfortable. She's not quite sure what she's supposed to be doing while the other women are dancing and, essentially, selling themselves. One thing that stands out for me in concern to this video is India, never looks at them with disdain or judgment. India never looks down on them, and that's an element of the song that I love. She's not saying that her way of living is right, and that anything outside of that is wrong. India is using "Video" to say that being happy with your perfectly imperfect self is what works for her own personal sensibilities. "Video" peaked on Billboard Hot 100 at 47 and got all the way up to 9 on the R&B charts.

"Brown Skin" is the 4th song on the album and the second single to be released. "Brown Skin" has a tribal chant to it. It's carnal. This is what an India Arie "baby making" song sounds like. She used this song to talk about how attracted she is to black men. On a deeper level how attracted she is to the reflection of herself that she sees in them. So much to the point that she doesn't know where their skin begins and hers ends. "Brown Skin" is a song I've always been able to associate with, because I **LOVE** black women. Yep. I **LOVE** everything about them. I LOVE how incredibly beautiful they are and how I can see the better parts of myself in them. I find them sexy. Of course none sexier than my psych...I mean my wife. My wife, but there's a universal beauty in all black women. "Brown Skin" is a song about India's sexual attraction to all the things that come with that "Brown Skin". The song was co-written and co-produced by India Arie and Mark Batson, a well-known producer across genres. India uses "Brown Skin" to question where her man's roots are, why his skin is so beautiful and why she can't resist it. "Brown Skin" is a good second single, proceeding "Video". "Video" is a declaration of independence, and bravery. What better way to follow up such a stance other than to claim domain over ones identity as a sexual being. The song isn't lewd or forward for that matter, but it is indicative of India and her more sensual side. The song wasn't a hit by the metric of charts or even money for that matter, but it was a much-needed statement in a time that attraction was being based on very loosely ethical things like money and materialism. "Brown Skin" didn't even break into the top 100 songs on the Billboard main charts, and only peaked to 39 on the R&B charts. "Brown Skin" wasn't nearly as strong a single as "Video", but it was a necessary step to introduce this fresh new artist.

"Strength, Courage & Wisdom" is the 5th song on the album. Of all the songs on the album that speak to individuality and the bravery that it takes to live as an individual in this world, this is the one that speaks the loudest. The song reads like a story of stepping out on faith and confidence to let the world know that she exists. India wrote this song, and co-produced with Mark Batson. "Strength, Courage & Wisdom" is a song that people have found value in as a mantra or anthem as they come out of a personal hardship. It's been the sunshine after the rain for many people. The album version is beautiful, but I enjoy India's' acoustic live version as well. It was released as a single in January of 2001 and peaked at 16 on the R&B charts.

"Ready for Love" is the 8th song on the album and also the third and last single to be released from *Acoustic Soul*. "Ready for Love" is a slow, intentionally dejected song. It's heavily acoustic led, and I love that because you're forced to get lost in her voice and her lyrics. My favorite vocalists can cover the act of pelting powerfully and simply delivering a song. India simply delivers this beautiful song. The sign of a great artist is being able to create something that no one else could recreate, and although India has hit that mark several time over her career, this was the first time. Absolutely no other vocalist could redo this song to the greatness that India had. There's so much left to the interpretation of this song. Like any good piece of artwork, there's just enough space to allow the patron to decipher what they choose from it. For me, I see "Ready for Love" as India inviting love to enter her life. Lyrically she's telling the cosmos that she's done her self work, and she's ready to love and to receive love. Some people hear this song and hear a desperation for love, but I don't. I hear preparedness and maybe even a hint of impatience in the waiting, but that's not desperation. That's different. "Ready for Love" isn't built like the average song. There's no real structure to the song. There's no repeated bridge, or a sanctioned hook/chorus. She's just delivering the song. Just speaking, if you will. It's a speech, or maybe more appropriately an invocation. "Ready for Love" is a spell, inviting love into her life. That's just my interpretation. The music video is a performance style video with India surrounded by a crowd of people. Some as couples. Interestingly enough the crowd has a few of my favorite voices in attendance, Glenn Lewis, Freddie Jackson, Anthony Hamilton, and India's' future boyfriend Musiq Soulchild. "Ready for Love" proved to be one of the strongest singles for India, peaking at 25 on the Billboard Hot 100 and all the way up to 12 on the R&B charts.

Acoustic Soul went double platinum album and finished at 97 on the Billboard 200 and 39 on the R&B charts. India also garnered 7 Grammy nominations for the album, including album of the year and Best R&B album. Seven. Not that awards or nominations are the scale of a great album, but it can be indicative.

Unfortunately India was completely fleeced of a Grammy for her first album. There were two moments in modern music history I can recall that music was taking a bad turn in the appreciation of what's important. The second time was the day that "Candy Shop" by 50 Cent (a song I love, might I add) went to #1 on 106 & Park, even though "Ordinary People" by John Legend had come out the same day. The first time was the night of the 44th Grammy awards, when I had to watch India Arie get robbed 7 times. I couldn't have been more disgusted, and it's the main reason that I don't really watch award shows or even care about music awards. There is precisely no way in hell that India Arie should've walked away with zero Grammy's that night. Nobody at the Grammy's will ever admit this but; India was very specifically put up against Alicia Keys, a fellow new artist. Alicia and India couldn't have been more different as artists. Alicia had a more ethnically ambiguous look than India, who was wearing her cultural ethnicity with way more intention. Alicia had a much more radio friendly, poppy sound to her music, while India maintained her soulful independent sound. Alicia's song lyrics were much lighter in context than those that India's lyrical content dealt with. India's album was about everything from romantic love, love of self, and self-actualization. Counted in all of those offenses that India had to suffer on that Grammy night, was her losses to Alicia Keys in the following categories Best R&B Album, Song of the year, Best R&B song, Best new artist and Best R&B vocal performance. Yeah. You read that right. India Arie lost best R&B VOCAL performance to Alicia Keys. I want to be clear here, Alicia Keys can sing. She can, but there is no way that she is a better vocalist than India Arie. Sorry not sorry. My personal opinion? I think Alicia Keys won because the people that voted found her look more acceptable than India's'. What a shame. The silver lining is India went on to make her sophomore album *Voyage to India* and finally got 2 of those elusive Grammy awards.

FUN FACT: India Arie is the daughter of ex NBA player Ralph Simpson. He was playing for the Denver Rockets of the ABA before they became the Denver Nuggets. India's musical influences as a singer songwriter came from her youth in Denver and the influence of her mothers' roots as a Motown performer. Groomed from a very young age, India always saw herself as a singer but didn't become a songwriter until college. India wrote on all but one song on her debut album of 16 songs.

1) What song from this album best describes India Arie as an artist?
   Answer:

2) Is it a stretch to suggest that India lost all those Grammys to Alicia Keys, based on image?
   Answer:

3) What is your favorite song on this album?
   Answer:

4) Do you prefer "Acoustic Soul" or "Voyage to India" as an overall project?
   Answer:

CHAPTER 23

WHERE I WANNA BE

There aren't many solo artists that I can point to in reference of making a perfect album. There are even less artists I can point to and say that they've done it more than once. Donell Jones is one of those chosen few. Donell's discography is a strong collection. Donell grew up on the rough south side of Chicago. He's the son of a gospel singer and he began singing at the age of 8. By age 12 he was sharpening his skills as a songwriter and he started playing the guitar at 14. He spent a little time in a group called Porché. After a strong run in the local circuit they put their energy into branching outside of the Chicago area. They went to a music convention in DC, where the group was discovered by producer Eddie F (from Heavy D and The Boyz fame) and signed to his new label imprint Untouchables Entertainment. The group broke up shortly after they signed with Untouchable Entertainment but it afforded Donell Jones the opportunity to work as a songwriter for LaFace, because Untouchables Entertainment had a venture deal with LaFace. Jones is an accomplished songwriter, getting his first taste of success, on a national scale, after co-writing Usher's first hit "Think of You" with none other than Faith Evans. It was the second single from Usher's debut album and climbed all the way up to 7 on the R&B charts and checked in at 58 on the Billboard Hot 100. The success of the song caught Babyface's attention. After giving the brass at LaFace an appetizer of his own material, LaFace decided it would be best if they allowed Donell to write and co-produce his debut album. Donell's first album *My Heart* was released in 1996. 1996 was a magical year for music. I like that album. I don't love it, but it's definitely a good album. Not great. Good. The album had moderate success charting in the top 200 on Billboard and up to 30 on the R&B charts. Between the sales of his debut and his work as a writer and producer Donell gave himself the opportunity to record his sophomore album and that's where we start tapping into his real brilliance. *Where I Wanna Be* was released in 1999. Donell Jones had his fingerprint all over the writing and producing of this album, and he took just over a year to create it.

"U Know What's Up" was the lead single off the album. An interesting choice to go with an up-tempo song as the lead single, since the little bit of success he'd found on his debut album came via a cover of Stevie Wonder's classic ballad "Knocks Me Off My Feet". The gamble went well because "U Know What's Up" is Donell Jones most successful single to date. "U Know What's Up" was co-written by a bevy of other writers including DJ Eddie F, Darren Lighty & Anthony Hamilton. At this time Donell Jones had a stronger association with LaFace than he did with Untouchables Entertainment, so it didn't take more than a phone call to get Lisa

"Left Eye" Lopes on the song. There is an album version, without her on it, but she definitely blessed that song and video with her presence. "U Know What's up" is a summer song. The old folks call it music for the jeeps, which means, any song that would be popular at a black barbeque. It's flirty. A song meant to be light hearted and fun. Donell paints the picture of enjoying his day with his friends until he sees a beautiful woman. They flirt. He macks. Again, the song is meant to be a lighthearted song with a sing along vibe. That's the blueprint for most successful singles. The strength of this song as a single was doubled by having a star studded music video attached to it. The video goes from room to room in a building appropriately being called The LaFace Place, giving a sneak peek of what each artist's suite would look like. It wasn't all hands on deck, but you do get an appearance from Left Eye, Usher, Big Boi (½ of the greatest group of all time Outkast. I SAID WHAT I SAID!) , Goodie Mob, The Youngbloodz and a young T.I. as more of a fixture than a feature. The single peaked at 7 on the Billboard Hot 100 and topped all the way to 1 on the R&B charts.

"Shorty (Got Her Eyes on Me)" is the second song on the album. Over time, this is the bag that I've seen Donell operate the best in. The fringe ballad, is a staple of a Donell Jones album. The song was co-written and produced by Donell Jones, Eric Williams from Blackstreet and Wesley Hogges. Slow tempo in nature but it still has a light aggression to it. Maybe that aggression is in the context of the song though. "Shorty (Got Her Eyes on Me)" is about wanting a night at the club full of flirting, to end in going to the hotel together and…you know * wink wink *. Anchored by a guitar lead and a walking bass guitar, this song is super sexy. "Shorty (Got Her Eyes on Me)" is the 1999 version of Teddy Pendergrass "Come Go With Me" in 1979. Both songs have the exact same premise. Donell is a bachelor trying to pull off one of the hardest things ever, which is detaching a woman from her friends in a club/party setting to retreat with him for the night. Many have tried, and many have failed. The whole song Donell is trying to get the woman he's been speaking to all night to come to the hotel with him, but the more important part is him telling her that, no matter what, he's going home with someone. Whether she's the lucky one for the night or not. Okay, so maybe this can be classified as "toxic" for today's ears, but whatever. Shut up. This song is incredible. One of the biggest differences in *My Heart* and *Where I Wanna Be* was the use of live instrumentation, especially the guitar. Donell has said that this song was built from the sound of the live guitar on up. The song did well peaking at 19 on the R&B charts and causing a pure ruckus on the quiet storm circuit, while landing at 80 on the Billboard Hot 100.

"Where I Wanna Be" was the last single on the album and the title track. I think it should've been a little further down the line of the album, but it was placed as the 3rd song on the album. It's a core protein of the album, so I'm not sure why it was so early in the playlist. It seems to be one of the more personal songs on the album, with the writing and the production of the song being done by Donell Jones and Kyle West. At the time, Donell Jones was in a long-term relationship with the mother of his children and they were growing apart at the time. The brilliance of this song is how Donell took a sentiment that a lot of people were feeling, but were never able to put into words and he made it a classic. He had the chords in his head, and called in West to help him build the music he was looking for. Once the live congas and guitar were added they knew they had something that sounded unique. Even to this day, I can't think of a song that takes shape in the manner that "Where I Wanna Be" does. The honesty of not being ready to fully commit to someone that you've already committed to is brave...or cowardly. I guess that truly depends on your personal perspective, but the question is laid out beautifully by Jones. Granted, from an intellectually and emotionally stripped down place, you'd hear this song and just think, "Damn. He spent all that time with her, just to leave her high and dry so that he can be a playa." Maybe there's some truth to that, but a deeper dive shows Jones wafting thru the confusion of his childhood love and his personal identity as a man outside of her. I have a LOT of lady friends that hate this song. Quite a few of them have been burned by this song or even the sentiment of it. They think that men have used this song to shirk monogamy, and I'm sure that's true to an extent, but it wasn't the purpose of this song's creation. The song peaked at 29 on the Billboard Hot 100 and all the way up to 2 on the R&B charts. The music video follows Donell Jones breaking the heart of his girlfriend and immediately going to a bar and having a night with a SEXY chocolate woman. Sheesh. His ex now, starts getting her life together and goes on a date with none other than Karl Kani, while Donell Jones ruins her date by being creepy and standing outside of the window that she and Karl are sitting near. The song and the video were groundbreaking, and the companion piece to this song came on his next album.

"Have You Seen Her" is the 4th song on the album. This song was created the same day that "Shorty (Got Her Eyes on Me)" was created. To be more exact, it was created in the same session. Donell Jones, Eric Williams from Blackstreet and Wesley Hogges put this song together in about 20 minutes. They were in a creative wave, and really felt like they should keep going forward, and this is what came out next. "Have You Seen Her" is about trying to re-create a serendipitous moment. I live in Atlanta, where it's easy to see a beautiful woman at Lenox, Greenbriar or hell even Kroger and NEVER see that woman again. "Have You Seen Her" is a ballad about that moment and hunting, for a lack of better words, to find that moment again and capitalize off of it by engaging that woman. He keeps passing by her on the road and every time he tries to pull up on her he loses her in the city. "Have You Seen Her" has a breathing bass line and live drums that are the life force of the song. It's a well-written song but this song holds its place on the album by maintaining the feel of the album. It was never officially released as a single but because of the sensuality of the song, it eventually crept its way into the heart of radio programmers and airwaves.

"Think About It (Don't Call My Crib)" is the 8th song on the album, but it was the first song recorded for the sophomore effort of Donell. It was totally written and produced by Donell Jones in his home basement studio. He'd been holding on to it since he'd finished up *My Heart*. You can tell that this song was made in a different time period than the rest of the album, because it's the one song on the album that doesn't sound like live instruments were used. It's funny because the average listener just hears another love song. A more concentrated look at the song, is Donell consoling his side chick. He's telling her that she's great, he wants to be with her and give her all the love that he can muster but now just isn't the time. He's begging her to be patient, and while she's being patient, don't call his house and ruin his REAL relationship. I'm sorry, but that's funny as hell to me. The sentiment of this song is one of the hidden messages of the album. The ending comes across as an outro or a separate song, but really it's all the same song. The ending is just Donell being as blunt as possible. He's saying, "You know what this is. Don't complicate it. Let's just enjoy each other when we can, but I don't need the pressure." Admittedly this is a little heartless at the framework of the song, because it's a little manipulative and, well, mean. It's still a strong offering in the middle of a perfect album.

Where I Wanna Be spawned 4 singles and the respect that Donell Jones always deserved. He'd created something that was special. Perfect in my opinion. Donell said "I wanted every song on the album to sound like it could be a single." and he almost pulled that off. "He Won't Hurt You" and "I Wanna Luv U" are two additionally strong songs that could have been singles. Donell's first album didn't move the meter of success by appreciation or monetarily. *My Heart* didn't even go gold, only selling around 200K copies. *Where I Wanna Be* broke the seal for Donell. He'd arrived as a serious contender for R&B royalty. By the end of 1999 *Where I Wanna Be* came in at 35 on the Billboard Hot 100 albums and all the way up to 6 on the R&B albums. It was certified platinum by the end of 1999 as well. Donell had a formula now. It would benefit him on his next album (*Life Goes On*), and in my opinion, to a much greater degree than the formula did on *Where I Wanna Be*.

FUN FACT: *Where I Wanna Be* as a collection of songs, is exactly how Donell was living at that time. Newly formed bachelorhood after a long, serious relationship. It chronicles a young man enjoying his first taste of success and bachelor life at the same time. He's not the only man to journal his discovery of self thru music, but his interpretation of that life definitely stands out and more importantly stood the test of time.

1) Which video linked to this album do you enjoy the most?
   Answer:

2) What song has the most replay value for your personal taste?
   Answer:

3) What is your least favorite song on the album?
   Answer:

4) Do you think that Donell does better with ballads or up-tempo songs?
   Answer:

CHAPTER 24

WHO IS JILL SCOTT?

It was the hottest day in the history of Atlanta. It was a dry 106 June 30, 2012 to be exact. I was still working as a bar manager in Buckhead and my wife was still working for HUD homes as a, I mean, shit I don't know. She's told me a million times but I just couldn't retain it. Sorry Tiff. The more important part is we were still new parents, and basically newlyweds too. We were both working a lot, and working opposite schedules. We were losing each other in the busy of life. All couples go thru it in some capacity. I was missing my wife and, I think, she was missing me too. We hadn't been out in the world enjoying each other's company in months. Tiffany loves Jill Scott. I'm a big fan too. It's kind of hard to not be a fan of Jill, but Tiffany's fandom far outweighs mine. I thought we'd do well to get out. I heard that Jill was coming in town, and started plotting on going months before to be off for that afternoon. This was not a small feat, since I was the closing manager of a bar that stayed open until 3AM everyday not named Sunday. My punishment for being the only sober manager on staff apparently. I said what I said. The night off was secured by closing the bar at 3AM, and coming right back to open it at 8AM. Again, my punishment for being a responsible adult. I was beyond tired, but we were headed to see Jill. We finally made our way to Chastain Park Amphitheater, where she was performing. The show was MC'd by none other than Jazzy Jeff, and opened by Kem, and Anthony Hamilton with the Hamiltones. It was an incredible evening. No other way to say it. Jill left everything on that stage. She didn't even leave the stage for an outfit change. She stayed right out there and suffered the 106° heat wave with us. Full crowd. We were all in it together. The one "outfit" change she did make was right on stage, when she put on her wig! Connected. It was an electric night. One of those moments that you could actually feel the current of life, pulsing thru the veins of the audience. We brought salads, fruit, water, and libations for Tiff, and even candles. That's how desperate we were to make the night memorable and it was. Jill performed EVERY song on her set list with the precision of a seasoned surgeon. Every song sounded exactly like the album version, and just as a random factoid, her background singers (all men) were incredible too. Our marriage rode high off of that one concert for half a year. It re-established a stillness that our young marriage had only experienced briefly pre-parenthood. We needed it. I mean, we needed something else the night of the concert as well, but a certain somebody, who's name starts with a T, went straight to sleep upon entering the house. Tuh huh. Jill took the poetry of her words and voice, and created a synergy in our marriage at a time of need. That's her power. That's Jill Scott. She came to national attention with the release of her first solo album *Who Is Jill Scott? Words and Sounds Vol.1*.

Who Is Jill Scott? Words and Sounds Vol.1 was released in July of 2000 on Hidden Beach Recordings. I was a little late to the party, because I've never been a fan of sampling all music. I'd much prefer that the music and I find each other organically. I didn't first hear Jill until around August of 2000, while sneaking into the girl's dorms of the illustrious Albany State University. It caught my immediate attention because it sounded like the music I grew up on, and I didn't know who it was. I quickly found out who she was, because I saw the music video the next morning. The entire album was recorded in Jill's hometown of Philadelphia. It comes in at just over an hour long at 72 minutes in the form of 18 tracks.

"Love Rain" was the first single off the album. Hidden Beach released it ahead of the album's release. For that time it was odd to release singles without a video attached to it. "Love Rain" is less song in the traditional sense and more of a spoken word piece. Spoken word is one of the many weapons in Jill's arsenal. The song was written by Jill Scott and Vidal Davis, and co-produced by the production duo of Dre & Vidal. "Love Rain" appears twice on the album, with the second version being a hidden track remix with none other than Yaasin Bey (Mos Def). On one hand Jill delivers this piece in a classic slam style, and one could really get lost in her flow. On the other hand, Jill delivered this wildly sexual "song" right up under our noses and we were in such a trance that we didn't even catch the sexual descriptions that she was dropping. I don't want to ruin that revelation for you. Just PLEASE read these lyrics as you listen to the song. Little Jilly from Philly is a grown ass woman. I SEE YOU MA!! The production is up beat and smacks of live instrumentation. I'd listen to this song as an instrumental. It falls into the category of "Get up and clean this damn house" music. The song charted very poorly. The radio just wasn't in the business of playing music that was outside of the current pocket that it was operating in, and there was really no way to push a single without a video at the time too.

"Gettin' In The Way" is the 4th song on the album and the 2nd single. It wasn't until the release of this song and video in November that the album started to pick up any real steam. "Gettin' In The Way" is one of the 8 songs that Jill put together with Dre & Vidal for the album. It's a sassy read, masquerading as a song. Jill uses this ballad styled production to tell a story of her warning the ex of her boyfriend to stop trying to cause trouble in her relationship. Jill wants her out of the way of the happiness that they're building and she's tired of being polite about it. Jill doesn't do any real singing on this song. She's delivering a declaration, so there was really no reason to show off her pipes on this song. The music video, shows Jill walking down the block to finally confront her man's ex that keeps calling her phone, hanging up and spreading rumors about her. It's a funny video. Hell, Jill even snatches ol' girls wig off. The song did well, and finally gave us a proper foreword on Jill and her particular brand of artistry as a writer/singer/performer. "Gettin' In The Way" peaked at 28 on the R&B charts and came very close to breaking into the Billboard Hot 100. This was Jill's first taste of national success.

"A Long Walk" is the 5th song on the album, and the 3rd single. The album's rollout was taking a firm shape with the success of "Gettin' In The Way", so another offering from Jill's work with Dre & Vidal was served up. A long walk is neither up-tempo nor slow. It's simply a vibe. No other way to describe. Vibe is that melodic cross between jazz, R&B, and Hip Hop. A cocktail, that very few artists can make. "A Long Walk" is the longest song on the album, sitting close to 5 minutes. This is the first single that Jill really gets to open up her pipes a little and sing. "A Long Walk" is a great song for people traveling down the road of that ever-infamous "talking" stage of a relationship. It's a song that says, "let's get to know each other". Not just thru words, or actions, but thru frequency. Vibration. What I love most about this song is how it speaks to one of my favorite mantras, which is "be in the moment". "A Long Walk" is a strip down of the moment that 2 people decide to trust each other and expose who they truly are without the assistance of a fancy night on the town or some other opulent experience. Bare-naked truth, built on something as simple as a walk in the park. "A Long Walk" was written by Jill and produced by Dre & Vidal. The song was already doing well on the radio, but the video is what gave us our first taste of Jill's personality and infectious smile. The video starts in black and white, and slowly fills with color. It's the subtle insinuation that, as their day fills with each other's presence, the more colorful (happy) the world around them appears. Brilliant really. The video is also shot from the perspective of Jill's paramour. He walks up on her and her friends on the stoop and they begin to take a walk thru the neighborhood, just enjoying each other's company. Talking about everything and nothing all at the same time. Shout out to Dj Jazzy Jeff for the brief cameo too. "A Long Walk" remains a staple of Jill's live performance sets. The popularity of the song helped it peak on the charts at 43 on the Billboard Hot 100 and all the way up to 9 on the R&B charts.

"The Way" is the 9th song on the album and the last official single too. Written by Jill and produced by main collaborators Dre & Vidal. Keeping with the spirit of songs that could be on the rush hour mix and the quiet storm, "The Way" is a vibe. A song meant to be heard and felt equally. The poet in Jill has a very brilliant way of hiding the sexual innuendo in her songs in plain sight, as evidenced by this song. "The Way" chronicles Jill's day. The same kind of 9 to 5 day that the average person lives. Punching a clock and waiting to be off and do the things that we actually want to do. Jill is questioning whether or not she can push thru the day, with all the harshness and difficulty of everyday life, because, frankly, she's getting it good and on a regular basis. It's all she can think about. So much that she's even skipping a night out with her friends, with plans of another lust filled night with her man. The hook is the song. It's easy to fall in love with this song, even if you didn't know any of the rest of the lyrics, there's no way you can listen to this song more than once and not sing the hook. It's simple. "The Way" is melodic and full of joy. I can remember a time that I was at an open mic event and a young woman sung this song. The gag is, she told the band to play the music, but she didn't know any of the lyrics to the verses. So instead she just vamped where the lyrics of the verse should be and sung the hook in all of it's glory, knowing that the packed house would sing right along, because while the lyrics of the verses help to paint the details of the song, the full view comes from the hook and the vibe. The song was appreciated by Jill's growing audience and peaked at 60 on the Billboard Hot 100 and got all the way up to 15 on the R&B charts.

"He Loves Me (Lyzel in E Flat)" has had a very strange existence. Of course the song was written by Jill Scott, but it was produced by Keith Peltzer. Jill wrote and recorded this song in dedication to her husband at the time Lyzel Williams. Unfortunately/fortunately the marriage ended in 2007 after 6 years. To this day, "He Loves Me (Lyzel in E Flat)" is a fan favorite for Jill. Artists feel in a way that other people don't. I can't imagine what it was like for Jill to perform this song professionally for her fans, while, on the other side of the coin, being the person that has to relive the feelings behind a relationship that failed after 7 years of dating and 6 years of matrimony. She did just that though. A pure professional. In addition to that, "He Loves Me (Lyzel in E Flat)" was a single chosen by the people. Hidden Beach decided to release it as an official single to promote the live album for Jill, but the people and the radio programmers had already thrown it into the airwaves. The song is undeniable. It had to be shared. It doesn't have any true composition from the traditional sense of songwriting. There are no true verses or hooks. It's as free as the wind and beautiful. Even though the song is about how he loves her, the truth is, the song is about her loving/appreciating how much he loves her. "He Loves Me (Lyzel in E Flat)" is a ballad, and even though it didn't fair as well as other singles on the album, peaking at 46 on the R&B charts, Jill did receive a Grammy nomination for Best female R&B Vocal Performance at the 2003 Grammy Awards.

Who Is Jill Scott? Words and Sounds Vol.1 could've been a much, much longer project. It's been reported that Jill wrote and recorded over 50 songs for the album. Maybe that's what the 26 silent tracks are supposed to represent on the CD. In the end, it was edited down to an 18-song masterpiece. Jill has said that around the time of the album, that she would just cry all the time. She was doubting herself. Saying that nobody was going to like the album. Can you believe that? She didn't know if there was a place in the industry for a curvier black woman, wearing her natural hair to succeed. *Who Is Jill Scott? Words and Sounds Vol.1* went on to sell 2.5 million albums and be certified double platinum. A huge success. The album was ranked 17th on the Billboard 200 for the year 2000 and it came in at 2 on the R&B charts. Jill had arrived, and if you have any taste, you're still riding with her. She's shared her truths and talent with us for 20 years, and we're expecting a new installment in 2020.

FUN FACT: Jill began solely as a spoken word artist. She was approached by Questlove of The Roots at an open mic, and he asked her if she writes songs as well. Jill told him that she definitely writes songs. The truth is, she had never written a song in her life. She lied, but she could tell that there was an opportunity hiding behind the question. Jill went on to earn a songwriting credit on the Grammy Award winning "You Got Me" with The Roots.

1) What song is your favorite on this album?
   Answer:

2) What music video is your favorite from the album?
   Answer:

3) Lyrically what song is the best written by Jill on this album?
   Answer:

4) Jill Scott graduated from Temple University. What was her major?
   Answer:

CHAPTER 25

TENDER LOVER

Not many people have been able to have a legendary impact on music in the ways that Babyface has. Babyface has crafted himself into a legendary songwriter, singer/performer, producer and executive. His dedication to his craft has allowed him to check off all of those boxes. Babyface has an endless stream of hits that he's either written, produced, performed or all 3 throughout the 80's to mid 2000's. Most people, including myself, see that time period as the golden era of R&B. Babyface and his partner LA Reid, were right there in the thick of it, and usually leading the charge on all fronts. Babyface grew up a shy kid in a big family. He has 5 brothers, and began writing songs at an early age. Babyface has been active in the music industry since the early 70's, but mostly in the capacity of a musician, playing guitar and keyboard for various groups. It wasn't until Babyface became a vocalist and keyboardist for 80's R&B group The Deele. Their biggest hit, "Two Occasions", came in 1987. The single peaked at 10 on the Billboard Charts and was written by Babyface, and co-produced by Babyface and LA Reid. This was nowhere near Babyfaces' first hit single though. After spending 7 years with The Deele, Babyface and his production partner LA Reid, left the group. Babyface got his first taste of life as a solo artist in 1986, when he released his first album *Lovers*. It was more of a side project for him, as he was taking a break from his group The Deele. In fact a few members were involved in the production process of the album. The album was neither successful or a failure by industry standards. Honestly, I'd rate the album a Meh. It's the audio equivalent of Transformers coming on TV on a rainy Sunday afternoon. You don't mind that it's on, and it may even hold your attention in spots, but ultimately it won't stop you from getting up and making lunch without pausing it first. Babyface has always written and produced, but it wasn't until the release of his 2nd album *Tender Lover* that we began to see Babyface and his brilliance as a solo artist.

Tender Lover was released in 1989. Babyface and LA Reid had been living in Los Angeles for a few years and were hell-bent on finding success as a production team. Babyface and LA Reid began production on the album in 1988, shortly after deciding to break ties with The Deele. The duo had been living in Los Angeles for a few years, and had already planted the roots of their burgeoning production careers there. By the top of 1989, *Tender Lover* was shaped into an 11 track album that plays at just under an hour. Babyface wrote the bulk of the album, and co-wrote the rest of the album. Always a writer first. Production on the album, was split with intention. Babyface would lead the production on the ballads, and LA Reid, would lead the production on the up-tempo songs, both with the assistance of the unsung hero of R&B Daryl Simmons.

The first single off the album was "It's No Crime". It's an upbeat song, falling right in line with the reigning sound of New Jack Swing of that time. Babyface has always had a witty way of taking random sayings and converting them into beautiful songs (End of the Road, Shoot 'em Up Movies, Ready or Not, etc.;). This is no different. The wordplay is simple genius. I love this song. Why not be brave and give love a try? Is it wrong that I love you? Well then charge me as guilty. Babyface's voice and vocal style is much more fostered for ballads, but he's always delivered on the up-tempo songs too. "It's No Crime" was Babyface's first single as a solo artist to crack the Hot 100, coming in at 90. It debuted and peaked to 1 on the R&B charts.

"Tender Lover" is the 2nd song on the album and the title track. The song was co-written by Perri McKissack, better known as Pebbles. SIDEBAR: Have you ever looked into her story? I'm not just talking about her dealings with TLC as their oppress…I mean manager. No. Have you ever looked into her life story? Jeeeeeeez. It's as shady as a magnolia tree. Anyway, Babyface and Pebbles wrote "Tender Lover" together. There were additional background vocals by R&B group TROOP as well. "Tender Lover" was the first, post-album release single, and the second number 1 single on the R&B charts. "Tender Lover" is up-tempo. The sound of the song falls in line with New Jack Swing. There are lots of electronic sounds and organized chaos. "Tender Lover" sounds one way and reads another way. At first listen "Tender Lover" sounds like a song about believing in love. A double take on the song, shows that it's a break up song. Babyface is saying, just because it didn't work out for us, doesn't mean that there's no love for you out there. Keep believing in love. A polite sentiment I guess. "Tender Lover" was a successful single, but it didn't do as well as "It's No Crime". The song peaked at 14 on the Billboard Hot 100 and got all the way to 1 on the R&B charts.

"Whip Appeal" was the 3rd single from the album. Released at the top of 1990 in February. Just in time for Valentine's day. "Whip Appeal" was the first ballad off of the "Tender Lover" album. It's the 7th song on the album, and kind of signifies where the energy of the album begins to take its shift. We were in Babyface's territory now. "Whip Appeal" was also co-written by the wicked witc…I mean Pebbles. Yeah. That's what I meant. Pebbles co-wrote this song. The idea of the song, comes from Babyface being called whipped by his parents when he was dating a young girl as a child. Whipped, meaning that he was super sweet on her, and would do anything she wanted, if it would make her happy. Older country folks, refer to it as "having your nose wide open". Horrible imagery. Same meaning. "Whip Appeal" is a sexy song. Made for the quiet storm, but delivered with a class that only an artist like Babyface could deliver. The music video is in a performance style, with Babyface performing in front of a crowd of women, after he's introduced by Holly Robinson Peete. It was during the casting process for the music video that Babyface met his first wife Tracey Edmonds. She won the role as the lead for the video, but had to back out at the last minute, because she was suffering with chicken pox. They reconnected months later in a chance encounter on the street. "Whip Appeal", to this day, is one of the main songs that people associate with Babyface as a solo artist. "Whip Appeal" peaked all the way up to 6 on the Billboard Hot 100, and landed at 2 on the R&B charts. The song did so well that Babyface got a Grammy and Soul Train nomination for R&B/Male performance. People loved this song worldwide, and it set the tone for what would be some of Babyface's more popular hits over the years.

"Soon as I Get Home" is the 8th song and by far my favorite on the album. What's an R&B album without the quintessential "YOU SHOULD BE WITH ME. I CAN LOVE YOU BETTER" song? I love that there are so many different approaches you can take to this sentiment. You can either beg your heart out devoid of all logic a la Keith Sweat and Lenny Williams, or you can take the approach that Babyface took, by explaining your stance of good intentions. "Soon as I Get Home" is a ballad. Easily the slowest, most mellow song on the entire album. Written and produced by Babyface with LA Reid. Babyface is saying that his love interest not only deserves more from her man, but more so deserves everything. Babyface takes a small sentiment and makes it as verbose as possible. Even proposing to pay her rent to take that off of her plate of stress and responsibilities. He just wants her to be happy. He wants to be her man so much, that he's willing to do anything and he knows he can be better for her than her current man. There's always a man floating around a good woman, biding his time and waiting for his chance at her. In Albany, GA they call this man Jody. More of a title than a name, but, every man should fear Jody. He's always around. "Soon as I Get Home" is the suggestion that, once he takes care of his responsibilities (at work), that he will dedicate his entire day to making her happy. There's a slight departure in the structure of the song here in comparison to a typical Babyface song. There's no bridge to drive home the point of the song, because the message is pretty straightforward. 2 verses and 2 hooks. But no worries, because you get some classic Babyface runs over the repeats on the hook. "Soon as I Get Home" was never truly released as a single but the strength of the record, pushed it onto the airwaves. It's about as quiet storm as a quiet storm song could be. A late night DJ wouldn't be worth their salt if they don't squeeze this song in.

Tender Lover only increased Babyface's persona as a solo artist, while simultaneously expanding the reach of Babyface, LA Reid and Daryl Simmons production arms. Business was booming in the wake of this classic album being released, and Babyface still found time to tour the album and do the occasional pop up on the late nights of Arsenio Hall. Over the span of his career Babyface is seen as one of the greatest songwriters and producers of all time. As he should be. The album sold 3 million copies and finished the year at 14 on the Billboard Hot 100, with two Grammy nominations for "It's No Crime" and 1 for "Whip Appeal". Tender Lover has amazing replay value and groundbreaking in the way of how R&B would be shaped for the next 20 years.

FUN FACT: The title track for this album "Tender Lover" was originally written for none other than Lionel Richie. Babyface and company had no intention of keeping it for Babyface's album. After Lionel Richie passed on the song, it was offered up to the Jacksons. The Jacksons ended up wanting the song, but they waited just a little too long. Babyface had already decided to record it and wanted the song for himself. After recording most of the album he decided that the song would also be the title of the album.

1) What is your favorite song on the album?
   Answer:

2) What is your favorite Babyface song written for other artist?
   Answer:

3) Is there a song on this album that best describes Babyface as a solo artist?
   Answer:

4) Do you prefer to hear Babyface deliver ballads or up-tempo songs?
   Answer:

CHAPTER 26

MARIAH CAREY

The Songbird Supreme, Mariah Carey, has been around since 1990. 1990. Do the quick math on that. That is a reign of 30 years. Well before she was a dominant, five-octave vocal force, capable of going platinum at the drop of a hat, she was just plain old Mariah from Long Island. For a while there was a bit of mystery surrounding Mariah. Everything from her upbringing to her ethnicity was under investigation. Everyone wanted to know where this beautiful woman with the magical voice came from. Mariah was raised in a house that valued music. Her mother was an opera singer and vocal coach. Her father was an engineer. Mariah's parents eloped, due to her maternal grandparents displeasure of her mother dating a black man. Her parents were only married for a short time. Mariah and her younger brother stayed with her mother after the separation. As the years passed, Mariah saw less and less of her father. For the bulk of Mariah's life, she was neglected by her mother's family. They had disowned her mother, which in turn, meant Mariah was disowned as well. Mariah had a natural shyness as a middle child of mixed ethnicity. In her childhood neighborhood, she wasn't black enough, and in her high school neighborhood, she wasn't white enough. It was a cocktail that made Mariah a pariah (see what I did there ☺). It wasn't until high school that Mariah started toying with the instrument of her voice. Her mother would give her lessons from time to time, but she never pushed Mariah to do anything with her gift. After high school, Mariah decided to pursue music as a career while she was attending cosmetology school in Manhattan. Writing and recording her demo with her high school friend the whole while. Failing time after time to get a foot in the industry door, Mariah's luck changed when she met and befriended Brenda Starr. Mariah began doing some background work for her and they became fast friends. Brenda wanted Mariah to succeed. She would take her to industry events, and introduce Mariah to people of influence. Mariah accompanied Starr to a showcase, where she had the chance to meet Tommy Mottola. Carey was giving her demo to another executive and Mottola intercepted it. Truth is he likely saw a beautiful young woman and wanted to broker a conversation with her. On his way home he listened to her demo, and was blown away. He was surprised at her talent. Mottola was running Columbia records at the time. Mariah was signed to Columbia records less than two weeks after that chance encounter. Mottola had big plans for Mariah in the pop sector. She had the voice, and more specifically, the look that VH1 and MTV were looking for at that time. Work on her debut went into immediate production.

Production for Mariah's debut album *Mariah Carey* began in 1988. Although she was a new and unknown artist, there were no expenses spared on her debut album. Carey began working with some prominent producers at the time, in addition to her high school collaborator Ben Marguiles. Carey was flying back and forth from New York to California, working with her new team. All four songs from Mariah's demo made the album, but they were re-worked for a larger more polished sound. The songs on the demo, had a dated, yet classic sound. It became quite the undertaking to modernize the songs, while maintaining their natural charm. Recording took just over a year. *Mariah Carey* was released in June of 1990.

"Vision of Love" was the first single released from the album. It's a ballad with a very 50's doo-wop feel to it. The song was released in May, just one month before the release of the album. Mariah had written "Vision of Love" with collaborator Ben Marguilles, while still in high school, at only 17 years old. The song was recorded in Skyline Studios in New York City. The song is an entendre of sorts. It can be perceived as a song about loving yourself thru strife or a song about the love she has of her man. It's open to interpretation, but Mariah has said that it's a little of both. She alludes to the love of self, on the second verse as she reminisces on her time as a young mixed woman and the stigmas that came with it in her childhood neighborhood. "Vision of Love" debuted at 73 on the Billboard Hot 100. Not bad at all for a new artist. Here's where things get interesting. Music videos were still a rather new expense in the music industry at the time. The empty suits in charge of branding/promotion didn't understand the weight that a music video could carry at then. Columbia was treating Mariah Carey like their franchise player. It ruffled a lot of feathers amongst the companies other artists and executives. She was being prioritized over other artists with a blatancy that some couldn't believe. Was it the talent level or the favoritism of her soon to be husband Tommy Mottola who was running the company at the time? Maybe both. Either way there were 2 different music videos shot for "Vision of Love". Mariah didn't like the original, so another director was brought in and they shot a completely different video for the song. Between the two videos, a whopping $450K was spent in production cost. A drop in the bucket, for what music video budgets would become, but at the time, this was a fortune! When the music video was released, 7 weeks after the single was released, the song shot all the way up to number 1. Columbia records had proven a stance that lives on to this day. Columbia records, like other labels, saw the talent of black music as more marketable if the talent was coming from a white person. Apparently the general public does too. If this wasn't true, then Jazmine Sullivan would be just as successful (if not more) than Adele. But I know you all don't want to go there soooooo...We all know that Mariah is a black woman NOW, but she was most certainly and very specifically marketed as anything but at the time, AND IT WORKED. I know that I was surprised when I saw the video for the first time and realized that a skinny "white woman" was singing this song that had been killing the airwaves for the past few weeks. After the video release, "Vision of Love" stayed at number 1 on the Billboard charts for a month, falling back down to 8 for the next 2 months. The song was a smash. It peaked at number 1 on the Billboard Hot 100 and the R&B charts. With concerns to how the song and Mariah as an artist herself were rolled out, it's no slight to her. I'm just calling a spade a spade. The fact that she was pawned off as a pretty talented white girl, to fool the masses, has nothing to do with the fact that she sung the sh*t out of this song. To this day, it's my favorite Mariah Carey song ever.

"Love Takes Time" was the second single to be released from the album. After the success of "Vision of Love" and the grand and purposeful reveal of Mariah's image, she remained on the ballad train. "Love Takes Time" was a shift from the positive tone that "Vision of Love" had. "Love Takes Time" is a sad song. Plain and pure. The song was written by Carey and Ben Marguilles when they were still in high school. Originally intended to be on her second album, but the label stopped the presses on *Mariah Carey* to ADD this song. The song was both recorded and released in 1990. In September it hit the airwaves. "Love Takes Time" was reworked on the production side by Walter Afanasieff. He'd become a longtime collaborator with Mariah as her career unfolded, and basically took the place of Ben Marguilles. "Love Takes Time" was written by Mariah when she was only 18. It speaks to time being the only cure for healing a broken heart. The song itself is the type of gray, sappy heartbreak song that pop has been known for. "Love Takes Time" only becomes an R&B song for the way that Mariah delivered it. Strong powerful vocals over electronic instruments. Songs like "Love Takes Time" from Mariah's catalogue are the very foundation of other artists like Christina Aguilera's career. The song performed well. It started a little slow, but by its second month on the airwaves "Love Takes Time" became Mariah's second number 1 single on the Billboard Hot 100. "Love Takes Time" didn't have the same energy as "Vision of Love", but it did the job in keeping Mariah at the forefront of people's mind.

"Someday" was released as the third single of *Mariah Carey* in December of 1990. "Someday" was a turn for Mariah as a new artist. Up until "Someday" people had only heard her sing ballads. She didn't have a voice, so to speak, as an artist that could deliver an up-tempo song. This was proof that she'd be capable of that as well. "Someday" was another song written by Mariah Carey and Ben Marguiles. "Someday" was produced by Ric Wake, who'd already had some success as the producer for other songstresses including Diana Ross, Sheena Easton and Taylor Dayne. "Someday" is about being able to tell the person that rejected you that they'll regret not giving you a chance. It's a young song. When Mariah recorded this song for her demo, it was her favorite. Mariah wasn't too pleased with how Ric Wake re-worked the song at first. He'd taken some of the more soulful elements out of the song and replaced them with other instruments. Mariah trusted Ric and re-recorded the song either way. All vocals, including background were done by Mariah. Mariah's famed whistle register was on full display for "Someday". "Someday" did better on the dance charts than it did on the R&B charts, but was still an overall success. The song peaked to 1 on the Billboard Hot 100 and dance charts, and got all the way up to 3 on the R&B charts.

"I Don't Wanna Cry" was the 4th single from the album. The song was released at the top of 1991. This was the first single that Carey wrote with someone other than Marguiles. "I Don't Wanna Cry" was co-written and produced with Narada Michael Walden. Walden had already had some success working with Whitney Houston, Aretha Franklin and Lionel Richie. It's one of the more soulful songs on the album. "I Don't Wanna Cry" is about a relationship gone awry. The relationship has hit a point that there is no course of reconciliation. It's a good song for your "Sad song" playlist. It's slow in tempo, fairly stripped down on the production side and has the big vocal moments that, by that point, we knew Mariah was capable of. Mariah delivered. For a while, Mariah kept this song out of her set, while touring. She didn't have many fond memories of recording the song, due to the production quarrels between herself, Columbia and Walden. "I Don't Wanna Cry" peaked at 1 on the Billboard Hot 100 and stopped at 2 on the R&B charts.

Mariah Carey had a release and rollout that spanned over 1990 and 1991, allowing the album to fall into different categories. In 1990 "Mariah Carey" finished as the 32nd ranked album on the Billboard Hot 100 and 30 on the R&B charts. In 1991 *Mariah Carey* finished as the number 1 album on the Billboard hot 100 and 6 on the R&B charts. The album rollout and run generated 9 million sold copies, 4 number 1 singles, and 2 Grammy Awards including Best New Artist. A star was born. Mariah had already begun working on her second album *Emotions* while promoting *Mariah Carey*. As much as Columbia Records wanted, Mariah never ran from her multi-racial background and *Mariah Carey* became the foundation of a long running career of hits. Mariah Carey is one of the greatest voices of all time and her success has become a case study of longevity thru adaptation.

FUN FACT: When Mariah signed her first recording contract with Columbia Records, it was for roughly $100K. After fulfilling her contract with Columbia Records and severing all ties with husband and manager Tommy Motolla, Mariah signed her second record contract with Virgin Records for a record breaking $100M dollars in 2001. When Virgin didn't make their money back on Carey's film *Glitter*, she was dropped from the company.

1) What is your favorite Mariah Carey song of all time?
   Answer:

2) How many octaves are in Mariah's vocal range?
   Answer:

3) How many songs from Mariah's original demo made her debut album?
   Answer:

4) What is your favorite song off of this album?
   Answer:

CHAPTER 27

PLEASURES U LIKE

Before we get to chopping this fable, I'd like to get a couple of things clear. It's necessary before we proceed. First and foremost, Jon B is one of a few R&B artists to make a perfect album. I went back and forth between whether he's made 2, but ultimately I decided that "Cool Relax" didn't make the cut. Still a good/great album, but not perfect. Secondly, Jon B is **NOT** blue-eyed soul. Stay with me for a moment. Blue-eyed soul isn't really a sub-genre of R&B, but it's a term that we've thrown around since the mid 60's. It became more prevalent in the early 80's with artists like Hall and Oates', Culture Club and Simply Red. It basically means soul music that is performed/recorded by white artists. Jon being the more modern artist, he's typically compared to Justin Timberlake and Robin Thicke. More so Justin Timberlake though. I really hate that comparison. It's shortsighted and unfair to all three of them really, but especially Jon B. When it comes to Jon and Justin, they're both incredible artist/musicians, but of the two Jon B is the only true R&B artist. He's never strayed from R&B, and he's never ventured into another genre for a hit, and there lies the difference. If R&B were a beachfront neighborhood Jon B would live there and be a regular at the local coffee shop. Justin, however, would only have a summer home there and spend 4 months out of the year there. I don't say that to slight JT, but he's simply NOT the R&B artist that Jon B is. Born Jonathon Buck in Rhode Island and raised in Pasadena with a musical family. Jon's mother was a professional concert pianist and his father was a professor of music. His siblings are musicians as well. Jon knew he wanted to be a singer early on. Finding inspiration in the works of greats like Marvin Gaye, Stevie Wonder and his soon to be early mentor, Babyface. Throughout high school, Jon was writing and producing his own songs. Performing at every talent show and expo that he could get in. After high school, Jon dedicated all of his time to writing and producing his demo tape, in search of his first record deal. Jon got the attention of record executive Tracey Edmonds. He was originally brought on as songwriter/producer. At the young age of 18 Jon was already an accomplished multi-instrumentalist. Early in his career he went on to write and produce for several acts including After 7, Color Me Badd and Toni Braxton. When Jon got his chance as an artist, he recorded his first album *Bonafide*. The album was solid and propelled forward by his duet with none other than Babyface. It wasn't too hard to secure this duet because the song is incredible, Babyface respected him, and Tracye Edmonds being Babyface's wife didn't hurt matters too much either. *Bonafide* went on to be a platinum selling album. Jon followed up *Bonafide* with his sophomore effort *Cool Relax*. The distance between the music and Jon's image on *Cool Relax* had slimmed. "Cool Relax" is a good/great album held up by some incredible and classic songs like "Don't Say", "They Don't Know", "Cool Relax", "Are U Still Down" and, my favorite off the album, "I Do (Whatcha Say Boo)". The album went double platinum, and Jon had arrived as a full blown R&B artist and a grown man. He was only 23 when he put out "Cool Relax" but those were grown man feels that he was talking about. After a 4-year hiatus, Jon put out, what I consider to be, the crown jewel of his catalog thus far with *Pleasures U Like*.

Pleasures U Like was released March 20, 2001. I was on the campus of Albany State University and recording my own music at the time. I was already of fan of Jon B. His work on *Cool Relax* was undeniable for me. As a singer/songwriter Jon had made an imprint on my mind. He was making incredible music at a very early stage of his career, and I'd taken notice. *Pleasures U Like* was Jon's first swing at the complete freedom to create, as he'd like. Jon has a writer and producer credit on every song for *Pleasures U Like*. Jon was ready to move on from his business relationships. He'd been under the wings of the Edmonds at Yab Yum for *Bonafide* and *Cool Relax*, and now under the wing of Tracye for her new venture Edmonds Record Group. It was a joint venture with Epic records. There was a rift bubbling between Jon and the brass at the label, and quite frankly they weren't trying to work with him anymore either. The rollout for this brilliant body of work was caught in the crosshairs. It makes sense. If your girlfriend is telling you that she no longer wants to be your girlfriend, then you're less likely to buy her that _____ that she's been eyeballing for 2 weeks, right? To that logic, Jon only got one single & video for *Pleasures U Like*. Talk about cutting off your nose to spite your face. Epic dropped the damn ball here. For an artist on your label to create a masterpiece like *Pleasures U Like* only to have the attention for the album be squandered, is the equivalent of buying a Lamborghini and only putting liability insurance on it. The album was recorded from 1999 to 2000. The overwhelming majority of the album was recorded at Jon's studio (Vibezelect Studios). Jon was focused on controlling his art and his finances.

"Don't Talk" was the only single to be released off of *Pleasures U Like*. The single was released on March 13th. Just one week before the album was released, in an additional attempt to squelch the success of the album. "Don't Talk" was written, produced and performed by Jon B. The single itself, was a turn from the norm for Jon. Jon hadn't been known for making up-tempo songs with club worthy replay value, but there he was, delivering a bop for the ages. Even today in 2020, if you drop that song in a party, people will instantly dance. "Don't Talk" is a fun song. It's a song that refuses to let you feel anything other than cheerful for the span of 4 minutes. It's a song about letting go of your tension, your trepidation your…whatever and enjoying the moment. In this case, enjoying the moment in a club. Just a feel good song. The video was a change for Jon too, because he's dancing all in the video. Having a good time, having drinks, with a faint smoke in the background. I'm sure that was all smoke machine though…right? The video is high energy, with an appearance by R.L. from the group Next. At the time, RL was spending a lot of time in LA, where the video was shot, because he was recording his solo album *RLements* for the Clive Davis' J Records. A good album. Couldn't make this list, but there is some real heat on that album if you've never heard it before. "Don't Talk" did well on the charts, despite the labels efforts to thwart its momentum. The song peaked at 58 on the Billboard Hot 100 and got all the way up to 21 on the R&B charts. If you're only going to throw one punch, I guess this was as good as any. The truth is, the album was full of songs that had single potential. *Pleasures U Like* is a perfect album, and I can play this album without skipping even once, but let's take a look a few more songs on the album.

"Finer Things" is the second track, and the first song on the album. It features rap legend Nas. If I were teaching a master class of what smooth R&B should be, I would definitely have this song in the lesson plan. "Finer Things" has the bones of a Curtis Mayfield jam session and the soul of a ted talk given by Billy Dee Williams circa 1976. Just smooth and ridiculously vibe. The song was produced by Jon B, and when he finished he thought that Nas would sound great on it. They had some talks about doing a collab before, and Jon reignited those talks. Nas was in L.A. and on a random day Jon B returned home to find Nas playing pool in his living room. They went into Jon's home studio and Nas wrote something on the spot. Jon thought the original verses that Nas wrote were incredible but Nas, being the perfectionist that he is, decided to write new verses and the two chose the second version. "Finer Things" is a song with Jon and Nas telling a PYT how her life would be better with him than without him. He can show her the better side of life. You know? The finer things. Jon and Nas walk all over the track with the guitar plucking and the bass line keeping the blood flowing. I love that Jon simply delivered the song. He put a little sauce on his vocals for the later verses, but never comes out of the pocket. The song remains smooth. The type of music you'd put on if you were having a small get together or a 1st date.

"Overjoyed" is the 6th track on the album. It's not a remake of Stevie Wonder's classic. They just have the same namesake. Jon B and Faith (Evans) got together and made "Overjoyed" one of my favorite duets of all time. Jon B wrote and produced "Overjoyed" with Denaine Jones. I'm not sure who invented the "talking" stage of new relationships but "Overjoyed" would be on the mix tape for it. Wait, do people still do that? Do people still make mix tapes for people that they're interested in? If that's not a thing anymore, we need to make it one. Back to the music... "Overjoyed" is a song about finally finding happiness in the exact person you wanted to find it with. That moment where the surprise of who a person is, matches exactly what you need. To be "Overjoyed" in the now that you've been waiting on. Faith is a siren and a powerhouse vocalist. What I love most about this song is that Jon did not get lost singing next to Faith. He not only held his own, Jon matched Faith's vocal power. I honestly didn't know that Jon was capable of it. When I first saw that this was a duet with Faith, I really expected her to wash him, the same way Jennifer Hudson washed Ne-Yo on "Leaving Tonight". Jon has always been more of a smooth, vocal tactician, and less of the type to run all over the place like Faith is prone to do. Jon's ability to deliver a song, is one of my favorite parts of his artistry, so I didn't know he was capable of cutting loose the way he did on this song. "Overjoyed" is a ballad with a piano driven production. The voices compliment each other and I think that this is one of the better songs on both of their resumes.

"Lonely Girl" is the 8th song on the album, and Jon got with Babyface to write and produce this ballad. "Lonely Girl" is slow, with violins and a soulful horn section. I'm a sucker for a good horn section on ballads. They seem to be at home on a well-built ballad like this. "Lonely Girl" isn't the typical song about being better for a woman than the man she's already with. Jon touches on quite a few things on the song. I think he and Babyface did a great job of describing the many different ways a woman can be lonely while IN a relationship. Lonely from being ignored by the man she's with, the intimacy that she deserves in his presence, and his lack of concern to please her in the moment of knowing her...biblically * wink wink *. "Lonely Girl" has a sing along quality to it that makes the song easy to love as well. Jon carries the song and sentiment without having to intensify the vocals. Still a strong showing by Jon, all in all.

"Pleasures U Like" is the title song and the 14th song on the album. "Pleasures U Like" and "Finer Things" are limbs on the same tree. Both are strangely mid-tempo and slow-tempo simultaneously. Easily categorized as either/or, and more importantly, smooth. "Pleasures U Like" feels like the follow up conversation to "Finer Things". Where "Finer Things" is the pitch, "Pleasures U Like" is the follow up with a course of action. "Pleasures U Like" has a Wurlitzer lead with light guitar strumming, and a bass line reminiscent of those that you would've heard on *Brown Sugar*. Production is minimal but evident throughout the song. Jon collaborated on the writing and producing of "Pleasures U Like" with a few people including Shawn

Rivera and Darryl Johnson of AZ YET. Although it is the title track for the album, "Pleasures U Like" is the shortest song on the album at just under 4 minutes. "Pleasures U Like" says "I want to do anything that you're into, and anything that would make you happy". It's not a desperate song. It's a love song presented as service to whatever will make Jon's woman happy, and his yearning to be the root of that happiness.

Listen closely. Since 2001, if I've ever made a slow jam mix/CD/playlist, "Inside" by Jon B made the cut. "Inside" is, hands down, one of the sexiest baby making songs of all time. The contrast of the guitar plucks leading the song and the heavy hi-hats keeping the pace with Jon setting the scene is incredible. Jon wrote and produced the song. I knew that Jon was a multi-instrumentalist but, I was still surprised when I found out that he's playing the guitar lead. "Inside" is the most important song on this album for me. I'm not saying that it's the best song. *Pleasures U Like* is a perfect album. One of the few, and more often than not, there is no best song on a perfect album. I will only say that it's the most important song, because Jon tapped into something special on "Inside" that he'd never tapped into before. Jon was no longer the kid that made nice songs on *Bonafide* or the young man on *Cool Relax*. *Pleasures U Like* was a declaration of his full bloom into manhood and "Inside" is a song that the previous 2 versions of Jon, couldn't have made. "Inside" with all of it's sexual innuendo and cleverly hidden descriptions of certain...acts * wink wink * is one of the first songs I point to when discussing the transition of Jon as an artist.

Pleasures U Like did well despite the lack of support from the Edmonds Music Group. A shame that radio couldn't be a bigger part of the success of this album, but the silver lining is, the music did all the work. Jon put his energy into making an album that was full of singles, and because the music was amazing the album sold organically. *Pleasures U Like* peaked at number 6 on the Billboard Hot 100 for the year and came in at 3 on the R&B charts. The album was certified gold, and eventually platinum. Jon was able to get out of his deal with the Edmonds Music Group. He was a free bird. *Pleasures U Like* didn't have any of the radio hits that his first two albums did, but the artistry was able to outshine the business. That was very important then, and even more important nowadays when there is constantly a room full of empty suits telling the artist what can and can't be marketed. Jon's publishing checks must have been crazy, with him having a hand in all the writing and production as well. He did good business and made one of the few perfect albums ever in the genre of R&B. One last thing, again, let's stop comparing Jon B and other white singers that do R&B. He's earned our respect. Jon B does not DO

R&B. He is R&B, and *Pleasures U Like* is the only proof you'll ever need to distinguish between the two.

FUN FACT: After leaving The Edmonds Music Group following *Pleasures U Like* Jon B, signed with Sanctuary Records. Sanctuary was known for its rock oriented artist as a major independent label. To develop their "urban" (because anything for or beloved by black people is termed "urban") arm of the label, they brought in none other than Matthew Knowles (Beyoncé's dad), and it was him that signed Jon B to a deal. At Sanctuary for his 4th album *Stronger Everyday*, Jon worked with a whole new team including a young musician and songwriter we've all come to know as Tank. I have another fact, that's not so fun, but it's worth mentioning. Jon B has NEVER won an award for his music. He's had a few nominations, but never won. THAT'S F*CKING CRIMINAL! HOW?!

1) What is your favorite song from this album?
   Answer:

2) How were you introduced to this album, considering the lack of radio play attached to it?
   Answer:

3) Which rapper had the best feature on this album?
   Answer:

4) What is your favorite Jon B song ever?
   Answer:

CHAPTER 28

DIARY OF A MAD BAND

Jodeci were the often imitated, never duplicated R&B bad boys hailing from Charlotte, NC. They were two duos of brothers that formed as a group, thanks to sharing a mutual acquaintance. Forging their way thru the industry and cultivating a sound that we'd never heard of before from an R&B group. Signed as a young act to Uptown Records and developed by company intern Sean Combs (Diddy). Jodeci put out their monstrous first album *Forever My Lady*. The album hatched 5 singles, 4 of which were hits, and established a standard that very few could duplicate. Only two groups I can think of honestly. The album had the gigantic hits "Forever My Lady", "Stay", "I'm Still Waiting" and "Come & Talk to Me", after their first single "Gotta Love" failed to chart. *Forever My Lady* went on to be a triple platinum selling album and garnered the group awards for Best R&B album, Best R&B song and Best R&B artist. R&B fans all over the globe rejoiced, and we all knew that something special had just happened for us but could they do it again? As it turns out, yes. Yes they could. More importantly? They did.

The one advantage that Jodeci, walked away from their rollout of *Forever My Lady* with was niche. They knew what people wanted from them now. Jodeci's very first single was "Gotta Love". An up-tempo, new jack swing song. Not a bad song at all, but it was a flop. The song didn't even chart. The world didn't know who Jodeci was until 6 months later when "Forever My Lady" was released as a single in a final attempt to save the project thanks to the vision of Diddy. What they learned is, their audience needed to hear ballads from them. The type of ballads that only Jodeci could deliver was the target moving forward and they built a career off that reality. Jodeci was known for working extremely fast on their projects. They began recording their second album in the summer of 1993 and finished by early November. Jodeci released their second album *Diary of a Mad Band* just a month later in December. The album was released to mixed reviews, and some of them were down right bad. They didn't know what the hell they were talking about though. The album was recorded in New York at the famous Hit Factory. Production and writing was handled by Devante Swing, just as he did on the first album. Devante has always been the "Rza" of Jodeci. The silent leader and the main decision maker, in reference to art and presentation.

"Cry for You" was the lead single released from the album. The song was released in November of 1993, just one month before the album released. People were happy to see the group. Albeit while wearing leather in the desert, but still, they were back. They had new music, and we couldn't wait to go buy the tape. Yes I said tape. "Cry for You" is a slow ballad straight out of the Keith Sweat handbook of begging. "Cry for You" isn't just about begging your woman to come back to you. It's about being willing to share yourself totally to regain your woman's trust and affection. Even if it means being vulnerable enough to cry for her to know that she's important to you. The song shot to number 1 on the R&B charts and stayed there for 5 weeks straight. It peaked at 15 on the Billboard Hot 100. Devante wrote the song and played every instrument on the song as well.

"Feenin'" was the 2nd single from the album. The genius here is that they took a common street slang term and transformed it into a sensual and romantic turn of phrase. "Feenin'" was written and produced by Devante Swing. The single was released on March 8th 1994. "Feenin'" is a slow tempo ballad with the signature sound that Jodeci has come to be known for. There have always been the talks of some ghost production being done by Timbaland and Missy for Devante Swing. The very first song I point to as evidence of that likelihood, is "Feenin'". "Feenin'" just feels like a Timbaland produced song. The infectious drums, the hard slaps, the guitar loop. It's all indicative of all the things that Timbaland injects into his production to this very day. I don't care what Devante or Timbaland say. Timbaland, at the very least, co-produced this classic. 2:23 to 3:08 has got to be my favorite portion of this song. The bridge is high energy and gives Jodeci a chance to tap into their gospel root superpowers. The music video follows the album title *Diary of a Mad Band*, which is a play on Ozzy Osborne's 1981 album *Diary of a Madman*. The music video has appearances by Snoop Dogg, Treach, and the legendary music video director Hype Williams as well. The bad boys of R&B are on a bender when the police bust in and have them committed into a mental institution...because they've gone MAD with their addiction to their ladies. See what I did there. They're thrown in straight jackets and tossed in their padded rooms. The institution tries electro shock therapy, isolation and nothing can shake Jodeci's addiction. It's one of their more well executed music videos, and rumor has it that Devante Swing co-directed with Hype Williams. "Feenin'" was an incredible hit for the group, and remains a fan favorite. The song peaked at 25 on the Billboard Hot 100 and got all the way up to 2 on the R&B charts.

"My Heart Belongs To U" was never released as a single, but it's an incredible song. It's the first song on the album. "My Heart Belongs To U" makes sense as the first song on the album, because it sets the tone. On *Forever My Lady* they got a hefty dose of New Jack Swing, and *Diary of a Mad Band* was simply not going to be that. "My Heart Belongs To U" is more mid-tempo than anything, and it must be played aloud. This is another song that I'd point to, when discussing Timbaland and his ghost production. I mean, c'mon. Listen to the beat. It's even got the same constant that he used on "Cheers 2 U" five years later. "My Heart Belongs To U" is the promise of only giving your love to your lover. Painted with heavy synthesizer sounds and a thumping bass line. "My Heart Belongs To U" was the exact statement that they needed to make in that moment.

"What About Us" was the 3rd and final single from the album. "What About Us" was released in August of 1994. It's a Devante Swing produced song that seems more like an album song than a single to me. If I were rolling out the album I would've trotted out "My Heart Belongs To U" or "You Got It" featuring Redman. "What About Us" worked though. "What About Us" plays as a good summer song. JoJo sung the entire lead on both verses. That was a rare occurrence. "What About Us" is about giving the thought of "us" a chance with your lover. Taking the relationship more seriously or at least taking things to the next level as instructed in the 2nd verse. HA! As most of the album, "What About Us" was recorded in the Hit Factory in NYC. With some heavy west coast influence in the approach to the song, it played well in the summer. The song peaked at 14 on the R&B charts and up to 48 on the Billboard Hot 100.

It was the end of a successful rollout. The album finished at 3 on the Billboard Hot 100 and number 1 on the R&B chart for 1994. *Diary Of A Mad Band* went on to sell double platinum. Jodeci was not a flash in the pan, and they weren't the subjects of favor from the nuances of their style. Jodeci, had a brand of music that was long lasting.

FUN FACT: *Diary Of A Mad Band* has the first official professional credit for Timbaland & Missy. Timbaland is credited with drum programming and scratches. Missy is credited as a performer. At the time they were both in a collective that Devante Swing was putting together called the Swing Mob. It was a crew, but really more of an incubator for young talent. There were all these different artists writing, recording, creating and perfecting their craft together, supposedly, under the tutelage of Devante Swing. Timbaland as a producer, Missy (with her group Sista) as a singer/songwriter, Ginuwine, Playa and Magoo.

1) What's your favorite song on the album?
   Answer:

2) Do you think that Timbaland did some ghost production on this album?
   Answer: This is rhetorical. **OF COURSE** he did. Don't be naïve ☺

3) Which album is better between "Forerver My Lady" & "Diary Of A Mad Band"?
   Answer:

4) What is your favorite music video attached to this album?
   Answer:

CHAPTER 29

II

I use music for many things, including comfort. Earlier today, I found out that a good friend (family really) transitioned. Kendall Johnson (Kenjo) is one of the most brilliant music minds that I've ever known, all while being one of the most humble people I've ever known. Before I push on to talk about this album, let me just say, Rest In Peace Kenjo. This world will definitely miss your voice, your laughter and your insight. #LONGLIVEJO

When I think about Boyz II Men, I immediately have 2 thoughts. The first is, has anyone outside of Boyz II Men ever been interviewed about what Shawn Stockman was like in high school? I only ask, because I need proof that he's human. Shawn is an absolute vocal surgeon. The second thing I think to myself is that, Boyz II Men came out with *Cooleyhighharmony* a classic album by any standard, and had the temerity of following it up with their sophomore effort *II*. Boyz II Men started out in the Philadelphia High School of Creative and Performing Arts. Founded originally by Nathan Morris and Marc Nelson (AZ Yet) and performing under the name Unique Attraction. After a slight shuffle Wanya and Shawn Stockman, and Mike McCrary were added to replace the original members. They were a quintet. Sharpening their skills in talent shows, corners, and school bathrooms. Fans of the showmanship of New Edition, they eventually changed the group name from Unique Attraction to Boyz II Men, with reference to New Editions' hit song "Boys to Men". As the story goes they hustled up an impromptu audition with Micheal Bivins. Bivins and his business savvy were in its blossoming stage, but he wanted to work with them, and decided to manage and produce them. Marc Nelson took issue with how long it was taking for the group to record their own material and decided to leave the group and go solo. The 4 left (Nathan, Michael, Shawn and Wanya) were the ones that found fame with their debut *Cooleyhighharmony*. Boyz II Men took the vocal precision of Doo-Wop from the 60's and paired it with the R&B/Hip Hop sound that Bivins and BBD had been cultivating. *Cooleyhighharmony* was a moment in R&B history. *Cooleyhighharmony* reset the standard of what we were going to be expecting from our male (R&B) groups from here on out. That had only happened 3 times throughout the course of music history. The Temptations set that bar, and then the Jackson 5 reset that bar. After that New Edition created a new bar, and Boyz II Men reset that one. Bottom line, you had to be able to sing your face off, harmonize and perform well live if you were a male group and wanted to play in the same sandbox as Boyz II Men. They, to this day, are a class of their own. *Cooleyhighharmony* has sold over 9 million copies worldwide. The group members did most of the heavy lifting on the writing side along with Dallas Austin at the production wheel for the bulk of the album, they were in great hands, and created a true work of art. The majority of the album was recorded right here, in good old ATL at the legendary Doppler Studios. *II* was their second act. They were still fresh off the success of their debut and tour.

II is Boyz II Men's growth album. After the success of *Cooleyhighharmony*, a world tour arose, and Boyz II Men took a small break from the tour to record "End of the Road". One of the greatest songs in the history of mankind on thee greatest soundtrack of all time (*Boomerang*). To top that all off, they even found time to record thee GREATEST Christmas album of all time with their *Christmas Interpretations*...I said what I said. They were on fire. They'd gone from an R&B favorite to household names. "End of the Road" stayed at number 1 on all charts for 13 consecutive weeks. While the iron was hot, Boyz II Men came off the road and started production on their 2nd album. Technically their third, since they'd put out the Christmas album. II would be their 2nd R&B album. Boyz II Men began recording *II* in December 1993 and finished in May of 1994. They'd already proven that they could deliver every type of song from ballads to jeep music and everything in between. Tim & Bob recorded well over 2 dozens songs with Boyz II Men for *II* but not many made the cut, and in fact 2 of the songs landed on 112's classic debut album *112*("Now That We're Done & "Can I Touch You"). *II* was about the attempt of being bigger than they already were and maaaaaaaaaaaaaaaan...

"I'll Make Love To You" was the lead single off the album. It was released in July of 1994. It was written and produced by Babyface. This had to be an easy collaboration to explore for both parties, after the shared success of "End of the Road". "I'll Make Love To You" is a slow tempo ballad. With all the tinks and orchestral drama that all the boy bands of the 90's like Backstreet Boys, N'Sync and 98 Degrees would use to sell a bazillion records. Boyz II Men did it first. Never forget that. We all know what the song is about * wink wink *. It was done tactfully and tastefully as only Boyz II Men could do. From a production stance, it really doesn't sound like a Babyface joint. I can only assume that the choice to have the instruments sound totally electric was on purpose. Maybe they thought it would give the song a broader reach for casual listeners. Yes, I'm talking about Pop fans. Fight me. Either way suffices to say, the gamble worked. "I'll Make Love To You" debuted at number 1 and stayed right there for 14 consecutive weeks. Yep. Read that again if you need to. I'll wait here for you. That's number 1 on the Billboard Hot 100, R&B, Mainstream and Adult Contemporary charts. The song was everywhere, all the time and none of us were ever tired of hearing it. The harmonies and the subtle power of the song would become the song that everyone was putting on mix tapes for their wives/husbands and everything in between. I think the easy sing along value of the song dampens the proper respect that the vocal performance deserves. I can tell you as a singer myself. Pick a part. Any part of all 4 members and I assure you that it's wildly technical. "I'll Make Love To You" broke records left and right, and is widely considered one of the greatest songs of all time. A great way to let the world know that you're here to stay and that you haven't even tapped into your full potential. By the way, if you don't do the Wanya from 3:35 to 3:45, you need to get your sh*t together.

"On Bended Knee" was the second single off the album. Released in November of 1994. "On Bended Knee" would be a new move for Boyz II Men in tone and reception. It was written and produced by Jimmy Jam & Terry Lewis. Jimmy Jam & Terry Lewis never got a chance to work with Boyz II Men on *Cooleyhighharmony* and were eager to get with them. Jimmy Jam said of the group "Boyz II Men make good begging songs". When Boyz II Men, played Jam & Lewis the album, they asked them to add something to it, and "On Bended Knee" was where they started. "On Bended Knee" is a song begging your lover to come back to you and give you another chance. It's begging for sure, but with a grandeur that only Boyz II Men could perform. "On Bended Knee" debuted at number 1, taking over "I'll Make Love To You". This was the first time an artist usurped themselves at the number 1 spot on the charts since The Beatles did it in 1963. "On Bended Knee" sat at the top of the charts for 6 consecutive weeks. Another big difference between *Cooleyhighharmony* and *II* was budget. Their success afforded them access to bigger budget, and at that meant bigger videos. "On Bended Knee" music video co-starred Kim Fields, Lark Voorhies, Victoria Rowell and Renée Jones. The video doesn't work without them. Unfortunately they shot the video in that nasty wasteland of a city, New Orleans. I said what I said (LET'S GO FALCONS!!)

"Water Runs Dry" was the fourth and final single released from the album in April of 1995. Written and produced by Babyface. This had much more of the Babyface sound to it than "I'll Make Love To You". Heavy on the strings of violins and cello, and guitar. Light drums and a stand up bass hiding in the corner. Love songs are typically written in the before and after of an event. What I love about "Water Runs Dry" is that it was written from the present tense. The song is about taking the opportunity in NOW, to fix the things that are hurting the relationship. The communication issues, the contempt, etc.; Let's be adults and figure this thing out before we don't even care enough to fight for US. I don't know many songs like that. Leaving the door open for hope to walk in. It's a beautiful song. Babyface gave this to the right act, because nobody else could have done these vocals. "Water Runs Dry" did well on the charts with the assistance of the video of Boyz II Men in the desert of New Mexico. It peaked at number 2 on the Billboard Hot 100 and floated around the top 20 for 5 weeks after that.

"Yesterday" was Boyz II Men's a cappella offering for the album. Never released as a single, but an amazing cover. Written by Paul McCartney and John Lennon for The Beatles in 1963. The very group that Boyz II Men would smack around with their record breaking efforts. "Yesterday" is one of the most covered songs of all time, with well over 3000 versions. With that said, make no mistake, Boyz II Men owns this song. Like Luther Vandross, Boyz II Men, have a way of making someone else's song theirs. "Yesterday" is a glum song. It's about a man feeling empty because his woman, abruptly left him and he has no idea why. He just knows it's his fault. The bulk of Boyz II Men's interpretation of the song is sung in total 4 part harmony, with the exception of a few spots on the song. A cappella songs are Boyz II Men's way of paying homage to their high school roots of singing, and never forget, it's what got them in the industry in the first place.

II changed things for Boyz II Men. They were household names. A brand. *II* sold 12 million copies and was the 3rd highest grossing album of 1995. Boyz II Men walked away with two Grammy awards including Best R&B Album. Boyz II Men had not only picked up where they left off of their debut, they pushed the envelope forward. Their sound quickly grew from young men doing a high talent version of New Jack Swing, to grown men bringing you the finest version of R&B available.

FUN FACT: Not only did Boyz II Men win a Grammy for Best R&B album, the important part is the award was inaugural. Nobody had ever won that award before because **it didn't exist**. *II* was such an incredible album that the Grammys' had to **CREATE** an award to recognize *II* properly. As a side note Boyz II Men, also had the best song on the two best soundtracks of all time (Boomerang & Soul Food). Alright so let's check the score here. The first Grammy for Best Rap Performance was won by Dj Jazzy Jeff and The Fresh Prince, and the first Grammy for Best R&B Album was won by Boyz II Men. I see you Philly!!

1) What is your favorite song on this album?
   Answer:

2) Who is your favorite singer in the group?
   Answer:

3) What music video do you like the most from this album?
   Answer:

4) Do you prefer Boyz II Men doing up-tempo or slow songs?
   Answer:

CHAPTER 30

NEVER SAY NEVER

Before Brandy was the vocal bible, she was just a talented kid making her way in an industry that wasn't quite ready for her. Brandy knew from an early age that she wanted to be a singer. She grew up in a musical household with her dad being a gospel singer and choir director. Taking on every talent show and competition that she could, Brandy eventually got signed to Teaspoon Productions. It was being run by Chris Stokes at the time and Brandy began to do background vocal work for Immature (later known as IMX). Brandy starred as Denesha on "Thea" for 1 season before reasserting her energy into her singing career. Although the show was short lived, it did provide her a nice springboard to the public eye. At 15 Brandy finally released her solo debut on Atlantic Records. Her debut *Brandy* was released in September of 1994, with the eternal bop "I Wanna Be Down" leading the charge. The album spawned 4 singles (5 if you'd like to count the remix of "I Wanna Be Down"). Brandy showed some incredible vocal poise and star power on the charts and for Atlantic Records, which was the home to Aaliyaah as well. The album *Brandy* peaked at 20 on the Billboard charts and got Brandy her first 2 Grammy nominations. Brandy sold 4 million copies of *Brandy*. She wasn't going to just be a teenage sensation. She had the drive and the talent to be much more. Brandy got a little pre-occupied with the success of her new show "Moesha" in 1996, but eventually returned to the studio in late 1997 to begin recording for her first adult album *Never Say Never*. I use the word adult loosely, because Brandy was only 19, but she'd accomplished so much up to this point.

Never Say Never was released in June of 1998. Like all artist that show a potential for high record sales, the label brought in a pop producer to give *Never Say Never* less of a hip-hop sound. In this case they brought in David Foster, famed pop songwriter and producer, to soften the production side in the attempts of an expanded audience. Foster, who is indeed a brilliant writer and producer for what he does, was tapped by Atlantic to oversee and mentor the young producer Rodney Darkchild Jerkins for the album. Brandy remained in the spotlight between *Brandy* and *Never Say Never* thru her work on the sitcom "Moesha" and her 2 hit singles "Sittin' Up in My Room" from the Waiting to Exhale soundtrack and the collaborative effort of "Missing You" from the Set It Off soundtrack. Brandy's first single for herself in almost 4 years would turn out to be a duet, with co-star Monica.

"The Boy Is Mine" was the lead single off of Monica's sophomore album. It's a mid tempo song, with heavy electronic instrument influence throughout it. Strange to lead an album rollout for an artist with a duet, and even stranger to lead off with an artist that's basically known for the same thing that you do. "The Boy Is Mine" was co-produced by Jerkins and Dallas Austin. The main producer per each of the artists. The not so secret competition between the two young songstresses was played on and exploited by the record companies for the betterment of their own personal sales...sound familiar? The song came to be the sound that Darkchild would be known for. It's a song about two women fighting over a man. A shared boyfriend really. Recording was quite the process. Originally they recorded together in the studio in Los Angeles, but the separate parties weren't satisfied with how they were being portrayed on the song. Monica got back in the studio with Dallas Austin and re-recorded her vocals and Brandy did the same with Rodney Jerkins. The song had to be mixed over a dozen times before it met the satisfaction of Brandy or Monica's camp. Nobody wanted to be outshined on a song that would be appear on both of their respective albums. For the most part, that worked out. Neither of them has a vocal moment that truly surpasses the other persons. "The Boy Is Mine" did well, with a music video assist starring Mekhi Phifer as the two timing boyfriend. "The Boy Is Mine" entered the charts at 23 on the Billboard Hot 100 and immediately shot to number 1. It stayed at the top of the mountain for 13 weeks. Brandy and Monica received a Grammy for Best R&B performance by a duo or group and the launch for Brandy's career as an adult singer had begun.

"Top Of The World" was the second single from the album. It's an up-tempo song featuring Mase. It was released in July of 1998. I know this, because I'll never forget my brother Derek singing this at the top of his lungs in the dorm room next door our first week at the unsinkable Albany State University. Darkchild produced the song. "Top Of The World" is a song about people perceiving that your life is easier than it actually is. It's a misconception that most of us probably have for anyone famous or successful. This collaboration made sense, because Mase was everywhere at that time. Brandy still needed a song that she could perform to, and this was it. "Top Of The World" wasn't the commercial success of her past songs, but it's a cultural gem. BBQ's abundant made sure that this song spun at least once in the set. "Top Of The World" peaked at 44 on the Billboard Hot 100 and got all the way up to 4 on the R&B charts.

"Have You Ever?" was the 3rd single from the album. This ballad was written by Diane Warren and produced by David Foster. That's a lot of firepower. Warren is famous for so many songs that have stood the test of time, including "For

You I Will", "Because You Loved Me" by Celine Dion, and "Un-break My Heart" by Toni Braxton. Brandy has been on record with saying that she'd never been in the studio with a producer like David Foster before, and that he required things from her vocally that she'd never had to do before. "Have You Ever?" was released as a single on September 29, 1998. Just in time to be the soundtrack for all those suffering from summer heartbreaks. "Have You Ever?" describes the helplessness of loving someone that won't love you back. The song captures the thoughts that haunt you when you're trying to figure out why you're just not good enough for them to love you back. Brandy didn't write this song, as we know, but is it really far fetched to think that this song might be based on the relationship that Brandy had with Wanya Morris from Boyz II Men? After all, that relationship had ended earlier that year in 1998, and it ended because Wanya ended it. Who knows? No way to verify, but I think attaching that thought to the sentiment of this song helps to enjoy it. There was a little something extra on this when Brandy sung it. Maybe it was working with Foster. Maybe she was purging her young pain from heartbreak. "Have You Ever?" did well. The song peaked at number 1 on the Billboard Hot 100 and R&B charts.

"Almost Doesn't Count" was the 5th single. It was released in April of 1999. Written by Shelly Peiken and Guy Roche. They were the same production duo to put together hits for Christina Aguilera, Jessie J, and Meredith Brooks. There was a very pop-like sound in their approach to production. It's light in tone and minimal. "Almost Doesn't Count" is a mid-tempo ballad and Brandy had to be the one to make it an R&B song. "Almost Doesn't Count" has two song meanings. From Brandy's perspective, it means that she can't be satisfied in a semi-relationship. She's saying that she can't allow herself to give 100% to someone that isn't giving her the same effort. The other side of this song is from the man's perspective, and the message is that he can't see her as someone close to what he wants. She has to be as perfect for him as she thinks he is for her. It's a pretty gloomy song, but there's a beauty in how finite the song lays out. There's no muss and no fuss to it. Brandy makes it clear that, this isn't going to work out. She won't settle. This my 3rd favorite Brandy song ever. The song peaked at 16 on the Billboard Hot 100 and got all the way up to 2 on the R&B charts.

Never Say Never was a coming of age declaration for Brandy. She wasn't a teen singing about butterflies and crushes anymore. Brandy was a young woman that had experienced real things both personally and professionally. Never Say Never was a progress report of such, on all things Brandy. It was a well-executed, well thought out venture that worked out for everyone. Never Say Never sold over 5 million copies and finished at 29 on the Billboard 200 for the year. Brandy embarked on a world tour and sold out arenas in several different countries. *Never Say Never* kept Brandy busy for almost 2 years and was a major success.

FUN FACT: *Never Say Never* is Brandy's highest grossing album, but when asked what her personal favorite was, she said *Afrodisiac*.

1) Do you have a favorite video attached to this album?
   Answer:

2) What song on this album, speaks the most to Brandy's growth between her debut and "Never Say Never"?
   Answer:

3) What song is the best produced on this album?
   Answer:

4) What song do you think Brandy sings the best on this album?
   Answer:

CHAPTER 31

VOODOO

D'angelo entered our music lives in 1995 with his perfect debut album *Brown Sugar*. He shook the world up with his style, and his approach to music. D'angelo took a step back from the spotlight to live, create and be. D'angelo was doing this before Beyoncé made public scarcity between albums so vogue. The recluse in D'angelo was always part of his mystique as an artist. There wasn't an abundance of interviews on him. All we had was the music, and that was enough. D'angelo was still a stranger to most of us. D'angelo toured *Brown Sugar* for almost 2 years, pushing his artistry to the forefront for all musicians/singers of that time. D'angelo was fighting writer's block. He had trouble, figuring out what his next plateau, as a songwriter/artist should be. In the interim of *Brown Sugar* and tour life D'angelo gave us a couple of covers and collaborations, including "Nothing Even Matters" with Lauryn Hill. D'angelo has been on record with crediting the cure for his writer's block to the birth of his son. D'angelo used that inspiration and traveled from NYC (where he was then living) back to his hometown of Richmond and rural South Carolina. He used that time to re-discover his love and the soul of black music. D'angelo used that time to study Sly and the Family Stones, Jimi Hendrix, Curtis Mayfield, and an array of golden age Pentecostal Gospel.

Production began on *Voodoo* in 1998. *Voodoo* was released in January of 2000. The bulk of the album was recorded at the world famous Electric Lady studios in New York City. D'angelo wanted to make sure that *Voodoo* showed he was capable of pulling back a few more layers of the onion. He made plans to work with some of the most creative musicians available, including Questlove of the roots, Q-Tip of A Tribe Called Quest, Raphael Saadiq, Roy Hargrove and Pino Palladino. Outside of D'angelo's success up to that point, he was already a highly regarded musician and artist. People were lining up to work with him on his next project and D'angelo was very selective of who he would allow into his creative space. D'angelo wanted to make sure that his love for the music was reflected in the album.

"Left & Right" was the first official single for *Voodoo*. It was released in October of 1999, prior to the album's release. "Devil's Pie" was released 2 years earlier for the *Belly* soundtrack, although the song still made the album. "Left & Right" features Method Man & Redman. At the time, the duo was a highly successful act, between their albums, performances, movie, and short-lived sketch show. Past all that, Meff and Red are just dooooooooope together. "Left & Right" is an up-tempo song. It leads with a funky guitar lead played by D'angelo. The song was written by D'angelo, Method Man and Redman, and produced by D'angelo, with the slight assist from the legendary producer J Dilla. "Left & Right" are some of the things you tell the person you're trying to leave the club with. It's smooth and casual. "Left & Right" is D'angelo watching a woman dance provocatively and him asking himself "But can she do it on the di..." never mind. You get my drift. It's a sexy, fun and flirty song. Another important element of "Left & Right" was the music video. It was the first time that the world took notice to D'angelo getting in the gym. It was also the world's first time seeing D'angelo develop his performing repertoire. He wasn't just a chubby 19 year old stuck behind a wurly anymore. D'angelo was front and center performing with a guitar in all the majesty of a 60's rock and roller. "Left & Right" peaked at 80 on the Billboard Hot 100 and got all the way up to 14 on the R&B charts. D'angelo was back, and people didn't know what to expect after "Left & Right" hit the airwaves.

"Untitled" was the second single. This incredible song, is unmatched. There is no song in the history of music that has both the mystery and sexual energy of this song. Even if there were no vocals on this song, you'd know exactly what it's purpose is. "Untitled" was written and produced by D'angelo with Raphael Saadiq. Raphael Saadiq played the guitar and bass, but D'angelo played all the other instruments. It's also one of the longest songs on the album, because they knew what they were doing. "Untitled" was released on January 1st 2000. Only a few weeks before the album was released. "Untitled" is a slow brooding song with a truly quiet power up until the bridge. "Untitled" is about making love, and I don't mean in the casual way. This is the song for you and your loved one to engage to. The lyrics are slightly explicit, but D'angelo's delivery is the smoothest veil. The music video, directed by Paul Hunter, was groundbreaking. It was the brainchild of Paul and D'angelo's manager at the time. It was a one shot video, and they wanted to make the video feel intimate. There was no storyline, no set/background, and no leading lady. It was just D'angelo in a void looking at the camera. His manager wanted to turn him into a sex symbol on top of his artistic gravitas. D'angelo was initially nervous about the idea, because he'd only been in this shape for about 4 months out of his whole life. This was all a new experience for him. The video was wildly successful, both to his detriment and pleasure. More on that later. "Untitled" peaked at 25 on the Billboard Hot 100 and got all the way up to 2 on the R&B charts. The video pushed D'angelo into a much broader spotlight and sparked a whole new wave of fandom for him.

"Send It On" is the 4th single from the album and it was released in March of 2000. This was the first song D'angelo recorded for *Voodoo*. He was in his hometown of Richmond, VA with his newborn son and his child's mother/girlfriend at the time, Angie Stone. D'angelo was celebrating this new life, and new reality of fatherhood. The footing of the song was created in Richmond on a visit home, but the life was breathed into it in NY at Electric Lady Studios. "Send It On" was written by D'angelo, Angie Stone, and D'angelo's older brother Luther Archer. The very birth of *Voodoo* was a family affair. D'angelo produced and arranged the song, but the musicians that were on hand to create his vision are a veritable all star team. He had Questlove on drums, Pino Palladino on bass, and Roy Hargrove on the horns. D'angelo played all the other instruments. "Send It On" sounds like a song from straight out of the 70's. There's a soul and funk tone all rolled into one. "Send It On" is about offering your loyalty and faith in love, no matter the circumstance. It was as good a choice as any to be the follow up to "Untitled", on an album as incredible as *Voodoo*. "Send It On" peaked at 33 on Billboard. The music video is a collage of live performance footage from the Voodoo Tour, and if you look and listen closely to the background singers, you'll see Anthony Hamilton singing background for D'angelo.

"One Mo' Gin" is the 7th song on the album. I love this song because it unfolds out of nowhere. It comes on slow and unwittingly. The bass line almost sounds like it's searching for where to land. Pino Palladino was tapped again for the bass and D'angelo played all the other instruments. "One Mo' Gin" is about the one that got away. D'angelo's been wanting to bump into her, and catch up. This is one of the few songs on the album that D'angelo doesn't do his typical vocal collaging act. He doesn't turn the heat up too much on the songs energy either. D'angelo has a deep respect for music and the vibe that it can create. He's obedient to it, and simply delivers the song here. With the 3 verses of the song, D'angelo steps away from the basic song structure and the song feels more like a story.

Voodoo debuted at number one for the Billboard 200 and the R&B charts. People had been waiting for that moment for 5 years. The musicians that got to work on the album with D'angelo, had been afforded the opportunity to make art and make something lucrative. All too often artist have to make a choice between the two. *Voodoo* went double platinum and D'angelo walked away with a Grammy for Best R&B album in 2001. The same year D'angelo won a Grammy for Best R&B vocal performance. Unfortunately all the success and accolades pushed D'angelo into an even longer hiatus from the spotlight. He was suffering with addiction and identity issues. It wasn't until 2014 that we got new music from D'angelo with his *Black Messiah* album. A damn good album.

FUN FACT: At the time that D'angelo was recording *Voodoo* at Electric Lady studios, there were several other artist recording their, soon to be classics, as well. Erykah Badu was recording *Mama's Gun*, Common was recording *Like Water For Chocolate*, and The Roots were recording *Things Fall Apart*. So there were 4 classic albums being created in the same studio, at the same time. Additionally D'angelo used the same Fender Rhodes that Stevie Wonder used on "Talking Book".

1) Which D'angelo album is your favorite?
   Answer:

2) What is your favorite song on "Voodoo"?
   Answer:

3) What song gives you the best memories?
   Answer:

4) Do you have this album in constant rotation?
   Answer:

CHAPTER 32

CHEERS 2 U

First and foremost, R.I.P. to Stephen Garrett, better known as Static Major. One of the most criminally slept on R&B albums of all time is *Cheers 2 U* by Playa. Playa came together in their hometown of Louisville, Ky. The trio were active in their respective gospel circles when they formed. Static Major and Smokey were good friends as children and began creating together in school. They met Black later on thru a mutual friend that thought they should all know each other. They became fast friends and started performing as a group under the name A Touch of Class. Each member brought a different aspect to the group. Black was more of the traditional soul vocalist with heavy gospel overtones. Smokey was the musician with more of a funk in his vocal approach. Static was the main songwriter and arranger of the group with a traditional R&B vocal style. Together they were something fresh and they were making the kind of music you'd hear at a neighborhood cookout. After an impromptu audition with Devante Swing, backstage at a Jodeci concert, they were signed to his label Swing Mob. Swing Mob was a joint venture with Elektra records. Swing Mob was a strong collective of talent and served to be an incubator for Playa. They learned how to properly build a song, production practices and performance routines. Unfortunately the biggest accomplishment they had while with Swing Mob was a small amount of production for Jodeci. Timbaland and Missy had already moved on from Swing Mob and were in full swing of making hits for other acts. Simultaneously Def Jam was putting a lot of energy into developing the R&B arm of their company (Def Soul), and Playa was able to make the jump with them. Playa left Swing Mob with quite a bit of material and were already well down the road on almost 3 albums worth of music. Official recording for their debut album began in July of 1997 and ended in January of 1998. Finally, after years of perfecting their craft, and industry bullshit, Playa released their debut album *Cheers 2 U* in March of 1998.

"Don't Stop the Music" was the first single off of the album. It was released in September of 1997. Let me be honest. I don't like this song a lot. It's an okay song, but that's it. Just okay. It's the only song on this album that keeps me from calling this a perfect album. I've had this album in steady rotation since 1998, and when I play the album, it's the only song I skip. "Don't Stop the Music" just didn't seem like the right song for them. The production on the song was incredible and it's well put together, but the song itself is very hollow. Some people do well with making party songs, but that just wasn't going to work for me with Playa. "Don't

Stop the Music" did receive some airplay. "Don't Stop the Music" is a cover song, originally done by Yarbrough and Peoples in 1981. Playa didn't stray too far from the original, but unfortunately, this song didn't even chart. There was a video shot for the single and everything. From what we know about the music industry, one would have to assume that their album was in trouble at this point. Def Jam put money into the production and a video, for a song that couldn't even crack the top 100 chart? That's dangerous territory.

"Cheers 2 U" was the second single and the title track. The album had a different name originally, but after they recorded this song, Static thought it was a good idea to use it as the name of whole album. "Cheers 2 U" was written by Static Major and produced by Timbaland. Everything about this song is in the right place. A lot of what became Timbaland's signature sound is in this song, right down to the same sounds used on "Nigga What, Nigga Who". This isn't one of Static's more lyrically written pieces, but the sentiment conveyed is huge. "Cheers 2 U" is about celebrating a new relationship while coming out of a bad one. It takes a certain range of courage to get in a relationship after coming out of a bad one that you've devoted yourself to. I think Static captured that courage with the simplest of words. "Cheers 2 U" is a ballad that found it's way in all airplay from the traffic jam mix to the quiet storm. The song has a versatility to it, because the production is grappling and the hook is easy to sing along with. "Cheers 2 U" was Playa's first, and arguably only, taste of commercial success. "Don't Stop the Music" didn't get my attention, but I knew something different was happening when I first heard "Cheers 2 U" and I was right. I bought this album, solely off of the strength of this song, and it was a worthwhile gamble. "Cheers 2 U" peaked at 38 on the Billboard Hot 100 and got all the way up to 10 on the R&B charts.

"All the Way" was the 3rd and final single off of the album. It was written by Static Major and produced by Timbaland. I'd love to talk about this song too because I love it, but I wouldn't have chosen this as the 3rd single. Pay close attention; because I'm about to drop a gem on those that didn't already know. I say this as humbly as humanly possible. I make the best slow mixes known to man. A reach? No. Not at all. Bryan Michael Cox MIGHT be able to contend with my prowess, but even that is an unfair fight because Cox could teach a master class in R&B. Anyway my point is this, "Push" by Playa is a song that should be on everyone's slow jam mix. After seeing the success of Playa and their ability to deliver a ballad, "Push" just seems like it would've been the right choice to continue their momentum. "Push" was written by Static Major and produced by Timbaland. "Push" starts with birds chirping in the background, a slow synthesizer and a flirty electric guitar. I'm a fan of letting a song build up to it's highest point of energy and tone, but that is not what happens here. The whole song is high emotion and energy. Static sings the first verse with impact. He didn't walk onto the song. He ran. Somehow it was still appropriate. Black, who usually does the heavy lifting on the vocal side for Playa, brought in the 2nd verse and Smokey carried the bridge. Considering the purpose of "Push", I'd think that the song would be longer, but the point still gets across. "Push" is a mid-tempo song, and would've likely done very well on the charts if it had been released after "Cheers 2 U".

I had trouble deciding what the last song to feature should be. There's only one song on the whole album that I skip. Should we talk about "One Man Woman" featuring our beloved Aaliyaah? Should we talk about "I-65" and how they could've taken the breakdown and made another dope ass song with it? We could even talk about "Together" and the vibe that they were able to catch on that song. Instead, I chose "Buggin' Over You". I love this song. It's mid-tempo and one of the most human songs on the album. There's no language in the song about being misunderstood. "Buggin' Over You" says I messed up, and I just want things to be the way they used to be. "Buggin' Over You" is a piano lead song with plenty of synthesizers and organs to fill the production out. Playa shows their harmonizing skills off on this song. Smokey opens the song up. Black rounds the second verse out and Static leads the bridge. It was produced by Smokey.

Cheers 2 U never got its proper respect. The album did well enough for the group to start recording another album. They were already in the practice of constantly recording and constantly creating. Unfortunately that music never saw the light of day. Each of the members went on to pursue solo careers, and Static put energy into his songwriting ability as well. As an album, Cheers 2 U, finished the year peaking at 86 on the Billboard 200 and 19 on the R&B charts. The album drifted away with no awards, and not enough fan fare to guarantee another album release on Def Jam. They will mostly go down as one hit wonders in the history books when the truth is, that's far from the truth. Cheers 2 U was the right R&B album from a male group for their time. It would have been great to see what they could cook up on another go around.

FUN FACT: The majority of the songs on *Cheers 2 U* were created while they were still a part of Swing Mob. After the group disbanded Static Major went on to do some heavy song writing for quite a few hits, including numerous hits with Aaliyah ("Are You That Somebody"/"Try Again"/"Rock the Boat").

1) What was the first song you ever heard on this album?
   Answer:

2) What is your favorite song from Playa to come after the album?
   Answer:

3) Do you prefer Timbaland or Smokey's production on this album?
   Answer:

4) What is your favorite song on "Cheers 2 U"?
   Answer:

CHAPTER 33

LIFE GOES ON

Donell Jones made a huge leap as an artist and star between his debut album and his FIRST perfect album, *Where I Wanna Be*. The lyrics got sharper, the content got deeper, and the production got realer. He wasn't a bubble gum R&B artist. Donell had reset the standard on what we, as fans, were expecting out of his music. With his third album *Life Goes On*, Donell widened that expectation. After the success of his 2nd album, Donell toured and continued to write and produce. Official recording for this album started in summer of 2000. Donell was a success and the stakes were higher. Donell did NOT disappoint. *Life Goes On* is my favorite album from Donell.

"You Know that I Love You" was the first single. Released in April of 2002. A perfect song for the spring. It's a light and airy mid-tempo song that just makes you feel good as soon as the music drops. One of the few songs on the album that Donell didn't write. It was written and produced by the production trio of Chis Absolam, Richard Smith, and Jamie Hawkins. "You Know that I Love You" is Donell Jones reassuring the love of his life that their situation has changed, but not the love. He'll always love her. Rumor is that this song was a dedication to his long time girlfriend. They had four daughters at the time, but were no longer together because Donell was asking himself "Where I Wanna Be". There's always a beauty to the music when it's based in truth. "You Know that I Love You" became my favorite song for the spring and let the world know that the Chicago's favorite crooner, was indeed back. "You Know that I Love You" finished at 54 on the Billboard Hot 100 and got all the way up to 16 on the R&B charts.

"Put Me Down" was the 2nd single off the album, and I always found that peculiar. I always thought the 2nd single should've been "Where You Are (Is Where I Wanna Be)". "You Know that I Love You" let us know that Donell had a new plate for us to eat off of, but after the success of "Where I Wanna Be" as a single, I wanted to know what happened next! "Where You Are (Is Where I Wanna Be" was the answer that we'd been waiting for. It's a ballad that starts with a light wurly and mild percussion. Truth is, there isn't a full production soundtrack on this song until the hook. I love it. I love that the song goes from intimate conversation in the verses and bridge, to pleading from the mountaintops in the hook. The dramatic approach to delivering the song resonates with the desperation. "Where You Are (Is Where I

Wanna Be) is about Donell wanting to come back home. He was confused about whether he wanted to be in a relationship or not on "Where I Wanna Be" and after being in the streets coming to the realization that by his woman's side is where he wants to be. A powerful song. It takes a man to not only admit that he was wrong but that his life is better with the person that he disappointed. Over time I've come to respect this song even more, because men aren't making these songs anymore. The pathway of music has made it so that there really is no window for men to be apologetic and sincere in their proclamations of love. Donell isn't saying that he deserves another chance, he's not really even explaining himself. He's saying "Baby I messed up, and I want to be back with you." The song was written and produced by the same team of Jones, West and Goode that created the sister piece "Where I Wanna Be". It's fitting that they got back together to round the story out for us. Not only a gem on the album, also a jewel on Donell's entire discography.

"Guilty by Suspicion" is one of the more interesting songs on the album. It's as croon worthy as some of the other songs on the album, but the air is different. Guitars, violin strings and slow snaps. Yeah. "Guilty by Suspicion" is definitely a mood. The song is Donell asking his woman to let him work thru his issues with infidelity. He doesn't want to lie to her anymore and he already promised that he wouldn't cheat again. The song is strange because it's both an admission and denial of infidelity. In the end he just wants her to focus on how much he loves her and wants to provide everything she needs to be happy. I don't even know what to say about that, but damn. "Guilty by Suspicion" was both written and produced by Donell with the assist from longtime collaborator Sheldon Goode on the guitars.

"Comeback" was written and produced by Donell Jones. This song is the stuff that open mics and coffee shop stages dream of. It's minimal. 80% guitar. "Comeback" is the song you send to your loved one, when they're headed out of town. "Comeback" is a ballad. It's an "I miss you, and can't wait for you to get home to me". Being that Donell wrote it, and kept it for himself, I've got to believe that he wrote this from a personal place. From the first verse, it seems as if "she" is leaving for an extended time. It's a sweet song. Very light and Donell didn't have to do much to deliver it. It's a crooner's song and nobody has made a career of crooning more than Donell Jones. Artists become powerful when they find the pocket that they can always reach in for inspiration. Crooning is Donell's.

"I Hope It's You" is the last song on the album and the longest. Donell once described his music as mellow, smooth, purpose driven music. That's what "I

Hope It's You" is. It's mellow. It's definitely smooth, and once the beat drops you'll have no confusion whatsoever on what the songs purpose is * wink wink *. How in the hell does Donell make these songs so easily? "I Hope It's You" was both written and produced by Donell Jones. Best way to describe this song? It's what two people spending their first night together and hoping that it goes the way that they've been dreaming of sounds like. "I Hope It's You" is oozing with lust, sex and moments. I remember I used to play this song so loud at my 1 bedroom hole in the wall that the damn floors would shake. The bass line thumps and the violin highs give this song a balance of smooth and aggressive. Trey Songz did the same thing with "Neighbors Know My Name". Both are songs that are begging to be played really loud! Donell chose this as the last song on the album, and I think that makes sense. "I Hope That It's You" is a catch all of the underlying theme of the album, which is to be alright. For things to work out, and see that *Life Goes On*, even if only for an intimate moment with the one you love.

Life Goes On only had 2 singles off of the album, even though there was a list of others that could've set the airwaves ablaze as well. I'm not sure what the politics behind that was but, truthfully, Donell has never been in a position that the record label has put the support that he deserves behind him. As an album *Life Goes On* peaked at 3 on the Billboard charts, and 2 on the R&B charts, in spite of so few singles. *Life Goes On* has sold just over 500K copies and is certified Gold by the RIAA. Many people think that *Where I Wanna Be* is his best album, and one could argue that the metrics say that as well. I've always thought that *Life Goes On* was the better album to point to, when defining who Donell is as an artist.

FUN FACT: The second single off this album, was "Put Me Down", which was written and produced by Eddie F and Darren Lighty. The single that was actually released was a remix with Styles P of The Lox, and Lady May featured on it. This version does not appear on the album.

1) Do you prefer *Life Goes On* or *Where I Wanna Be*?
   Answer:

2) What's your favorite ballad on this album?
   Answer:

3) If you were to pick a 3rd single for this album, which song would it be?
   Answer:

4) "Where You Are" is the follow up to "Where I Wanna Be". Do you think that these songs fit each other for a full story?
   Answer:

CHAPTER 34

FAITH

Faith Ev...Jordan. Faith Jordan. Still getting used to that. When she was Faith Evans, she was the first lady of Bad Boy Records. She was the first female artist to be signed to Bad Boy Records. Faith was born in Florida, and raised by her 2nd cousin and her husband as her foster parents in Newark, NJ. Faith's foster parents were deeply into the church, and with Faith's birth mother being a singer herself, it wasn't a far stretch for Faith to be touched by the gift of music. Faith started singing in the church by age 4. Faith attended college for a year after high school, while recording and perfecting her craft as a songwriter as well. Faith and her boyfriend, at the time, were expecting a child so Faith left school to focus on being a mother and a singer. Faith was living in Los Angeles and working as a background singer for Al B. Sure when Diddy discovered her. Diddy signed Faith to Bad Boy Entertainment in 1994, and she began working immediately. Diddy put Faith in the studio with his in house production team and they worked on her debut album from November of 1994 to June of 1995. Faith's debut album *Faith* was released on August 29, 1995.

"You Used to Love Me" was the first single off the album and it was released in July of 1995. To this day it's one of my favorite songs by Faith. "You Used to Love Me" was co-written by Faith and Chucky Thompson, and produced by Chucky Thompson and Diddy. Originally recorded in Daddy's House recording studio. Faith was one of the first artists to record at Daddy's House studio. Daddy's House was Diddy's original recording studio. "You Used to Love Me" is about a relationship going awry because one person is invested and the other isn't anymore. Contrary to popular belief, this song isn't about Faith catching Biggie with one of his mistresses. It's a mid-tempo song. This song is recognizable as soon as it drops. In the end "You Used to Love Me" peaked at 24 on the Billboard Hot 100 and got all the way up to 4 on the R&B charts.

"Soon as I Get Home" was the second single on the album. The song was released in September of 1995. It was our first time hearing Faith's voice on a ballad. The album had only been out a month but it was growing. "Soon as I Get Home" was co-written by Faith and Diddy produced by Chucky Thompson. "Soon as I Get Home" is an apology of sorts. Faith is saying that even though she's been busy at work and with life, that she never stopped loving her man. She'll make up for her absence when she sees him again. The vocal arrangements on the bridge and hook speak to Faith's gospel roots. There's a choir like quality in the vocals on the bridge. The song peaked at 21 on the Billboard Hot 100 and got all the way up to 3 on the R&B charts where it floated in the top 10 for 5 consecutive weeks.

"Ain't Nobody" was the 3rd single off the album. Co-written and Co-produced by Faith, Chucky Thompson and Diddy. Bad Boy was known for making songs for the clubs. It was Diddy's specialty. He always knew what would work in the clubs. "Ain't Nobody" was one of those songs. Smooth, and mid-tempo, but had the type of sound that would do well in the clubs. Faith said that she wrote "Ain't Nobody" because she wanted to make a love song that ladies would find easy to sing along to in the club. At the time Faith was only 22 years old and still enjoying her life as a young woman so naturally she'd want a song like that. "Ain't Nobody" didn't do as well as the other singles though. The song peaked at 67 on the Billboard Hot 100 and got up to 14 on the R&B charts, where it stayed for 3 weeks.

"Come Over" was the 4th single off the album. This is, even to this day, my favorite song by Faith. This song is so sexy. They even pulled the organs out for this one! The song was released at the top of 1996. "Come Over" was written by Faith and & Floyd Howard, and again produced by Chucky Thompson. They do us the favor of sharing what the song's about in the first 35 seconds * wink wink *. I.LOVE. THIS.SONG. They knew what they were doing with the 30 second intro, unfolding slowly. Cozily. Starting the song with the hook. Oh yeah. They knew exactly what they were doing. They recorded this at a session in The Hit Factory, and Faith wrote right on the spot. I always wished this song were a little longer. It's just begging for an extended version with a breakdown in the middle of the song. You fumbled the ball on that opportunity Diddy. This was the first peak at what Faith could do with the power of her voice. She really went all in on this song, but she didn't over sing on it. Faith was patient and let the song build where it should naturally. Faith applies steady pressure up until the 2nd bridge, and then she goes for it.

Faith peaked at 22 on the Billboard 200 and got all the way up to 2 on the R&B charts. *Faith* was certified platinum. The church girl from Jersey made her stamp, as the first lady of a flourishing young label. Thru her songwriting and strong vocal performance Faith was able to deliver us a classic album. She followed it up with a classic as her sophomore album as well. A good album, but not cracking this list. Faith worked with Herb Middleton, Mark Ledford and Jean-Claude Olivier

(Poke) on this album. Chucky Thompson took the lead on the production because he was Faith's personal choice. She knew that their work together could lead to something distinctive, and she was exactly right.

FUN FACT: On the first pressings of *Faith*, "Love Don't Live Here Anymore" was a duet between Faith and Mary J. Blige. The album had already been out for a couple of months, when Faith got a call from the General Manager of Bad Boy (Harve Pierre I believe) telling her that Mary said she doesn't want her vocals on the album. Faith had to get back in the studio, begrudgingly, and re-record the whole song. Faith shared this story, years later, and Mary refuted it. Mary said that she loved the song, and more importantly, never said that. Nobody knows the real story, but any tape/cd with Mary on the duet, could be considered a collectible.

1) What is your favorite song off of this album?
   Answer:

2) Did you follow Faith's music past this album?
   Answer:

3) Faith has 7 albums in her discography. Which is your favorite?
   Answer:

4) How much did Faith's, newly wed life weigh in on her writing for this album?
   Answer:

CHAPTER 35

TONIGHT

Silk is one of my favorite groups of all time. I've got them ranked 5th all time on my personal list behind The Temptations, Boyz II Men, New Edition, and 112. Silk has been criminally slept on their entire career. I know it's hard to align a platinum-selling group with being undervalued, but it's true. Silk began their career on the Atlanta music scene in 1989. Keith Sweat discovered them. Apparently the group called his hotel room and sung over the phone for him. Shortly after that they were signed with Keith. They'd seen success with their debut *Lose Control* being a double platinum seller and their sophomore album *Silk* going gold. Truth be told, *Silk* should have gone platinum too. I'm still trying to forgive you all about that. The woes of the industry were weighing on them after the second album. Silk wanted more control over their sound and, frankly, bigger budgets for their projects. It's a natural progression for artists that want to grow. Silk severed ties with their management after their second album. Silk started recording their 3rd album in early 1998. Most of the recording was done in Atlanta at D.A.R.P. studios and in NYC at Quad Recording Studios. In the short stint of their creative output, Silk proved that they have a proclivity for making what we in the culture call "baby making music". On March 23rd 1999, Silk released their most important work to date, with the heavy assist from producer Darrell Delite Allamby. It was their 3rd album, *Tonight*. An album, totally dedicated, to that which they do best.

"If You (Lovin' Me)" was the first single off of the album. It was released on February 23rd 1999 and produced by Darrell Delite Allamby. This was Silk's first time back in the spotlight in years, and they were sounding completely brand new. It was a collage of strings, pianos, synths, and drums. John-John sung the first and second verse, with Lil G bringing us the bridge. "If You (Lovin' Me)", is a song about letting go of that angst you have when you know you're sexually attracted to someone and letting the moment happen. This is also the longest song on the album, checking in at 5:37. I can understand the logic of picking this as a lead single for a reemerging, talented group. "If You (Lovin' Me)" answers a lot of questions about the album and about Silk. What will the album sound like? What will the tone of the album be? Can Silk still deliver? Silk dropped "If You (Lovin' Me)" as a resounding yes. The song peaked at 4 on the Billboard chart and got all the way up to 2 on the R&B charts.

"Meeting In My Bedroom" was the second single off the album, and rest assured, I'd never heard anything like this. By any standard of slow jam philosophy, "Meeting In My Bedroom" is an mind-blowing song. Everything from the production, the lyrics, the vocal arrangements. "Meeting In My Bedroom" is the Silkiest song Silk has ever sung. Try saying that 3 times fast. The song was produced by Delite, and written by Link. Link wrote "My Body" for the R&B super group LSG. "Meeting In My Bedroom" is dramatic. The way the song unfolds from the top to the bottom is evidence of such. Delite really got to show off his production skills here. The song has a heavy piano presence and synths to match the mood. John-John sings lead on the entire song, but Lil G leads it out. After all what's a Silk song if Lil G isn't putting the finishing touches on it? When "Meeting In My Bedroom" dropped, it was played at every party and every quiet storm radio show that could get their hands on it. The music video was so vaunted that it became a staple on the popular late night video show Midnight Love on B.E.T....when it was still black owned. Tuh Huh. As a sidebar, that top note on the hook is a REAL note that Lil G hit. That is not studio magic. Lil G, really hits that note. Feel free to Google a live performance of "Meeting In My Bedroom" and see for yourself. "Meeting In My Bedroom" peaked at 15 on the Billboard Hot 100 and spent the next 20 weeks floating around the top 25.

"Let's Make Love" was the 3rd single, released in February of 2000. Just a week and some change before Valentine's Day. Well played Silk. Well played. "Let's Make Love" was written by Link, and produced by Delite. This mid-tempo song is more fun and flirty than the deliberate energy of "Meeting In My Bedroom". The message is the same though. Making love. Silk didn't stray very far away from the theme of the album. The song is built to reveal the whole production in the hook. The instrumentation is minimal in the verses and doesn't open to full bloom until the hook and bridge drop. John-John sings the verses and Lil G puts the finishing touches on the song in the bridge until the end. The vocal arrangement on this song is what gives it the feel of a mid-tempo song. The full vocals give your mids, highs and subs their fair share of work to do for 4:40 seconds. By this point the album was already making its rounds on the charts and in homes. This was the final single off of the album. "Let's Make Love" never broke the seal on the Billboard charts, and it peaked at 58 on the R&B charts.

"Sexcellent" was never released as a single, but it definitely had single appeal. It was written by Link, and produced by Delite. Sexcellent is a mid-tempo song. It leads with heavy synth and guitar. John-John sings the first verse and Lil G sings the 2nd verse and bridge. "Sexcellent" gives me the same feel that their past hit

"Hooked On You" gave me. A fun song, with easy sing along value, and the gentle reminder to the listener that Silk is capable of much more than the swarm of steamy ballads that, ultimately, became their staple. "Sexcellent" is the shortest song on the album. In the album's sequence it's tucked right between the hidden gem "I Wonder" co-written and co-produced by Lil G and John-John, and the apex of vibe for this album in "Love You Down".

Tonight is Silk's masterwork. They put quite a bit of work in this project. At this point of their career it was the one work that they had the most creative control over. The gamble worked out perfectly. Tonight introduced us to a fold of production that we'd never heard before. Delite and his 2000 Watts cohorts turned out to be the perfect pairing for what Silk wanted to do. With Tonight, Silk was able to reclaim their careers post Keith Sweat while succeeding at making the music that they want. Tonight is Silk's second most successful album, behind their debut. Tonight peaked at 50 on the Billboard charts and got all the way up to 4 on the R&B charts while going platinum. Silk was able to follow up Tonight with their 4th album Love Session. It's another multi-layered collaboration with Delite and Link. It's a good album, but one of its glaring downfalls is that they put it out after Tonight.

FUN FACT: When Silk was in the fight to reclaim the control of their sound and career, one of the biggest moves they made was changing management. After their second album went gold, Silk really wanted to move in the industry with more freedom. They switched managers, and had the terms of their next album negotiated by their new representation. That new manager was none other than Sonja Norwood. The mother and MOMager of the vocal bible we all know as Brandy. The album that she negotiated the terms of was *Tonight*. Silk's greatest body of work to date.

1) What's your favorite Silk song ever?
   Answer:

2) This album came out in 1999. What memories does this album give you?
   Answer:

3) Do you enjoy Silk songs, if it's not a ballad?
   Answer:

4) What is your favorite Silk album?
   Answer:

CHAPTER 36

DANGEROUSLY IN LOVE

Inevitable. Inevitable is an adjective meaning, unavoidable, or certain to happen. Inevitable, is a bit of a phenomenon, because it speaks to the natural order of things in the universe. It's inevitable that the sun will rise in the east and set in the west. It's inevitable that a Quentin Tarantino movie will be riddled with racial epithets, and it was inevitable that Beyoncé would be a solo artist. We all knew it was coming, just like we knew Sisqo from Dru Hill and Justin Timberlake from N'SYNC would go solo. Something's are simply aligned with the natural course of the cosmos. We were introduced to Beyoncé when she was with Destiny's Child. They were a young girls' group coming out of Houston, Texas. Originally the group was comprised of 6 members and was whittled down to four. The group's original name was Girl's Tyme, and there were points that they went by other names until deciding that Destiny's Child was the best way to go. After some trials and tribulations, the group became a huge success, under the management of Matthew Knowles (Beyoncé's father) and the front WOman abilities of Beyoncé. Destiny's Child went on to make record breaking sales and an impact on the music industry, while going thru two more iterations of what the group would be. Destiny's Child ended with Beyoncé, Kelly Rowland, and Michelle Williams being the 3 members remaining by 2001. The group took a hiatus, and released solo albums. Beyoncé was able to fully spread her wings and began recording her solo debut in March of 2002. After just under a year of recording Beyoncé released *Dangerously In Love* in June of 2003.

"Crazy In Love" was Beyoncé's first single off of the album. It's a collab with Jay-Z. It wasn't too far off the heels of their original collaboration "'03 Bonnie & Clyde" from Jay-Z's album *The Blueprint 2*. That song was a success for them, and a great chance to cross-pollinate their individual fan base. It was also a chance for them to put a little more gasoline on the rumor that they were dating. Something that was also a good business move for them. There was no reason to think that "Crazy In Love" couldn't do the same thing. "Crazy In Love" was released as a single in May of 2003. It was written by Beyoncé, Jay-z, and Eugene Record. The song was produced by D.C. based producer Rich Harrison. "Crazy In Love" has similar horns and drums of a good go-go record. It's a popular style of music coming out of the DMV club scene. "Crazy In Love" was an important step for Beyoncé, because she was still transitioning her artistry from young girl music to young woman music. "Crazy In Love" was a good bridge to that walk. "Crazy In Love" is about being so head over heels with someone that your behavior changes. Everything about you seems off. It's a very young love, type of song, but when it was meshed with the production and the incomparable H-O-V, it became something greater. "Crazy In Love" took off like a rocket. It's one of those songs that sounds better loud, and more importantly it was the moment that we all knew was coming. Beyoncé was now a solo artist, and she was being escorted into that moment by THE GREATEST RAPPER OF ALL TIME (DEBATE YOUR MOTHER. NOT ME). "Crazy In Love" peaked at number 1 on the Billboard Hot 100, R&B charts and the mainstream 40. The music video was shot in Los Angeles, and got all the critical acclaim it could garner for everything from Beyoncé's beauty to the dance routine.

"Me, Myself and I" was the 3rd single off the album. Beyoncé recorded this song in Miami, with famous producer Scott Storch. It was written by Beyoncé. The song was released as a single in October of 2003. Perfect timing since October is the very last month of the holiday bae tryouts. It doesn't work out for everyone though. Destiny's Child, had a few songs that were seen as vehicles of women empowerment, so Bey wasn't a stranger to providing that kind of content in her artistry. "Me, Myself and I" is a song about a cheating boyfriend, and women being able to find the comfort they seek from others, in themselves. Of all the songs, that Beyoncé has done, this is the one I point to that can be marked as the shift to grown woman music. "Me, Myself and I" was able to help quite a few people thru a hard year. "Me, Myself and I" peaked at number 1 on the Billboard Hot 100 and R&B charts, and served as Beyoncé's 4th consecutive number 1 song.

"Yes" was never released as a single, but it's one of my favorite Beyoncé songs ever. Beyoncé once told a story about some of the best advice she'd ever received. She said that she was watching an Oprah special, and that Oprah was talking about the power of the word NO. Oprah was saying that for women especially (not sure how she would know that) the word NO could be a powerful tool of independence and dignity. Bey said that she had to learn how to say NO, to protect herself from being used for her kindness and to maintain her boundaries and integrity in both business and her personal life. "Yes" is part story and part song. "Yes" is about Beyoncé meeting a man and slowly giving in to the idea of becoming more and more personable with him. Everything is going great between the two of them. Beyoncé said yes to dinner dates, meeting his parents, hanging out in private and everything. There was never a hint of a problem until she said no to being...intimate * wink wink *. She'd set a boundary and all of a sudden there was a problem. She even makes a comment about how she's confused at his immaturity being that he's grown/older. After listening to this song a few times, it was easy to come to the conclusion that she was likely talking about her early relationship with

Jay-Z. After all, by his own admission, he's got no passion and he's go not patience… (I hope you all get that reference). Low and behold, who co-wrote this song with Beyoncé? HOV did. Interesting how life can hide in the art right? The song was produced by Focus and recorded in Miami. The production is minimal with a synth lead and vocals that sound canned. Beyoncé proves on "Yes", that she can, not only, pelt and powerhouse. It proves that she also has the discipline as a vocalist to simply deliver a song. In this case, a great one.

"Signs" found Beyoncé in the good hands of Missy Elliot. "Signs" was co-written with Missy Elliot, Beyoncé, and Nisan Stewart. "Signs" is one of the songs that Beyoncé put together while recording in Miami, where Missy (and Timbaland) have been based out of for many years. "Signs" is a mid-tempo song. Mostly a groove. Beyoncé weaves a tale of looking for the right person to love her based on their astrological sign and the traits that are typically assigned to them. A lot of people don't put much in to astrology, but rest assured it is a science and the alignment of the planet and stars, at your birth definitely matters. The song does a good job of saying nice things about each sign and the qualities that Beyoncé finds attractive. She could have shown us Leos a little more love, but that's fine. Beyoncé makes many references to Sagittarius. Saying that she was in love with one, once before. People always assume that she was talking about her high school sweetheart and boyfriend, but she could have just as easily been talking about Jay-Z, who is also a Sagittarius. It's one of the shorter songs on the album, but seeing Beyoncé and Missy together was a welcomed sight on an album that needed a sprinkle of Missy's creativity on it.

Over the years, and especially after her marriage to HOV, Beyoncé has been more and more open with her sexuality as a woman. She's discussed her role, and her joy in it. I'm not talking about her surfboarding * wink wink *. I'm talking about her acknowledgement of self as a sexual being and as a woman. Beyoncé explores that premise on "Speechless". Man oh man did she explore that thing on "Speechless". "Speechless" is by far the most sensual song on the album. It's a ballad and it comes as no surprise that it's the longest song on the album too. Beyoncé has always had a tactical approach to ballads. The song swells and swells over 6 minutes as if it were building up to a…climax * wink wink *. You get what I'm hinting at here, and I'm sure that it was on purpose. The brilliance of the song is that she's describing the night of lovemaking without using any words. Especially in the hook. It's as if she's, wait for it, speechless. The song was written by Beyoncé and produced by Fanatic (producer of "Crush On You" by Lil Kim). The song has a heavy guitar presence as the lead, and a pocketed Jazz like drum pattern with heavy synth use. You can tell that the spirit of the Isley Brothers was at least channeled for this song. "Speechless" could have been a song released in the mid 70's when people were still doing deep listening to whole albums. "Speechless" has a trance like value, and Beyoncé, here more than any other song on the album, goes places vocally that she hasn't before. People get engulfed in Beyoncé's beauty, her show stopping abilities and her overall mystique as a person and tend to forget one small, but wildly important thing. Beyoncé can sing her ass off and she does just that on this song.

Dangerously In Love debuted at number 1 and sold close to 350K copies in its first week. The album went on to sell 11 million copies worldwide, and is still Beyoncé's highest grossing album. She walked away from Dangerously In Love with huge album sales, more than a handful of awards from every arm of tastemakers from ASCAP to The Grammy Academy, the most ravenous and illogical fan base throughout the course of history (I said what I said) and more important than anything, the foundation of what has become a long fruitful solo career.

FUN FACT: Beyoncé's debut solo album *Dangerously In Love*, was listed as one of the top 200 definitive albums in music history by the Rock and Roll Hall of Fame.

1) What is your favorite song off of this album?
   Answer:

2) Do you prefer Beyoncé singing her big stadium, up-tempo hits or ballads?
   Answer:

3) What is the best Beyoncé written song on this album?
   Answer:

4) Do you know any fan base as, horrid, aggressive or illogical as the Beyhive?
   Answer:

CHAPTER 37

ENTER THE DRU

Dru Hill came out of nowhere. They had the voices, the stage presence, the songs, and the flashy front man in Sisqo. They snuck on the charts and into our hearts with their first single "Tell Me" from the *Eddie* Soundtrack. Before that they were just a young group out of Baltimore making their way as new artists in the industry. They released their solo album *Dru Hill* in November of 1996. The album had 4 singles, including the cult classic "In My Bed". The group was a success. They'd established themselves as incredible performers, a unique talent collective and they sold just over a million copies of their album. They were a platinum group from their very first release, and with that came expectation. Expectations ruin the potential of plenty of artists. They'd spent their whole first campaign being compared to the legendary likes of Jodeci and 112, and still found a way to set themselves apart. After the album, the group had another smash single from the *Soul Food* Soundtrack in "We're Not Making Love No More". The single was certified gold, and peaked at 2 on the Billboard Hot 100. By early 1998, Dru Hill was back in the studio, curating the piece that would come to be known as *Enter the Dru*.

With the success of their first album, Dru Hill asked for more creative control. There were a line of producers waiting to work with them, but this served as a great opportunity for the group members to leave their imprint on the production side as well as the performance side. *Enter the Dru* was released in October of 1998. *Enter the Dru* was a play on Bruce Lee's movie *Enter The Dragon*, since Dru Hill's symbol was the Chinese dragon. The first single off the album was "How Deep Is Your Love".

"How Deep Is Your Love" is an up-tempo song, with a Spanish guitar on the lead. It was released in June of 1998. It was co-written by Sisqo and Nokio, and produced by Nokio, Dutch and Warryn Campbell. It wasn't really a gamble for Dru Hill, because they'd already proven that they could deliver every type of song. They weren't confined to any particular sound. "How Deep Is Your Love" is pure machismo. I love it. The whole song is saying, "I'm a better lover than that other guy you're messing with". HA!! Just full blown macho shit, but it's necessary. Sometimes you have to talk your shit and that's what Dru Hill was doing. Sisqo sings the lead on the whole song, they shot their first big budget video as well. It's funny really. A couple of brothers singing a song with strong Spanish guitar elements, and the video was shot and based in Hong Kong. "How Deep Is Your Love" was also featured on the *Rush Hour* Soundtrack and that's the link, but still. Stretch much? The song peaked at number 1 on the Billboard Hot 100 and the R&B charts. It stayed there for 3 weeks and sold over 500K copies nationally.

"These Are the Times" was the 2nd single off the album. This was an curious choice, because it was Dru Hill's first attempt at a crossover hit. They needed something that the suburban soccer mom could play in her minivan and not feel guilty about loving it. At the same time, they wanted to maintain their integrity as R&B artists. There's really only one person to call when you want to check those boxes off at the same time and that's Babyface. "These Are the Times" was written and produced by Babyface and Damon Thomas. It was released as a single in November of 1998. "These Are the Times" is about being in the moment and being happy with whatever that moment brings. The moment can be a night of passion or a night of passionate conversation. Patience gets lost in anxiousness. The verses are split in half between Sisqo and Jazz. Dru Hill, unlike most groups, has two powerhouse vocalists in Jazz and Sisqo. There's usually only one. This song is a very light ballad, using a lot of electronic sounds and synth elements. Those are all the things that pop acts use to construct their ballads, and Dru Hill still managed to make it an R&B song with their talent. The video was an interpretation of the movie *The Man in the Iron Mask* with Leonardo DiCaprio, and Lark Voorhees plays the love interest of Sisqo. The song did well, but likely didn't hit the mark as the pop crossover they wanted it to be. They put just a little too much sauce on it. "These Are the Times" peaked at 21 on the Billboard Hot 100 and got all the way up to 5 on the R&B charts.

I love the fringe conversation of top 5 this, and top 5 that. Especially when it comes to music. Most times it helps me contextualize a conversation and a person's music taste. One of my favorites is the best bridge singers of all time. Bridges used to be important. Hell they used to exist in general, but not so much anymore. My favorite bridge singer is Musiq Soulchild, but for a while it was a tossup between him and Sisqo. One of the main reasons I couldn't decide was "Beauty". What Sisqo did with the bridge on "Beauty" is damn near scriptural. "Beauty" was never truly released as a single, but the album had been out for a couple of months and it was already being signaled as one of the gems on the album. It wasn't going to be denied it's run on the radio. "Beauty" is a ballad. Very minimal in production. It's got some light strings, and a piano as the lead. The song took about a year to write and produce because Nokio was living it in real time. It was co-written by Nokio, Guy Roche, and Phil Weatherspoon, and produced by Nokio and Guy Roche. When Nokio first presented the song to the group, they weren't fans of the song. It wasn't until Nokio got in the studio on his own time, demoed the song and brought it to them, that they changed their minds about recording the song. "Beauty" spent 5 weeks on the chart and peaked at 68 on the Billboard Hot 100. I think it's the strongest song on the album, but it didn't do as well as other songs. However, even without the backing of the record company, "Beauty" went on to be one of the R&B songs of the year with ASCAP.

Dru Hill recorded *Enter the Dru* at a fairly vigorous pace. The entire album was recorded in Los Angeles over a 3 week span. In that time, they were able to put together a few songs, with the legendary duo of Diane Warren and David Foster. They're known more for their iconic pop hits, but are respected industry wide. There were two songs put together by Warren and Foster for Dru Hill. One of them was "If I Was the One" and it ended up in the hands of another Baltimore based group (Ruff Endz). The song that did make the album is the power ballad "What Do I Do with the Love". This unassuming song was tucked towards the end of the album. "What Do I Do with the Love" is an thought-provoking song, because it questions the act of being full of love and being satisfied with giving but not receiving vs. needing the ebb and flow of sharing love. "What Do I Do with the Love" has that big sound of all the epic pop love songs from the 80's. If this song was sung by any boy band instead of these Baltimore crooners it would have likely been a diamond selling single. Jazz sings the first verse and Sisqo sings the second verse. This was never a single, but I can only imagine the damage it could have done on someone's soundtrack.

After a long drawn out battle with their label, Dru Hill came back with this album and established that they'd be around as long as they choose to be. *Enter the Dru* gave Sisqo, Nokio, Jazz and Woody their first executive producer credits, and became a vehicle for their maturation as artists and businessmen. They all oversaw the writing and producing of the album to varying extents, and as performers they'd seen the world. They even performed at Nelson Mandela's birthday party. They bet on themselves and won. *Enter the Dru* went on to sell over 2 million copies and ended the year peaking at 2 on the Billboard charts.

FUN FACT: Well. Not so fun fact really. This truly took the wind out of the momentum that Dru Hill was working so hard for and building up to. Dru Hill locked in to the studio in Los Angeles and knocked the album out. After the album was finished Dru Hill was in Africa singing at Mandela's birthday party, when they got the call to come and shoot their video for "How Deep Is Your Love" in Hong Kong. They left Hong Kong to return to Los Angeles and shoot the video for "These Are the Times". Shortly after that Woody, abruptly left the group to pursue a solo career in gospel music. That's why Woody wasn't in the last video for this album "You Are Everything (remix)" featuring Ja Rule. With Woody leaving the group and a regrouping happening, they lost a little support from their company and the album faded away much faster than it should have.

1) What is your favorite song off of this album?
   Answer:

2) Who is your favorite singer from Dru Hill?
   Answer:

3) Do you prefer Dru Hill doing ballads or up-tempo songs?
   Answer:

4) Woody eventually rejoined the group as the 5th member. Do you think that if Woody never left Dru Hill would have been more successful?
   Answer:

CHAPTER 38

FROM THE MINT FACTORY

The 90's were the golden age of R&B. For all the talent that came out of the 90's, there were two acts that held a very particular distinction from the pack. Tony! Toni! Toné! and Mint Condition. While the rest of the R&B landscape were a collection of solo artist and groups, Tony! Toni! Toné! and Mint Condition were actual bands. Musicians in the most direct sense of the word. Mint Condition came out of Minneapolis, Minnesota and consisted of 5 original members (Stokley, Homer, Larry, Jeff and Keri). Minneapolis is known for its fertile music grounds and it's the home to quite a few incredibe vocalists like Prince, RL (from Next), and Alexander Oneal. Mint Condition burst onto the national music scene in 1991. They were discovered a few years earlier by the legendary duo Jimmy Jam and Terry Lewis, and signed them to Perspective Records. Mint Condition had been making their rounds in the Minneapolis music scene, perfecting their craft and honing their sound. After finally breaking thru to the big stage of the First Avenue nightclub in Minneapolis. The same club used in the movie *Purple Rain*. Their debut album *Meant to be Mint* was released in 1991. It served as a polite, introduction to the band, and their abilities. Their breakthrough hit was of course, the ballad "Breakin' My Heart (Pretty Brown Eyes)" that wreaked havoc on the charts for 34 weeks. The band had enough momentum to push forward with their second album efforts. In October 1993, Mint Condition released their sophmore album, and the statement piece of their discography, *From the Mint Factory*.

"Nobody Does It Betta" was the first single off the album. Releasing this as the lead single, served three purposes. 1) It was Mint Condition's way of saying we're back. 2) Mint Condition needed to toy with the idea of landing an up-tempo song because, although it was very early in their career, they knew they could deliver a ballad. 3) It was their way of stepping away from the New Jack Swing sound that they'd flirted with on their debut, and was slowly fading away from it. "Nobody Does It Betta" was a kiss goodbye to the old guard, and the ushering in of what they would come to be known for. "Nobody Does It Betta" was written by frontman Stokley Williams. Stokley had quite a bit of imprint on this song, outside of his regular lead vocals. He was also the drummer of the band, and had a hand in a good bit of the production on this song, including some keyboards. "Nobody Does It Betta" is a slightly up-tempo song about being the one completely resolved to pleasing your lady. The song is so melodic, and the lyrics are so graciously written that it may escape the casual ear. Make no mistake about it. This song is about sex.

Stokley has a way of unlocking these different textures, depending on the song and depending on where the song's progression is. He dug in is funk bag, for "Nobody Does It Betta". This is a song that you could see Morris Day taking a swing at in his hay day. The song served it's bigger purpose, and peaked at 45 on the R&B charts.

And then there was "U Send Me Swingin'". HO-LY-SHIT! Every part of this song was carved to perfection. "U Send Me Swingin'" was released in October of 1993. Mint Condition recorded this song at Jimmy Jam and Terry Lewis' Flyte Tyme Studios in Minnesota. It was written by band member Keri Lewis. "U Send Me Swingin'" is one of Mint Condition's more popular songs. They have songs in their discography that are more poetic in lyrics, but what sets this apart is, well, frankly, Stokley sang the shit out of this song. Not sung. SANG. "U Send Me Swingin'" is a love song. Plain and pure. It's a love song about, the act of being in love. The sense of fulfillment and passion that comes with new love. There are a few things that stand out to me about this song that make it unique to Mint Condition. On the production side, there's the compliment of electronic and live instrumentation. You can hear the synth and keyboards, on top of live drums, stand up bass and guitar. In the vocal arrangement you have elements of harmony and collaging. It's a pratice made famous by collaborations with Babyface and LA Reid. After stumbling out the gate a little with "Nobody Does It Betta", this was the shot in the arm that the album needed, and the reassurance the fans needed of knowing that the ballads would keep coming. "U Send Me Swingin'" peaked at 33 on the Billboard Hot 100 and got all the way up to 2 on the R&B charts.

"Someone to Love" was the 3rd single off the album. It was written by band member Larry Waddell. "Someone to Love" has a little fusion of jazz and R&B in its DNA. There's a heavy saxaphone presence from band member Jeff, throughout the song. Every R&B group worth their salt have to go out to the desert to sing. This was Mint Condition's moment. "Someone to Love" is a complimentary ballad. "Someone to Love" is one of the easier songs to sing along with on the album. The song is about wanting to be the person that is receiving a certain kind of love. One of those crush meets reality moments. Stokley always finds a way to take the most mellow songs, and open them up with his vocal ability. "Someone to Love" peaked at 28 on the Billboard Hot 100 and got all the way up to 6 on the R&B charts.

"So Fine" was more of a fringe single than an actual release. It was written by band members Stokley and Homer. It's a ballad with funk & R&B

elements in it. If ever there were a song in Mint Condition's history that was specifically made for slow jam playlist and quiet storm radio, it would be "So Fine". It's also the longest song on the album at just over 6 minutes long. I see what you did there guys. You ain't low. "So Fine" isn't such an on the nose sexual song that you'd feel uneasy listening to it in front of your mother. That's never really been Mint Condition's style. "So Fine" plays as more of an appreciation of a woman's beauty as opposed to the more common version of wanting to conquer that beauty. One of the defining components of this song is the guitar solo by Joe McCreary and Homer Odell. In the calm of the song, is this storm of aggressive yet dulcet guitar, helping to amplify the passion of the song. "So Fine" peaked at 29 on the charts in 1995.

From the Mint Factory peaked at 104 on the Billboard 200, but faired much better on the R&B charts getting up to 18. Those aren't stratospheric numbers. I know. Gaudy record sales, aren't what makes this album so special. The combination of the songs we'll play forever like "U Send Me Swingin'" and the journey into other genres on songs like "Fidelity" are what make this album special. No matter where the musicality takes you, it's still digested the same. This isn't Mint Condition's highest selling album. In fact, *From the Mint Factory* barely went gold, but it was the bridge to the artistry and momentum they needed to create their most successful album *Definition of a Band*. Mint Condition made *From the Mint Factory* an easy play.

FUN FACT: Mint Condition started in 1984 with the original members being from the twin cities St. Paul and Minneapolis at Central High School and one of the original members of the group was Ray Lynch. Ray is the son of Roger Troutman from Zapp and Roger fame. Band member Keri Lewis and Toni Braxton were married for 12 years, and even reconciled (as boyfriend and girlfriend) for a full year and a half after the divorce.

1) What's your favorite Mint Condition song?
   Answer:

2) Do you prefer Mint Condition doing ballads or up-tempo songs?
   Answer:

3) What is your favorite Mint Condition album?
   Answer:

4) Have you listened to Stokley's solo debut? No? YOU SHOULD!
   Answer: No. Seriously. Go listen to it. It's reeeeeaaaaally good.
   You're welcome ☺

CHAPTER 39

THE MISEDUCATION OF LAURYN HILL

Lauryn Hill is **the most talented woman of all time.** It's not up for debate, and Beyhive stans can argue with their mother if they choose, but facts are facts. Acting, dancing, singing, GOD level emceeing, musician, songwriter, performer (I know, I know. We'll get to that a little.). It seems the only thing Lauryn Hill can't do, is be on time for her shows. Okay. Everybody good now? We've had a comment about her tardiness. Let's move forward now.

Lauryn Hill grew up in Newark, New Jersey. As a kid, Lauryn's parents had her involved in everything from acting, to cheerleading. Her love for music, came from simply being in a house that was filled with it. Lauryn's mother and father were professional class people making a way for their family, and the children were an important piece of that. They invested in Lauryn and her brother. Lauryn even took acting lessons on the weekend in New York, where the family lived briefly. Lauryn's mother and father were semi professional musicians as well. Singing in clubs and on the local gospel circuit. Lauryn was in middle school, when she performed at the apollo. It didn't go very well for her, and she was discouraged for a time over it. It wasn't until high school that Lauryn linked up with Pras and Wyclef to form the Translator Crew. Later on changing their name to Fugees, short for refugees. After signing to Columbia records they saw very minimal success with their debut album, but they'd begun building a reputation for their showmanship and use of live instrumentation to fuse with other genres like reggae and afro-punk. It wasn't until their second album *The Score* that the Fugees saw true success. Hailed as one of the best Hip Hop albums of all time, selling 17 million copies worldwide, 6 million domestically. There were quite a few successful singles off that album, but it was Lauryn's rendition of "Killing Me Softly" that blew the top totally off. We all knew she'd have to eventually go solo. Beautiful and talented with a built in dynamic following? Yeah. Even as a kid the math was pretty easy to do on that one. They even won a Grammy for best R&B performance with that song. Lauryn and Wyclef's romantic relationship was marred by new found success, young love and Wyclef being married, certainly didn't help things either. The group eventually broke up to pursue their own projects. From the ashes of a hard breakup, and the new reality of being a star, Lauryn created one of the finest projects to ever grace our ears.

Lauryn began recording *The Miseducation of Lauryn Hill* in 1997. The album name is a play on *The Mis-Education of the Negro* by Carter G. Woodson and the 70's film *The Education of Sonny Carson*. Lauryn wrote the album while she was pregnant with her first child. She'd written over 30 different songs, and has said that the overwhelming flow of creativity that she was in, was induced by her pregnancy. Hill recorded the majority of the album at Tuff Gong Studios in Jamaica. The recording home of Bob Marley who is the father of her, then boyfriend and co-parent Rohan Marley. Lauryn chose to go to Jamaica and record because she felt the pressure of being too accessible to people in America. She needed the artistic freedom of distancing herself from people. Lauryn took her time. She'd fought and won the right to have total control over her album. By the summer of 1998, Lauryn's album was done, she was a new mother, and was ready to share her vision of that which was and will be with the world. On August 25th, 1998, just a few short weeks after her son Zion's first birthday, we opened our arms and received *The Miseducation of Lauryn Hill*.

"Doo Wop (That Thing)" was the first single off of the album. It was released in July of 1998. Lauryn wrote, produced and recorded the song. It's an up-tempo song with elements of Doo Wop, R&B and Hip Hop. "Doo Wop (That Thing)" is one of the truest representations of Lauryn Hill and her boundless artistry. Lauryn has always professed to be a lover of God and all things created by God. This song kind of speaks to that sentiment. Lauryn spends the first verse compelling women to have more respect for themselves, and to find their beauty and value within themselves, as opposed to waiting for a man to tell them their value. The second verse is a wakeup call to men, to focus on the important things in life, over image. Kind of a call to the altar for men that find joy in bragging about their money and things when they're really just living in their mothers house and shirking their responsibilities. "Doo Wop (That Thing)" is an accountability report on the current war of men and women in relationships. The song debuted and peaked at 1 on the Billboard Hot 100 and R&B charts. It was an actual rocket that shot straight to the top. This was the first time since 1989, that a woman debuted at 1 on the charts with a song that she'd written, produced and recorded on her own. She was no longer just L Boogie. She was becoming Lauryn Hill.

"Ex-Factor" was the second single off of the album. It was released in the winter of 1998. More specifically in December. Right in the midst of holiday season and the loneliest time of year for a lot of people. I pity you if you'd broken someone's heart around this time, because I can assure you that your victim had this song on repeat. Around the time that Lauryn wrote "Ex-Factor" she'd been on a little bit of a tear as a writer and producer. She'd recently written for Aretha Franklin, CeCe Winans, and Whitney Houston. She was in a good creative space at the time. Initially "Ex-Factor" was written for another artist, but after Lauryn demoed the song, she decided to keep it for herself. It was just too personal for her, and she wanted to be the one to tell that story. Lauryn never fully confirmed that she wrote this song about her relationship with Wyclef Jean, but you'd have to pretty much be dumb, deaf and blind to not see the deep and apparent correlations. Lauryn produced the song as well. "Ex-Factor" is about having your heartbroken and being confused at the actions of the person that you've poured so much of yourself into. The part of the song/story that doesn't really get discussed much is the mind games that she dealt with. In the bridge Lauryn talks about how she knew the relationship/situation she was in was wrong. It was bad for both of them, and every time she'd try to make some distance between herself and him, that he'd beg her to stay. He'd just keep begging her to stay and make him happy, but wouldn't commit to her happiness in return. It's a selfish act that everyone has either been on the receiving or giving end of. The same sample used in Wu-Tang Clan's "Can It Be All So Simple" was used in the song, which Lauryn eludes to in the first line, were taken from a Gladys Knight & the Pips song "The Way We Were". "Ex-Factor" peaked at 21 on the Billboard Hot 100 and got all the way up to 7 on the R&B charts. It spent about 7 months on the charts.

"Everything Is Everything" was the 3rd single from the album. It was released in May of 1999 and by this time, the album was already a success. Lauryn took this turn of phrase meaning, everything is alright, to paint a picture of overcoming some past pains that she endured. Lauryn once referred to "Everything is Everything" as a return to a brighter space. The album deals with so much pain and Lauryn put just as much energy into adding space for hope on the album. She says that she wrote the song for people in their youth, but it could really apply to anyone looking to find their way in the world. "Everything is Everything" is a song about deciding your fate instead of letting lifes ills decide for you. Lauryn reminds you that what's meant to be will happen and that its inevitable. It's as if she wrote this for Zion to lean on when he became a young man. The song peaked at 35 on the Billboard Hot 100 and got all the way up to 14 on the R&B charts. The video shows Lauryn walking in New York as if she's in search of her happiness, and New York is on a record. The video was lauded pretty well and even nominated for a Grammy, Soul Train, and MTV award.

I have a certain appreciation for love songs that are just love songs. Over time, R&B has strayed away from it's roots of deep sentiment and emotion, to this crass, exploitation of shallow, sexually charged anthems. Honestly, think for a moment. For those of you that still listen to the radio, when was the last time you heard a love song devoid of some sexuality in it? It's just where the music is right now, and it's partly why the dynamic of men and women is where it is right now. Is the music a report card on reality or is reality a report card on the music? Not sure either way, but the lack of love songs, has made me truly appreciate the real ones. When I think of love songs that are purely love songs, I think of two songs. "Spend My Life with You" and "Nothing Even Matters". This couldn't be more perfect for me. D'angelo just as much then as now, was my favorite singer, and the woman I once told my mother I was going to marry did a song together, and it came out absolutely perfect. "Nothing Even Matters" is presumed to be Hill's nod to the happiness she found with Rohan. I'm sure it's true. It speaks to a love being so full and wholehearted that the day to day ups and downs of life, can't even disturb its flow. Lauryn and D'angelo wrote the song together. Their connection was James Poyser, who was D'angelo's keyboardist, and he had been working with Lauryn on her album and D'angelo on his upcoming album *Voodoo*. Lauryn served as the producer here as well. I've been listening to this song for over 20 years, and I still can't believe the strength of what D'angelo sings in that 4th verse. That's deep. Lauryn, being a fan of old soul, said that she always wanted to do a duet that reminded her of Roberta Flack and Donny Hathaway singing together. I think they did just that. Nobody is trying to outsing the other person here, and nobody is trying to steal from the feeling of the production. "Nothing Even Matters" is a completely symbiotic song, that didn't dissapoint in even the slightest way. It was never officially released as a single, but once we got ahold of it, you would've thought that it was. *The Miseducation of Lauryn Hill* ended 1998, ranked 24 on the Billboard 200, and that ranking jumped to 11 in 1999.

FUN FACT: While Lauryn was recording her album, she was impressed with a cover she heard of a Stevie Wonder song from a 19 year old. She loved his approach to playing the piano. She was even more impressed when she found out that he was a junior at the University of Pennsylvania at the young age of 19. Lauryn was so impressed by the prodigy that she asked him to sit in and play on the album, and he played piano on "Everything is Everything". That young student, went on to become John Legend. He's credited in the production notes under his government name of John Stephens.

1) What is your favorite song off of this album?
   Answer:

2) Have you ever seen Lauryn Hill live in concert?
   Answer:

3) What song on the album should have been a single but wasn't?
   Answer:

4) Do you consider this an R&B album?
   Answer:

CHAPTER 40

THREE KINGS

Tyrese, Ginuwine and Tank have all had different paths to stardom, and different courses in their career. Ginuwine has the hits out of the group. Tyrese has the popularity of the group. Tank, in my opinion, is the most talented of the 3 as an overall artist. They've all been underrated in their career as well. They decided to join forces and when that finally came to fruition, the timing was perfect. They've all been personal friends for years, and the idea of forming a super group bloomed well before the album. The idea of TGT started in 2007. It was going to be more of a campaign than a project at first. They intended to put a tour together called the single ladies tour, and fuel it with a solo project from each member. There was just too much red tape between schedules, labels, and overall timing. It wasn't the right time. It wasn't until 2012 that all 3 members sorted their business and schedules to the point that they could follow thru and begin working on their TGT album. They recorded for a year between LA and NYC and each member appears on every song. In August of 2013 TGT released their album *Three Kings*.

"Sex Never Felt Better" was the first single off of the album. It was released on February 14th of 2013. Valentines' Day. A little on the nose, but it was important. TGT wanted to let people know what they could expect from the album. Tyrese, in his salesmanship and colorful commentary categorized the songs on the album as "leave it in" music. Yep. That's a quote. "Sex Never Felt Better" delivered. It was written by Tank, Tyrese, Lonny Bereal, and Doe Smith. "Sex Never Felt Better" is a ballad, but the production gives it a real flare. Between the synth sounds, guitar and the bass line, it comes across as a mid-tempo song. Ginuwine sings the first verse, with Tyrese singing the 2nd. Tank sings the bridge and pulls up the rear. The video is a performance setting, with TGT singing on stage in front of a crowd of women, swooning and throwing their panties at them on stage. "Sex Never Felt Better" peaked at 13 on the Billboard Hot 100.

"I Need" was the 2nd single off of the album. It was released on July 2nd 2013. Keeping with the theme of the album and it's grown man business ethos, half of the album is an ode to sexy time and the other half to let's figure this thing out. That's where "I Need" falls. It's a ballad. We've got to have some begging right? This is R&B right? "I Need" was written by Tank, Ginuwine, Tyrese and Brandon Hodge and it was produced by The Underdogs. "I Need" is saying that I can't live without you and being with you is more important than being right. Pretty important message, because being at that stage is not only a testament to a relationships strength, but also personal development as an adult. Women are usually the last to reach this level of thinking in a relationship...I said what I said. Tank opens the song with the first verse and Tyrese is on the 2nd verse. Ginuwine sings the bridge, but it really feels like more of a long verse. "I Need" peaked at 29 on the R&B charts.

"Next Time Around" was the 3rd and final single from the album. It was written and produced by Tank. There's a heavy guitar and synth presence on this song. At first listen it kind of reminded me of "Motivation" by Kelly Rowland. Tyrese opens the song with the first verse, Ginuwine is on the 2nd verse and Tank sings the bridge and vamp. "Next Time Around" is about getting past mistakes that you've made in your relationship and doing things better if you were to get a second chance. What I really love about this song is how the vocal arrangements change throughout the song. The first second and third hooks, all sound different. Even though their singing together the top vocal keeps switching between the three of them. This may be the one song on the album that Tank allowed himself to stand out a bit more than Ginuwine and Tyrese. "Next Time Around" was an early release in 2014, but the album was already in people's hands at that point. It peaked at 6 on the R&B charts, but it was only on the charts for 5 weeks.

"Hurry" is probably my 2nd favorite song on the album. It was written and produced by Tim & Bob with Stevie J. Which makes total sense, because it has a 90's R&B vibe to it. "Hurry" is some of that "leave it in music" that Tyrese was talking about. "Hurry" speaks to wanting to get right to business in the bedroom. Skip the foreplay, forget all the prepping, we don't even have to cut the lights out. I WANT YOU RIGHT NOW. "Hurry" is all passion. Tank sings the first verse, with Ginuwine on the 2nd verse and Tyrese on the bridge and vamp. My one complaint with "Hurry" is that it's only 3 minutes long. I would've loved it to be more around the 4 to 5 minute mark. Of all the songs on the album, I like the vocal arrangement on "Hurry" the best. It's the one that most makes them sound like a group.

Three Kings, debuted and peaked at 3 on the Billboard 200, and it got all the way up to 1 on the R&B charts. *Three Kings* wasn't just about the music. It wasn't just about the 3 amazing solo artist that decided to weld their talents together for a collaborative album either. *Three Kings* was about timing. At the time that *Three Kings* came out, it was the most important R&B album in nearly a decade because, frankly, there wasn't much real R&B being made at the time. Radio and the landscape of R&B music was either some watered down lyrically deficient pop masquerading as R&B, or a fusion of rap and R&B. *Three Kings* came out and we were once again hearing real singers, delivering songs with adult content. Unfortunately, it looks like *Three Kings* will be the last TGT album that we'll ever get. It took 6 years to materialize and it's over that fast. Grand opening. Grand closing. There were internal disagreements that were rooted in business, and spilled over into personal. Each member has a different account of what happened, but either way it looks pretty bleak on a reunion.

FUN FACT: During promotion for the album, TGT had a bad performance on television. They were performing "I Need". Tank was playing the piano and Tyrese and Ginuwine were in front of him. It was a lifeless, horrible performance. This is the performance that Tyrese points to as the downfall for the group. Tyrese says that Ginuwine showed up to the performance drunk, and was forgetting his lyrics. Ginuwine says that it's not true, and honestly...yeah. I don't know. You can Google it and watch it on YouTube for yourself. All I know is, Tyrese looked like he really wanted to slap the shit out of Ginuwine.(Google TGT+Bad performance). It looks bad.

1) Which member of TGT is your favorite?
Answer:

2) What is your favorite song on the album?
Answer:

3) When this album came out, did you buy it?
Answer:

4) If there were going to be 3 other R&B solo artist to form a super group, who would you like it to be?
Answer:

CHAPTER 41

CONFESSIONS

The work was put in. The talent has always been there and in fact sharpened over time. The legacy is set in stone. There's no way in hell URSHER, yeah URSHER not Usher, was going to miss his place on this list. Usher was born in Dallas, Texas and raised between Chattanooga and Atlanta. He discovered his love for singing while in his youth choir in Chattanooga. Usher had a small stint with a singing group when he was ten, but his MOMager knew that wasn't the best route for him. Usher and his family moved to Atlanta to explore bigger and better opportunities for Usher. Usher continued to do talent shows and, showcases once he came to Atlanta. Usher really began to make noise around the city when he won the Atlanta Talent Search in 1992. Usher signed with LaFace records shortly after that win. Usher has had a brilliant career, making the quick shift from child star to heartthrob, to superstar. His breakthrough album was his sophomore release *My Way* in 1997, which was curated by Jermaine Dupri and sold well over 6 million copies. *8701* was Usher's 3rd album released on 8/7/01. My girlfriend at the time bought it for me as one of my birthday gifts. Usher was no longer making heartthrob music. Usher was a young adult at 23 and his music now reflected that. It was vibrant, emotional and fun. *8701* sold 5 million copies and sent Usher home with 2 Grammy awards, 3 Billboard awards, A BET award, and a Soul Train award. With all this success, Usher still hadn't seen his ceiling. There was so much more for him to explore as a creative. It wasn't until Usher's 4th album, that he entered a new stratosphere as an artist, celebrity and a man. He began recording the album in 2003 and finished at the top of 2004. On March 23, 2004, Usher released *Confessions* and the R&B world hasn't been the same since. Usher had the usual cohorts on hand for the album and it's production in Jermaine Dupri, and called a few extra favors in to Jimmy Jam & terry Lewis, Just Blaze, Lil Jon, James Lackey (his younger brother), and the ever so important Brian Michael Cox (R&B's Neo). The album was swirling with rumors of the album's theme being a recollection of Usher's personal life. It's never been confirmed by Usher and in fact Dupri has said that the album is more of a reflection of his own past experiences, but I think we can all reasonably rationalize that it's probably a bit of both.

"Yeah!" featuring Ludacris, was the first single off of the album. It was released in January of 2004. It was produced by Lil Jon and at the time he was still in the beginning stages of the short lived genre Crunk&B. "Yeah!" was written by Sean Garrett, James Phillips, Ludacris, and Patrick Smith. "Yeah!" was a sound that we'd just never heard before. Most of the pull of the song is the curiosity that the song makes. You wonder where it's going as soon as it comes on. "Yeah!" is a club banger, because it's high energy and melodic at the same time. All of us got so caught up in the song that we never really even thought about what the song means. "Yeah!" is about young URSHER spending a night out at the club with his boys and getting seduced by a woman that used to be good friends with his current girlfriend. She's seducing Usher with her dancing and all the sweet nothings she keeps whispering in his ear. Usher already knows he's wrong for even dancing and flirting with her, and the song ends with him trying to figure out whether he should go and do the damn thing with her. The song ends before we find out how the night played out, but based on the recurring theme of the album, it's safe to say that it went down. "Yeah!" almost didn't make the album. Usher was concerned that it sounded too much like "Freek-A-Leek" by Petey Pablo and produced by Lil Jon. "Yeah!" peaked at number 1 on the Billboard hot 100, R&B, R&B/Hip-Hop and Mainstream top 40, where it remained for 12 consecutive weeks. **Side note for the ladies**: Every woman has a friend or ex-friend (like the one on this song) that will sleep with your man if given the chance. Again, EVERY WOMAN ☺.

"Burn" was the 2nd single off of the album. It was co-written by Usher, Bryan-Michael Cox and Jermaine Dupri, and produced by Bryan-Michael Cox and Jermaine Dupri. The song came about around the time that Usher and Chili were breaking up, so the speculation has always been that it was written about Chili. "Burn" is about how Usher feels he needs to breakup with his woman because he doesn't think that the problems they've been having will get better. Every relationship has a point of no return and he thinks they've crossed it. This is a very grown-up song, because you have to be an adult to understand that you can love someone and still know that the relationship can't go any further. The real lesson here is that Usher feels like he threw the relationship away to early and he wants her back. The context of the song changes thru the course of the song from needing to let the relationship run it's course and "Burn" away, to being in so much emotional pain from her absence that he feels like he's actually "Burn"ing. Pretty brilliant, but I've come to expect such things from anything that Brian-Michael Cox touches. "Burn" dethroned "Yeah!" after 12 weeks at the top of the charts and peaking at number 1. "Burn" spent 7 consecutive weeks at number 1 before moving.

"Confessions Part II" was the 3rd single off the album. It was released June 1, 2004. "Confessions Part II" is the companion piece to "Confessions" on the album. "Confessions" is more of a ballad describing Usher's cheating and "Confessions Part II" is more of a mid-tempo song explaining of his actions. It's less of a singing song than "Confessions" too, because Usher is telling the story of how he came clean. Jermaine Dupri has stepped in front of the barrage of speculation that this is about why Usher and Chili broke up, by saying that it's based of his own life experiences. "Confessions Part II" was written by Usher, Jermaine Dupri and Bryan-Michael Cox, and co-produced by Jermaine Dupri and Bryan-Michael Cox. "Confessions Part II" debuted at 48 and eventually peaked at number 1 on the Billboard Hot 100 and R&B charts, making this Usher's 3rd consecutive number 1 single. It stayed at the top of the charts for 3 weeks and in the top ten for 13 weeks.

"Simple Things" was never a single, but it's a very important song. Usher got together with Jimmy Jam & Terry Lewis in their home studio in Santa Monica to make this gem. "Simple Things" is about remembering to spoil your lover with more than just material things. Usher warns to spoil with your attention, moments and your love. "Simple Things" is that mid-tempo vibe that's been popular in modern R&B. Usher had a lot of true moments of perspective on this album and "Simple Things" is one of the more important ones, because it speaks in the present tense as a precautionary tale, as opposed to being a story of regret. I think it's an interesting concept. Jimmy Jam & Terry Lewis made use of all their typical elements to create this song, with a heavy keyboard and guitar presence to drive the song.

"Can U Handle It?" is one of my favorite songs on this album because, honestly, when Usher decides to make a song for bedroom activities it damn near becomes an anthem. It was written by Robin Thicke, Usher, and Robert Daniels, and produced by Robin Thicke and Pro J. Many people don't know that Robin Thicke got in the game by being a songwriter and producer before launching his own solo career, and thank goodness that he never stopped creating for other people. I don't think anyone else could have done this song besides Usher. The vocal ability that it takes to sing in your falsetto with this much power and clarity is a rare gift. "Can U Handle It" is the longest song on the album at almost 6 minutes. Perfectly unfolded at the right pace for a song like this. Robin built the music with strings, guitar, an infectious bass line and the snaps. I mean, what's a bedroom centric song without the use of snaps to set the pace? The beautiful Paula Patton, Robin's ex-wife, is the woman doing the backing vocals on the song. I wonder if she got a plaque too. Never the less, "Can U Handle It" is a must hear on an album packed with hits.

Confessions ended the year as the number 1 rated album. It debuted at number 1 on the charts and it made URSHER the first solo artist to ever have 3 songs on the Billboard Hot 100 simultaneously. It was just out of control how successful *Confessions* was, and it wasn't without warrant. *Confessions* was a phenomenon at every juncture from it's folklore to the music itself, without even considering the gaudy record sales, in a time where bootlegging was taking a true chunk out of the music industry's pockets. *Confessions* sold 1.1 million copies in the first week. *Confessions* is a diamond album, selling 10 million copies domestically and 15 million worldwide. Usher won a Grammy, 2 Billboard awards, 2 American Music Awards, a Soul Train award and an MTV award. Every box was checked and *Confessions* continues to be one of the greatest R&B albums ever made, by one of the greatest R&B artists of all time.

FUN FACT: The video for "Yeah!" was shot in an art gallery in Los Angeles. The director had a vision of a sprawling dance floor, and laser lights filling the void of darkness in the club. It was a really big cast, and a long shoot. With the constraints of the music video budget, the production team had trouble feeding everyone and no vendors were brought in. Instead everyone feasted on peanut butter and jelly sandwiches and CRUNK Juice (Lil Jon's energy drink). HELLLLLLLLLLL NAAAAAAAAAW.

1) What is your favorite song on this album?
   Answer:

2) How many of this album's content/songs do you think stem from Usher's relationship with Chili?
   Answer:

3) What rapper do you think had the best feature on the album?
   Answer:

4) What song do you wish there was a music video for?
   Answer:

CHAPTER 42

CRAZY SEXY COOL

Rest In Peace Lisa "Left Eye" Lopes

Let's just assume you've been under a rock your whole life for a second. TLC came into our lives in 1992. They're a girl group rooted in Atlanta, Ga. The group consisted of T-Boz, Left Eye and Chilli. As a young talented group they signed an absolute DOG SHIT of a contract with Pebbitone, run by Pebbles Reid. They were then signed to a production deal on Pebbles' husband label LaFace, to be distributed by Arista, the parent company. They pretty much began working immediately on their album and in February of 1992 they released their debut album *Oooooooohhh...On the TLC Tip*. The album was this genre bending fusion of Hip-Hop, R&B and Funk. They were basically the female and more importantly better version of Bell-Biv- Devoe. That's not a diss either. I just need to scale how incredible TLC was. They washed us over with their flare, their performance, their risqué content and their cadence. They seemed like the girls you wanted to have a summer romance with, and in the minds of some weirdos, they were just that. It's me...I'm some weirdos. The debut had "Ain't 2 Proud 2 Beg", "Baby-Baby-Baby", "What About Your Friends", "Hat 2 da Back" and so on and so on and so on. It was just an amazing and fun album. I obviously wasn't the only one to think that because the album sold 6 million copies worldwide. TLC was a success. They were touring the world, opening for MC Hammer and performing in front of every camera that was pointed their way. They started recording their second album in 1993 and finished in the summer of 1994. On November 15, 1994 TLC released their sophomore album and classic, *CrazySexyCool*.

"Creep" was the first single off of the album. "Creep" was written and produced by Dallas Austin. He was a common collaborator for TLC from their first album, and he'd begun a romantic relationship with Chilli. "Creep" was released as a single on October 31, 1994. It's a song about a woman who cheats on her man, because he's cheating. That's the bones of the song, but there are also points that insinuate she's cheating because he isn't paying her enough attention. Jeez. Tough room. The song was written by Dallas Austin, but it was inspired by a personal situation with T-Boz. T-Boz shared the situation between her, Dalvin (Jodeci) and _____. Dallas turned it into a song. The song did well. "Creep" debuted at 71 and peaked at number 1 on the Billboard Hot 100 and R&B charts. It was their first Billboard Hot 100 #1. They were 1 on the Billboard Hot 100 for 4 consecutive weeks. To this day it's considered as one of TLC staple pieces of music. One of the important things that Left Eye wanted to show on this album, was their personal growth. She really wanted them to be seen as grown women, fully capable of wielding their sexuality as women. That thought is partially where the treatment for the "Creep" video came from. Left Eye saw the "Whatta Man" video with Salt-N-Pepa and En Vogue and told T-Boz and Chilli "that's what we need to do".

They got their first chance with "Red Light Special". It was the second single off of *CrazySexyCool*, and they released it on February 21, 1995. "Red Light Special" was written and produced by Babyface. T-Boz sings the first and second verse. Her raspy lower register sits squarely on top of the funky Isley Brotheresque guitar riffs. Chilli sings the bridge and gives the song a chance to transition. "Red Light Special" checks the box for the sexy element of the album. It's slow, full of both live and electronic sounds and very, very intentional * wink wink *. It's the longest song on the album and serves its purpose. The term "Red Light Special" is a turn of phrase that was casually used in Amsterdam in the 90's, when it was known as the sex capital of the world. "Red Light Special" is also their spiciest video ever. It's set in a brothel full of male prostitutes and Left Eye is playing their pimp. Chili and T-Boz are clients trying to win a game of strip poker. Famous director Billie Woodruff directed the video. "Red Light Special" peaked at 2 on the Billboard Hot 100 and got all the way up to 3 on the R&B charts.

"Waterfalls" was the 3rd single off the album. It was released in May of 1995. It was written by Marqueze Etheridge and Left Eye, and produced by none other than Organized Noize (Outkast, Goodie Mob, En Vogue). Ceelo even sung background vocals on the song. TLC was no stranger to discussing tough topics, even so early on in their career. On their debut they talked about safe sex, being liberated as women and the power of making your own choices. "Waterfalls" was different for them, because the conversations were life and death in a very relatable way now. The first verse tells the tale of a young man (Shyheim the rugged child for all my Hip Hop heads) falling victim to the pressures of the streets. His mom keeps trying to stop him from selling drugs, and he eventually gets shot down on the street corner (by Bokeem Woodbine). The second verse is about the dangers of unsafe sex becoming HIV or AIDS. In 1995 that was a major issue, and that's not to say that it isn't still in 2020. It is safe to say that people were operating with far less information about HIV at the time. The "Waterfalls" that the song talks about are things people can obsess over without thinking of the consequences that are attached to that obsession. In the first verse it was the money from dealing, and in the second verse it was the casual sex that he was enjoying. Both situations led to death. It was also a rough time for Left Eye, because she was still fresh off the drama of burning down her boyfriend Andre Rison's Atlanta Mansion, and being arrested, dealing with rehab, all while still being in the public eye. She was in a rough personal space, and she knew things were going to be better when a sign of things to come came as a rainbow she saw in the sky. Her verse on the song was real. It was a recollection for her. She needed to get that weight off her chest and it couldn't have been a better moment to do it. This was also the first single from the album that Left Eye had a verse on. I was going to say that "Waterfalls" WAS a great hit, but the truth is, it's STILL a great hit. From the mouth of Rico Wade of Organized Noize himself "I still get checks for "Waterfalls" to this day." It peaked at #1 on the Billboard Hot 100 and got all the way up to #4 on the R&B charts. "Waterfalls" spent 2 months at the top spot on the charts, and brought TLC damn near 10 different awards for the groundbreaking music video.

"Diggin' on You" was the 4th and final single from the album. It was written and produced by Babyface. "Diggin' on You" had a much lighter feel to it than the other singles. It was clearly a swing at the crossover song that so many R&B albums had to have on them. MTV was the main music video source at the time, and they had a demographic that was spending millions on boy bands every year. It was just good business to do songs that felt like pop, but were delivered by R&B artist. "Diggin' on You" is a song about having a crush on someone. Babyface did a good job of throwing around all the electric instruments that pop songs are typically built on top of. "Diggin' on You" peaked at 5 on the Billboard Hot 100 and got up to 7 on the R&B charts. Just as it was on quite a bit of the album, Left Eye's vocals were taken off of this song and replaced with Debra Killing's vocals. It's one of the main reasons that Left Eye sought to go solo.

CrazySexyCool debuted at 15 on the Billboard 200 and peaked at 5 on the Billboard 200. The album went platinum, even though the group filed for bankruptcy shortly after the album was released. Again, thanks to the evil that is Perri Reid (Pebbles) they signed an absolute DOG SHIT contract and they were broke. All in all *CrazySexyCool* sold over 14 million copies worldwide. TLC eventually got out of their contract and completed a 3rd album.

FUN FACT: The visuals for this album had many stories attached to them. Left Eye was opposed to the song "Creep". She thought it would send the wrong message and have a negative presence in her own personal relationship. She was however outvoted and TLC did the song. Left Eye eve threatened to appear on the video with a piece of tape over her mouth in silent protest. She ditched the tape idea and simply didn't lip sync on the song. If you watch the video, there is no footage of Left Eye singing the words to the song. "Waterfalls" almost didn't make the album, let alone a video. TLC had to plead to Clive Davis and LA Reid to give the song some promotion and a budget for the video. They knew that the song would be a hit, but had to convince the brass. They took a big poster board and wrote, "Believe in us. Believe in our vision" on it, and had it delivered to LA Reid, and he put the budget together for the video. "Waterfalls" video was shot at Universal Studios in the same pool they used to shoot *Jaws*. Chilli was terrified at the shoot, because she couldn't swim. They were all standing on this thin strip of hard plastic in the middle of tons and tons of water. Chilli said, "That's exactly why my feet were planted. I would not move. I was too worried about falling in." It's funny. I'd never noticed it before, but if you watch the video now that you've read this, you can see that she's clearly only moving her arms. Well played Rozonda. Well played. Also, it was MC Hammer that pulled them to the side while they were on tour and let them know that the metrics in their contract were not right. He's the one that opened their eyes to what the wicked wi...Pebbles. I mean Pebbles. Hammer was the one that let them know that Pebbles was fleecing them.

1) What is your favorite song on the album?
   Answer:

2) Who is your favorite TLC member?
   Answer:

3) What is your favorite music video from this album?
   Answer:

4) Have you ever heard the unreleased rap single from this album "My Secret Enemy"?
   Answer: HEAD ON OVER TO YOUTUBE THEN ☺

CHAPTER 43

IT'S ABOUT TIME

SWV rose out of NYC. They originally started off as a gospel group. The members are Coko, Taj and Lelee. Coko and Lelee were original members with Taj coming on to replace another young lady that didn't work out. SWV stands for sisters with voices. SWV was the first R&B girl group of the 90's to successfully connect with the New Jack Swing sound. 1992 was a good year for girl groups, with it being the same year that Xscape debuted. SWV was discovered after they got their demo together and their manager (even today) Maureen sent the demo out. SWV got invited to audition for RCA and were signed to a multi-album deal. The group was sent to California almost immediately and began recording their album in in October of 1991. By summer of 1992 they'd finished recording their debut. It was a mix of classic R&B and New Jack Swing. They had some difficulty getting out of the starting gates thanks to typical industry red tape. On October 27, 1992 their debut *It's About Time* was released.

"Right Here" was their first single off of the album, released August 20, 1992. It was written and produced by Brian Alexander Morgan and the group member Taj. Morgan was the main producer on the entire album. Taj said she was sweeping the floor of her apartment, the first time she heard the song, and started jumping up and down on the floor so much that her neighbors started banging on the ceiling. "Right Here" is about reassuring your lover that you're not interested in anyone else, as long as they keep making you happy. Young love is often hindered by insecurity. "Right Here" is an up-tempo song with Hip-Hop influence. It was Brian Morgan's interpretation of New Jack Swing. It passes the ear test, because it was well written and had the sing along value that we've all come to love in R&B. "Right Here" didn't get much airplay. It was drowned in all the other sounds on the radio at the time. "Right Here" never made the Billboard Hot 100 and it peaked at 13 on the R&B charts. That's a rough start for a group that already had trouble getting their album released in the first place. The album sales were stagnant to say the least. SWV didn't have a single that was pushing attention to their album. They didn't really start picking up steam until their second single.

"I'm So into You" was the 2nd single off the album and their first taste of success. It's another up-tempo song that gets a little closer to what New Jack Swing was. "I'm So into You" was written and produced by Brian Alexander Morgan. He pieced together the song with samples from several different songs. It's quite the quilt of production, but it came out beautifully. Morgan took the sentiment of being a side chick and romanticized it to the point that we didn't even notice that was the bones of this song. "I'm So into You" is about a woman having a relationship with a man that she knows has a girlfriend. Brilliantly hidden in plain sight and cloaked by the perfect harmony of SWV. It was the jolt the album and the group needed. It rolled slow, but "I'm So into You" eventually peaked at 6 on the Billboard charts and got all the way up to 2 on the R&B charts.

"Weak" was the 3rd single off the album and their first released ballad. They knew they'd be able to shine here. Brian Alexander Morgan wrote and produced "Weak". Originally Coko did not like the song. She had to be convinced by the producer to sing the song, and Coko gave him grief the entire recording session. "Weak" is about being so enamored with someone that you feel "Weak" at the knees from just being around them. I remember being a kid, and wanting to build the courage up to sing this to a girl I had a crush on named Benita. I never did, but the song translated for me even at such a young age. Like most of the album, "Weak" was built with electronic instruments, but it seems more intentional on this song. Morgan made the song intimate and thanks to their gospel roots, SWV pulled this song off with ease. They sung "Weak" a cappella on national TV and didn't miss a beat. It was their biggest hit. "Weak" peaked at 1 on the Billboard Hot 100 and R&B charts. It stayed at 1 for 2 consecutive weeks.

Likely my favorite song ever by SWV came on this album. "You're Always On My Mind" was the 6th and final single. "Weak" was Taj's favorite song off the album, but "You're Always On My Mind" was Coko's. One of the many disagreements they had early on. It's the longest song on the album, and written and produced by Brian Alexander Morgan. It's a duet with SWV and Brian Morgan. He sampled "Yearning for Your Love" by the Gap Band to make the song. Morgan thought the song would give him a chance to show his vocal ability as well, and that it would lead to more on that side of recording for him. It should have. Do you know how hard it is to show up Coko on a song? He did it though. The song was arranged in such a way that it keeps it's sing-along value while still giving Coko and Brian a chance to showcase their voices. The song only had moderate success, even with the music video, and peaked at 54 on the Billboard Hot 100 but got all the way up to 8 on the R&B charts.

Unfortunately life took quite a bit of steam out of SWV, after the album roll out. Coko and Taj were constantly arguing and at odds. They were no longer friends and didn't speak unless they were on stage. The album was a success though. *It's About Time* peaked at 8 on the Billboard Hot 200 and 2 on the R&B charts. *It's About Time* sold a little over 3 million copies and because of Coko's pregnancy and internal problems (specifically Coko saying that she wants ½ the money) it took 4 years for them to release their sophomore album. Thank goodness they could keep it together long enough to make this album first.

FUN FACT: SWV's signature song "Weak" was written and produced by Brian Alexander Morgan. His muse for the song was none other than the beautiful Chante Moore. He intended on giving the song to her for personal and professional reasons, but never mustered up the nerve to shoot his shot. That's when he presented it to SWV and fought for them to record it. Chante had him shook...I get it. I swear I do.

1) What was your favorite song off of this album?
   Answer:

2) Did you follow Coko's career as a solo artist?
   Answer:

3) There were 6 singles off of this album. Which was your favorite?
   Answer:

4) Have you listened to their (2nd) reunion album Still?
   Answer:

CHAPTER 44

I'M READY

Of all the child singers throughout the course of time, it's safe to say that the most vocally talented was Tevin Campbell. One could make an argument that the kid from Gary, Indiana was the most vocally talented, but I'd disagree. He was the most talented all round, for sure, but as far as good old fashioned ability to blow peoples socks off with a voice, we'd have to give that to Tevin Campbell.

Tevin Campbell was born and raised in Waxahachie, Texas right outside of Dallas, Texas. He was a child prodigy. Campbell was discovered by Benny Medina and introduced to Quincy Jones for tutelage. His first national song, "Tomorrow (A Better you, Better Me), came on Quincy Jones' Grammy award winning album *Back on the Block*. Tevin had the chance to work with Prince on the *Graffiti Bridge* Soundtrack, and finally started working on his debut *T.E.V.I.N.* in May of 1990. Tevin was paired with Quincy Jones, Al B. Sure, Prince and Narada Michael Walden. It was released in November of 1991. The album saw success with singles like "Round and Round", "Just Ask Me To", and "Tell Me What You Want Me To Do". The album peaked at 38 on the Billboard 200 and got all the way up to 5 on the R&B charts. *T.E.V.I.N.* sold over a million copies and Tevin Campbell was everywhere from xmas albums, to The Fresh Prince Of Bel Air (Partially based on the life of Benny Medina). He was a week away from 16 years old when the album dropped. It wasn't until October 1993 that we got a glimpse of Tevin as an adult when *I'm Ready* was released. He was 17, soon to be 18, and had a wider range of context that he could touch on. This time around, Tevin got in the studio with Quincy Jones, Babyface, Daryl Simmons too.

The first single off the album, is debatably the greatest R&B song of all time. It was written and produced by Babyface and Daryl Simmons and in the summer of 1993 "Can We Talk" was released. They recorded the song at the legendary DARP studios in Atlanta, Ga. Tevin recently said that "Can We Talk" is a song about stalking someone. He was joking, but we still rebuke that. We will not let Tevin's jokes put a damper on our childhood memories. That song was everywhere. You couldn't turn the radio on for 30 minutes and not hear "Can We Talk". Despite Tevin's description, I hear "Can We Talk" describing the situation of wanting to express your interest in someone, and not knowing what to say. "Can We Talk" is a call to the courage it takes to spark a conversation with a complete stranger.

Babyface has had so many strokes of brilliance over his career as a songwriter and producer, but even he realizes that he really captured something unique with this song. Tevin's voice was the difference. Tevin, even at the young age of 11, has always had incredible vocal control and power. But what he does from the 3:00 to 3:23 mark on this song is unbelievable. Being honest, listening to this song with me can be annoying, because I'll have to listen to the bridge at least 3 times before I can move on. Tevin sung the ever-loving f*ck out of this song. "Can We Talk" peaked to 9 on the Billboard Hot 100 and got all the way up to 1 on the R&B charts.

"Shhh" was the second single off the album, and Tevin's attempt to get into some grown folks business. It was written and produced by Prince. This is probably the most PG-13 ballad that Prince had in the stash to give Tevin. This wasn't nasty Prince. It was sensual. This was new territory for Tevin, so prince gave him the keys to his motorcycle, but it had training wheels on it. It was built on top of piano and strings. Quiet storm had a field day with this. Good thing Tevin is an incredible vocalist, because usually songs that Prince writes/produces for other people sound like they'd be better if he kept them. Tevin owns "Shhh". I don't think anyone, could've delivered this song better than Tevin did. "Shhh" spent 13 weeks on the chart and peaked at 12 on the Billboard Hot 100.

"I'm Ready" was the 3rd single and the title track off the album. The album had been out for a while and was making a steady run on the charts. The public was slowly accepting that little Tevin Campbell, was now a young man. "I'm Ready" was written and produced by Babyface with Daryl Simmons. It was recorded at Doppler Studios in Atlanta. "I'm Ready" is a mid-tempo song, and it's got a melancholic feel to it. It's really kind of sad. The song is about waiting for the person that you were once with to finally accept you and love you the way that you love them. It's well hidden in the melody of the song and of course Tevin sung the hell out of it. That's just a hard song to swallow. If you listen closely you can hear Babyface in the background. This was an important song for Tevin Campbell as he began to venture into the adult portion of his career. His handlers needed as wide a net as possible to reel in as many fish as possible. "I'm Ready" is an R&B song, but it has a pop appeal to it as well. It peaked at 9 on the Billboard Hot 100 and got all the way up to 2 on the R&B charts.

"Brown Eyed Girl" was the final single off the album. It was co-written between Tevin Campbell and Narada Michael Walden, who also produced the song. Walden had experience dealing with great talent from all his work with Mariah

Carey. "Brown Eyed Girl" is a ballad. There are lots of electronic sounds in the composition of it. Keyboards, synths and drum programming. I like "Brown Eyed Girl". I think it's a really good song, and it has a very broad feel about it. It's an R&B song, because Tevin Campbell made it that, but if you give this same song to the BackStreet Boys it could be a pop song. I think that "Brown Eyed Girl" would've been better on his debut album. It's a very innocent, and lighthearted song. Maybe it would've played better for a younger Tevin, but he still delivered it.

I'm Ready was a success. There were 5 official singles off of the album, and the world got their sneak peek at what Tevin could be as an adult artist. "Can We Talk" is one of the best marriages of song and artist across any genre and Tevin had the chance to work with other writers and producers while still being mentored by Quincy Jones. *I'm Ready* went double platinum, selling just over 2 million copies and the album was nominated for multiple Grammys, including Best R&B album-Male.

FUN FACT: Around the time that Tevin was recording his album, LaFace was at the beginning of their inner turmoil. LA Reid wanted one thing and Babyface was wanted another and they just weren't seeing eye to eye as much as they used to. LaFace was still grooming their own stable of artist at the time, while still producing for other people. Babyface was putting more focus on Usher's music at the time, and LA was more out and about selling their services. Through all the confusion, a song that was originally meant for Usher, ended up in Tevin's hands and made the album. That song was "Can We Talk".

1) What is your favorite song on the album?
    Answer:

2) Which song on this album do you have the fondest memories attached to?
    Answer:

3) How old were you when you first heard this album?
    Answer:

4) Is this your favorite Tevin Campbell album?
    Answer:

CHAPTER 45

LIVE FROM NEW ORLEANS

I'm one of those fortunate people that grew up in a house full of music. Whether it was Hall & Oates to Genesis or Earth Wind & Fire to Sam Cooke, my childhood home(s) were always lit up with music. I can remember pulling off from Perimeter Mall in Atlanta once, and on that particular day I just felt like listening to Maze featuring Frankie Beverly. I had "Running Away" blasting out of my trucks' speakers. As I was backing out an older gentleman with a child, walked by smiling and yelled to me "What you know about that, young blood?!" I get that all the time from older people when they hear me listening to "their" music. I smiled and said "I was just raised right!" Truth is, it's my music too. Less my music than theirs, but still, I'm invested all the same. I wonder what memories were conjured for the old head by hearing me playing that music. He was happy. That's the nature of music. The emotions attached to it. Maze was formed in the early 70's in Philadelphia. The founding member is Frankie Beverly and they used to perform under the name Raw Soul. They began recording in Philly, and saw moderate success as a regional band. It wasn't until they relocated to San Francisco that they began to see success on a larger scale. They'd met Marvin Gaye and were afforded the opportunity to be his opening act on tour. He was very impressed by the band's full sound, and song making. They put their first album out in 1977 and kept pushing the envelope with each release up to 1993. All together they have 10 projects in their catalog, and the most important is their first live album from 1981. Why they would choose to record an album in the most loathsome, disgusting, low brow city in America (New Orleans) populated by the ugliest, subhumans in this country's sordid history (Saints fans), I will never understand. They did just that thing though. On November 14th, 1980 Maze featuring Frankie Beverly performed and recorded their first live album *Live in New Orleans*. It was a "best of", of sorts, from their previous projects, sprinkled with a few new songs. In January of 1981, the live album was released.

"You" is a song off of their first album *Maze featuring Frankie Beverly* in 1977. The studio album version is almost 9 minutes long. Bands use to really take their time and show their chops as musicians. The live version is only about 6 minutes long. "You" was written and produced by Frankie Beverly. "You" is a mid-tempo song with a guitar lead. The song is about being able to find happiness with your woman, no matter what the world is throwing at you. It was a good choice to start the concert with. The song isn't too high energy and it's easy to sing along with. Frankie Beverly is a multi-instrumentalist and plays the rhythm guitar on this song.

"Joy and Pain" is the title track off of their 4th album *Joy and Pain*. It was their current album at the time of the live recording in that wretched little swamp (New Orleans). "Joy and Pain" is one of the songs that I always reach for when I'm walking, or being dragged thru life's storms. So I've been listening to it pretty f*cking often over these last 2 years...and counting. A completely different book. Tuh Huh. On the studio album the song is 7:30 long, but on this live album it's damn near 10 minutes long. It needs to be. Like any good chef, they cook this meal up very slow, like a great risotto. "Joy and Pain" was written and produced by Frankie Beverly. "Joy and Pain" is a reminder that the bad things that happen in your life are just as important as the good things, because all of them help you to grow. Frankie compares it to a flower needing sunshine (good times) and rain (bad times) to grow. It's all important in the process of growth. It's a perspective that gets away from me sometimes, but I think we could all learn to remember this. Even when a situation is at it's worst, there is still something there that will help you grow. That bass line is like an invocation. Even if you'd never heard this song before, you'd know that something special is happening when it drops.

"Happy Feelin's" is a song off of their first album as well. On the studio album the song is just over 7 minutes long, but it's a little shorter on the live album at 5:28. "Happy Feelin's" was written by Frankie Beverly. "Happy Feelin's" is based in, what has become, the fairly modern mantra of good vibes only. Frankie Beverly says that he believes in the power of spreading that good vibe all over the world to push for change in the frequency of the world. Real hippie shit, but the fact of the matter is, it's true. Your positive energy can resonate and inspire other people to do the same. If there's one thing I've learned in the quarantine of 2020, it's that we're all cosmically connected in some shape form of fashion and we all have the power to be the light in each others lives...except for Saints fans. They don't count. "Happy Feelin's" is a ballad. It's a love song dedicated to the good hidden in all of us...except for Saints Fans. They have no good in them. This is one of their most melodic songs. It's really hard to not sing along with it.

In the last year or so, there have been talks of redoing a few of my favorite movies growing up. Malcolm X, The Princess Bride, Robin Hood: Prince of Thieves to name a few. Some have actually gotten thru the cracks and been remade unfortunately. Movies like Carrie, Point Break, and Ghostbusters were remade/modernized. All of which were horribly received because frankly they sucked. That's less important than the main reason that these movies failed though.

They failed because the first version of these movies were already perfect. You don't mess with perfection, especially when dealing with art. Nobody has tried to redo the Mona Lisa, or Pietà. Why? Because it was done perfectly the first time. So imagine my surprise when Beyoncé remade "Before I Let Go". Like. WTF?! Why? Why mess with perfection? That song can't be made any better than Maze already made it. You're not at a black cookout, of any age group, if you don't hear this song. It's become the anthem of block parties, festivals, cookouts and get togethers alike. "Before I Let Go" wasn't performed for the swamp people of New Orleans. It was a fixture on the album, as a studio recorded song. It was written and produced by Frankie Beverly. "Before I Let Go" is a jam. Plain and simple. It's a song that incites joy and if the DJ doesn't stop the record while everyone in the spot sings along at the bridge, you're in the wrong place.

Live in New Orleans was a recap of their past projects, and the introduction to their new works. There aren't many bands like Maze with a front man like Frankie Beverly. Only Earth Wind & Fire, and Mint Condition are comparable, and the latter was likely inspired by Maze. The concert has always been an audio experience for me. I commend Maze for having the fortitude to choke back their vomit and perform for those troglodytes in New Orleans. They put on a hell of a show in the most uncivilized jungle in North America (New Orleans). The album was received well. Live in New Orleans peaked at 34 on the Billboard 200 and got all the way up to 3 on the R&B charts. Maze featuring Frankie Beverly were on a roll of Gold albums, and Live in New Orleans followed suit, selling just over 500 thousand copies. It would be 2 years before Maze released their next album We Are One. I thank my parents for keeping music in the house, and I thank the Army for sending us to Germany and making my parents cling to the music even more at that time to remind them of home. This album still goes, and it's 2020.

I know I took a couple of, debatably, unfair shots at New Orleans and the "people" of that town, so I want to clear that up really quick. There are two things to remember when I speak of New Orleans, and Louisiana in general. 1) I'm an Atlanta Falcons fan. A die-hard that lives in post Hurricane Katrina Atlanta. The city has been well infiltrated by a horde of people from Louisiana (Saints Fans), and the metrics of the city reflect that. 2)...I meant everything I said. The hell with Saints and all Saints fans ☺

FUN FACT: Maze featuring Frankie Beverly changed their name at the suggestion of Marvin Gaye. They were once known as Raw Soul. "Before I Let Go" is one of their most notable and iconic songs. The song was created from a real life situation that Frankie Beverly was going thru. Beverly was cheating on his girlfriend with another woman and they broke up. He said that it was hard for him, because he wasn't with the woman he loved, but he couldn't stay with the woman he was with. "Before I Let Go" is a song about breaking up, and we've been so lost in the groove of it for so long that we never even noticed.

1) How were you introduced to Maze featuring Frankie Beverly?
   Answer:

2) What is your favorite song off of this album?
   Answer:

3) Do you like Beyoncé's cover of "Before I Let Go"?
   Answer:

4) Have you ever seen this concert before?
   Answer:

CHAPTER 46

BADUIZM

1997. Erykah Badu has been a part of our auditory lives since 1997 and somehow, she's still a mystery to us. I mean really think about it. 23 years, 5 studio albums, 1 live album, 2 mix tapes and she still holds the same mystique that she did when we met her. At this point we'd have to get ahold of her NSA file to know anything past her favorite color and restaurant. We do know that Erykah Badu is a very soulful artist. She was born in Dallas, Texas and raised by her mother Kolleen Wright. Erykah was young when she came under the tutelage of he mother and godmother (Gwen Hargrove). Erykah showed a talent for singing and dancing. Originally Erykah put her focus on rapping. As a teenager she was part of a trio and they would perform throughout the Dallas/Fort Worth area. She went by MC Apples. After high school she attended Grambling State University to study theater. Badu left school to pursue her music full time and returned home. It wasn't until she recorded a demo with her cousin that an industry heavy hitter took notice. Erykah opened for D'angelo in Dallas and put her in the spotlight with his manager Kedar. Kedar Massenburg liked what he heard and got Erykah to do a duet with his artist D'angelo. She was signed shortly thereafter. Badu relocated to New York and begun recording her album at the top of January 1996. By October recording stopped and Erykah had completed her debut. On February 11th 1997 *Baduizm* was released.

"On & On" was the first single off the album. It was written by Erykah Badu and JaBorn Jamal and produced by Madukwu Chinwah. Alright, so there's a lot going on in this song. Without getting into the translation of Supreme Mathematics, and ideologies you can still enjoy the song. The song is so abstract that it's left to interpretation. I'll give you mine but you should listen to it yourself and come to your own understanding. It's about pushing thru life and accepting whatever lessons you've opened your heart to. She talks of being broke, but still being fulfilled because she's not bound to luxurious things. Erykah talks about earning your lessons through living life. Her wordplay is clever. It's as if every line has a dual meaning. Whether she was referencing her cypher to mean her life/anatomical makeup or being born underwater to signify natural birth/her zodiac sign, there was a lot to chew on. The music video was loosely based on one of my brother Derek's favorite movies *The Color Purple*. It gives us a chance to see the face of the person we'd been hearing on this lightly bubbling single. I don't know about you, but when I first saw the video, I couldn't get over how damn gorgeous this woman was. The hazel-eyed bandit stole our hearts and hasn't let go sense. She starts the video doing Celie-esque chores around the farm, but by the end of the video she's headlining at the juke joint and being smiled upon. Adorned in her wrap around dress and head wrap. Her original uniform for the public. "On & On" peaked at 12 on the Billboard Hot 100 and shot all the way up to 1 on the R&B charts.

"Next Lifetime" was the second single off the album. It was released in May 1997. It was co-written by Erykah Badu and produced by Tone the Backbone. "Next Lifetime" is a ballad. It's our first real chance to see that Erykah can really sing, and has the control to deliver a song. "Next Lifetime" is beautiful. There's a real dignity to the feelings be conveyed. The song starts with a man telling Erykah that he wants to be with her. He's grown feelings for her and decided to step out on faith and shoot his shot. With a hint of trepidation, you can hear Erykah saying that she can't do it. Not that she doesn't want to do it, but that she can't. That minor but major distinction is the blood of this whole song. "Next Lifetime" is saying now isn't the right time for us to be together, but hopefully the universe will give us another opportunity to explore these feelings. Even if only by reincarnation. Erykah recorded "Next Lifetime" at Battery Studios in New York. Like "On & On", "Next Lifetime" has 3 verses in its build. Not the typical 2 verse and 2 hook construction. Erykah has a way of breaking the rules of songwriting and making it seem right and exact. Production wise, there's a strong use of synths and a thumping bass line. Erykah's background vocals are throughout the song and play as additional production the way they sit in the song. The music video shows Erykah living a string of different lives with different partners. Moving from one to another as their interest peaked. It had Andre 3000, Pete Rock and Method Man as her love interests. "Next Lifetime" got all the way up to 1 on the R&B charts. It spent 28 weeks on the chart.

"Otherside of the Game" was the third single off the album, and probably my favorite song off the album as well. The song was co-written by Erykah Badu, Questlove, Richard Nichols and James Poyser. The song was produced by The Roots. Despite their many, many, well-earned accolades as a Hip Hop group, I think that people tend to forget the incredible band that they are. Under Questlove's leadership, they weaved together the soundtrack of a woman struggling with her man being a hustler while carrying his child. At the time she was actually pregnant with her and Andre 3000's son, Seven. Although the song isn't political it does give you the "Otherside of the Game". It speaks to black men feeling like hustling illegally (no matter what that may be), is their only way to success. Like she says in the song, he had education and likely could've done something else. It reminds me of the first season of Real World, when Kevin Powell, in the beginning stages of his young black brilliance, said that he considered selling drugs because he needed money to pay his rent. Kevin has since, moved on and become a successful writer and content creator but it could've gone either way. Another element of the song is Erykah talking about how she too, has become accustomed to the things that her husbands illegal dealings bring. She even refers to him as the Sun and her the moon. Meaning she's a reflection of him, and he is the center of her universe. The natural order of things. "Otherside of the Game" ends with no real resolution. It never became a mainstream hit, but it did peak at 14 on the R&B charts.

Baduizm took the world by storm. It was a hearkening to the past and a glimpse into the possible future. Erykah was the new beautiful abstract songbird. She followed up Baduizm with a tour and a live album that gave us jewels like "Tyrone" and her cover of "Boogie Nights". Baduizm sold over 3 million copies and made Erykah a staple of R&B. She's become a case study for artist looking to reach past the typical barriers of R&B. I struggled with whether Baduizm or Mama's Gun was the better album. In that struggle I never really got an answer, because both of them are phenomenal pieces of work. We can't even begin to understand Mama's Gun until we've listened to Baduizm. It's a 101 course on the artist that is still becoming Erykyah Badu. Baduizm ended the year at 20 on the Billboard 200 albums and launched her world tour.

FUN FACT: Erykah Badu's mother is the real "Ms. Jackson". The song was inspired by the strained relationship between Erykah's mother Kolleen and Andre 3000. She was unhappy with what she perceived to be Andre's character. He took it to heart and took it to the pen. Badu says that she appreciated 3000's verse because it was inspiring but she didn't like Big Boi's verse too much. Oddly enough the person that loved the song the most was Erykah's mother. She went and got a vanity license plate, coffee mug and headband with the words Ms. Jackson on it.

1) Which Erykah Badu album do you think is her best?
   Answer:

2) What's your favorite song on *Baduizm*?
   Answer:

3) What's your favorite music video for *Baduizm*?
   Answer:

4) What song makes you the happiest from *Baduizm*?
   Answer:

CHAPTER 47

NEW YORK: A LOVE STORY

Music and film are linked more than ever. Some people do music to get into film, and some do film to get into music. You think about wildly talented people like Jamie Foxx, and remember his stories of only ever wanting to sing, but his avenue to those opportunities came thru standup comedy & film work. On the other side you have Will Smith, who got into film work by way of his music career. I guess there's no right or wrong way. The important thing is to do something memorable when you make that transition. There have been other successes in this exchange like Donald Glover/Childish Gambino or even our beloved Whitney Houston. One of the more recent and interesting stars of this subcategory is Tristan "Mack" Wilds. Coming out of Staten Island (Shaolin) Tristan saw a little success in roles on the small screen. He'd had a few credits from shows like *Law & Order*, *Cold Case* and *Miracle's Boys*. It wasn't until he landed the role of Michael Lee on *The Wire* (3rd greatest show of all time) that he really started to build some notoriety. Tristan became a fan favorite and his career blossomed with ease. After *The Wire* Tristan quickly pivoted to a new role on *90210*, making sure that he could never be typecast. His acting career was going well. That's why the interest in music was such a surprise. By way of a chance encounter Tristan met Salaam Remi, and they've been friends for a while. Wilds signed to Remi's Louder Than Life/Sony imprint and the two began recording in early 2012. Salaam was excited because Mack was the first artist that he'd be introducing in 20 years and Mack was excited to be working with such an accomplished creative. By early 2013, the recording was done and on September 30, 2013 *New York: A Love Story* was released. The album name has a double meaning. It's a story of Love & Loss in NYC, but it's also a love letter to the historic Hip Hop sound of NYC. After all Mack was born and raised in Shaolin (Staten Island). You can't expect Mack to not be a Hip Hop fan when he was born and raised in the same housing projects as RZA and the Ghostface Killah. The music represents that.

"Own It" was the lead single. It was written by Ne-Yo and produced by Salaam Remi. Nobody knew what to expect. "Own It" is an up-tempo song, with a sample from "Eric B. Is President". "Own It" is about being young and living in the moment. It's a good summer song, because it's young and even though it was built on top of this Hip Hop beat, there's a smoothness to it. Mack really let the track breathe. The heavy strings and kick drums walk over the song. "Own It" was the only single off the album that charted. It peaked at 35 on the R&B charts. All together "Own It" spent about 5 weeks on the charts.

"Henny" was the second single off the album. The song was built on a sample Havoc produced for Mobb Deep's song "The Learning Burn". As far as the album and its production schedule, it was the first song recorded for the album. "Henny" was co-written by Mack and Salaam, and co-produced by Havoc and Salaam. The album came from an experimental place. Salaam was sending different tracks to Mack and had him write and record to them. Salaam just wanted to see what he could do with the music. When Mack sent the track back for "Henny" Salaam was impressed. He shared the song with Havoc and Havoc was so impressed that he sent Salaam the original instrumental to work with. "Henny" is Mack spitting game at a young lady. He's a young man. There's no such thing as a young man worth his salt, that doesn't talk his shit. Mack is comparing a night with him to a shot of Hennessy. The song is really bare. There aren't any attempts at vocal gymnastics on this song. He's just talking his shit. I love it.

"Magic" is my favorite song on the album. It doesn't remind me of any other song that I've ever heard. The song was written by Rico Love and produced by Salaam Remi. "Magic" is just hard to explain. Is it a ballad? Is it mid-tempo? Honestly, it's both. Mack got his grown man on. "Magic" is a song about his woman's power to please him. I like how the song was written. I think all the comparisons to a cause and cure make this song really easy to put to memory. The production is incredible on this song. I never play this song, unless I can play it as loud as possible. The sounds Salaam used, remind of the music that dropped when Sho' Nuff asked Leroy "You warmed up yet?" (I hate it for you if you need that line explained). The chaos that was taken to create the music melts well with Mack crooning on the song. I like that Mack delivered the song without trying to take it over. It's definitely a great moment on the album.

There are so many standouts on this album. "Wild Things", "NY Love Story", "Don't Turn Me Down" is a vibe, and "Duck Sauce" is a good curveball too. That said, there's something incredible about a person that can do justice to a Michael Jackson cover. "Remember the Time" is a cover of the MJ hit by the same name. The music is completely different, and the vibe has a little more machismo to it than the one that Teddy Riley laced the King with. Salaam and Havoc co-produced the track. They took harps and strings with some aggressive drum programming and made a banger. MJ is a hard act to follow, but I really, really like Mack's version. It's a different song. As the story goes, Salaam sent Mack the track and told him to sing "Remember the Time" over it. Mack couldn't really hear what Salaam heard, but he did it anyway, and out of that came this.

Taking the chance to make a leap from one thriving career to start another with questions is commendable. It shows how dedicated Mack was to making this happen. Everything about this album came together from the theme to the music and features. There was no straying from what Mack and Salaam had in their crosshairs. Mack's first trot out and *New York: A Love Story* finished at 179 on the Billboard 200 and got all the way up to 28 on the R&B charts. Mack was also nominated for a Grammy in the Best Urban Contemporary category. It was one of the best R&B albums of 2013 and by some opinions thee best.

FUN FACT: Tristan decided to go by Mack for the music side of his career, because that's his family name. As far as he was concerned music is intimate and he wanted to show that. So by going by Mack, he was inviting us to be a part of his family.

1) What's your favorite song from the album?
   Answer:

2) Do you prefer Mack doing ballads or club bangers?
   Answer:

3) Are you a fan of the "Remember the Time" cover?
   Answer:

4) If you could've picked a 3rd single from this album, what would it have been?
   Answer:

CHAPTER 48

GUY

Guy is an R&B group founded by the brilliant Teddy Riley. The original group was founded in 1987 and consisted of Teddy Riley, lead vocalist Aaron Hall and Timmy Gatling. Growing up in Harlem together, Riley and Gatling had already had a stint in a local band. It wasn't until Timmy Gatling & Aaron Hall worked together at a popular clothing store that the idea to form a group came. They were eventually signed to Uptown Records. It was a hot up and coming label. Riley was still producing for other artists, and had begun putting songs together with Aaron Hall for other acts too. Guy began recording their debut album in October of 1987 and finished up a few months later in March of 1988. The entire album was recorded at Teddy Riley's mother's home on the first floor of the St. Nick Projects. The ENTIRE album was made on equipment that was donated to Teddy Riley. He was just finishing up Keith Sweat's album around the time that Guy formed. The album was finished, but due to the constant feuding of Aaron and Timmy, Timmy left the group shortly after the recording was finished to pursue his solo career. On June 13, 1988 Guy released their debut album *Guy*. It's a masterpiece of New Jack Swing.

"Groove Me" was the second single off the album. It was released in May of 1988. It was written by Aaron Hall, Timmy Gatling and Teddy Riley. Riley produced it of course. Even though Guy eventually re-recorded all the vocals at a bigger, fancier studio in the end they decided to use the original vocals recorded in Teddy's mother's home. "Groove Me" is up-tempo. It's a blueprint to New Jack Swing. It's got the heavy Hip Hop influence, and the harmonies of the group. "Groove Me" was close to being called "Do Me" because of the song's meaning, but in the end they all decided on "Groove Me" thanks to manager Gene Griffin's suggestion. Teddy started out making Hip Hop, so his production style began with that as the heaviest influences. It wasn't until "Groove Me" that Guy started to build some real momentum. Everything from how Guy's music is digested to how it's created starts with that in mind. "Groove Me" peaked at 4 on the R&B charts and spent about 5 weeks on the chart.

"Teddy's Jam" was the 3rd single off the album. It was released in September 1988. Aaron was always pushing Teddy to sing. In fact it was Aaron's idea for Teddy to be in the group. Aaron once said at the beginning that he wouldn't even be in the group unless Teddy was in it. "Teddy's Jam" was Aaron's idea. He heard the track and told Riley that he wanted to put a little singing on it, but that it should be kept as a mostly instrumental song. They didn't even have a real name for it. In the end "Teddy's Jam" just stuck for them. "Teddy's Jam" is a party song. People were still going to clubs to have a good time then. Men and women would get on the dance floor and enjoy each other instead of sitting in their sections exchanging stupid stares. "Teddy's Jam" peaked at 5 on the R&B charts.

"Piece of My Love" was never an official single, but it was not going to be denied its chance to shine. It was written by the Aaron, Teddy and Timmy and, again, produced by Teddy Riley. "Piece of My Love" is a ballad, but not a ballad at the same time. Guy was never really a ballad like group. "Piece of My Love" is a groove though. If you've heard it, even once, you recognize it as soon as the first note drops. It's the longest song on the album because Teddy knew what he was doing when he cooked this song up slow. "Piece of My Love" is about two people sharing a night together even though they shouldn't be, so that they can enjoy the time they're spending together. With all the party songs they were releasing as singles, this was one of the first instances that the public got to see that Aaron Hall could bobble just as well as Charlie Wilson. Aaron could really, really sing and he painted this whole song with his talent.

"Goodbye Love" was another ballad like song on the album. It's a break up song. Not the you did me wrong/I did you wrong type of break up song. Those are based in situations that we can all come to grips with. "Goodbye Love" is set on the premise of a relationship just not working out from disappointment and you're deciding to leave the situation. If you have a broken heart playlist this should probably be on it. Riley said that he wanted to make a song that he could've put on Keith Sweat's album. He wanted something that had the feel of some heartbreak in it. "Goodbye Love' was one of the last songs that they recorded for the album.

Guy released 5 singles from their debut album. *Guy* is one of the most influential albums of the genre. The sound was explosive yet melodic. The image was hip and urban, and the songs had all the soul of Motown and all the swagger of the NYC club scene. Guy finished the year with their debut peaking at 27 on the Billboard 200 and all the way up to 1 on the R&B charts and it held that position for 2 consecutive months. The album was certified double platinum by the next year.

FUN FACT: Guy got their name, from visiting a clothing store called Two Guys. They went with the derivative of Guy in the end. It was in this store that they got their sense of style and their first couple of performance outfits. Another strange coincidence is that, during the re-recording sessions the engineer for every song was Dae Bennett. He's the son to legendary jazz singer Tony Bennett.

1) What is your favorite song off of this album?
   Answer:

2) What is your favorite Teddy Riley produced song?
   Answer:

3) Did you know that for years it was assumed that Aaron was saying dumb bitch at the beginning of "Piece of my Love"?
   Answer:

4) Do you prefer Guy or Blackstreet?
   Answer:

CHAPTER 49

REALITY SHOW

She's probably the most underappreciated songstress in the last 20 years. Whenever people are discussing singers that can really sing, she's always an afterthought. Every blue moon someone will throw Keke Wyatt, or Fantasia in the conversation before they get to Jazmine Sullivan, and that's the problem. Jazmine is one of the greatest voices and songwriters that R&B has ever seen. Jazmine was born and raised in Philadelphia. Her mother was a professional singer too. Philadelphia has always been a hotbed of soul. Jazmine grew up singing in the church and was always known as the little girl with a grown woman's voice. Jazmine had her first record deal with industry giant, Jive records when she was only 15. She recorded an album, but it was never released and eventually Jazmine was dropped from Jive. After graduating high school, Jazmine continued to chase her career and found some work as a songwriter. It wasn't until she met Missy, that the winds of her career started to take a turn for the better. In 2008 Jazmine released her debut *Fearless* and the album went gold. She followed that up with her sophomore release *Love Me Back* and although it was a good album too, it didn't fair as well as *Fearless*. In 2011 Jazmine said that she wasn't having fun in the industry and she retired. She stepped away from it all. It wasn't until 2014 that we got the news that Jazmine had been recording for her new album. On January 13, 2015 Jazmine released her 3rd album *Reality Show*, and was signed to RCA. Jazmine came up with the album title, because she wanted it to reflect the times that we are/were living in. *Reality Show* was her thesis on society.

"Dumb" was the first single off the album. It was released in May of 2014 and it features her hometown friend Meek Mill. "Dumb" was written by Jazmine Sullivan, Salaam Remi, Dwane Weir II, and Robert Williams, and produced by Salaam Remi and Key Wane. "Dumb" is about Jazmine's man thinking he's smarter than her and that he's getting away with his cheating. Meek Mill's verse is basically from the point of view of the boyfriend. Meek isn't really defending himself, he's more so taking the stance of telling her not to worry about the other women because she's the one he loves. It's a fun song and that's what Jazmine wrote it for. She wanted to announce her return as well as put something kind of light hearted out. "Dumb" peaked at 45 on the Billboard Hot 100.

"Forever Don't Last" was the second single off the album, but as far as the recording schedule of the album, it was the first song recorded, and likely the reason that Jazmine started making another album. It was written by Jazmine Sullivan and produced by Chuck Harmony. Jazmine had just come out of a long relationship and she felt like she needed to do the song to fully let go of it. She needed to accept that "Forever Don't Last" and move on. This is a ballad. The type of song that Jazmine has always had her way with. Jazmine's background vocals are part of the production. What I like best about this song is, imagining Jazmine singing it at a live set with just her and an acoustic guitar. It's a very soulful song. "Forever Don't Last" peaked at 17 on the R&B charts.

"Let It Burn" was the 3rd single off the album. Co-written by Jazmine Sullivan and Key Wane. It was made from a sample of "Ready or Not" by After 7 and modernized by the production of Key Wane. "Let It Burn" is about giving into the process of falling in love with someone. Instead of letting your inhibitions or your fear get in the way, you just let the fire keep growing and "Let It Burn". "Let It Burn" is one of the most radio friendly songs on the album, but it still wasn't released as a single until almost a year later. "Let It Burn" did well as a single. In 2015 it peaked at 4 on the R&B charts and had a small resurgence on the charts in 2018 when it was played on an episode of Insecure.

"Mascara" is an important song. Jazmine dedicated a song to dealing with the judgment and insecurities that some women carry with themselves everyday. Jazmine said she got the idea for the song by looking on Instagram and noticing that all the Instagram Models/Influencers pages looked the same. She thought they all had the same bodies, the same faces and seemingly the same lives. Jazmine wanted to document this time in our history. Jazmine wrote the song, as if she were an Instagram model being defensive about the life and notoriety that her beauty had afforded her. I think that even though there are is a bit of jest used in the song, that there's still something very true in it. The song is called "Mascara" to infer makeup. Makeup helps to hide the imperfections on people's skin, or in this case, their lives. The saddest part about this song is the insinuation that the Instagram ladies always have to be on stage. They can't afford to have an honest moment, or they'll lose everything that's been given to them.

Reality Show spawned 3 singles and released to a bit of fan fare. Jazmine was re-entering the music world and we wanted to hear what she'd been up to. Turns out she was surveying US. Living, learning, loving and falling out of love.

Reality Show debuted at 12 and peaked at 12 on the Billboard 200 and it peaked at 2 on the R&B charts. We haven't gotten a new album from Jazmine since then, but we eagerly await the next stories that her pen and the that beautiful instrument of a voice can put together for us.

FUN FACT: Jazmine picked all of the tracks for the album off of cd's with no labels. She didn't want to know who did them. She picked what spoke to her and didn't want to be bothered with the politics of who did what. With this blind picking process, Jazmine still picked about 4 different tracks that were produced by Key Wane.

1) What is your favorite song off of this album?
   Answer:

2) Do you think that "Mascara" is an offensive song to women that make their living via Instagram?
   Answer:

3) What is your favorite Jazmine Sullivan song?
   Answer:

4) Why do you think that major success has escaped Jazmine thus far?
   Answer:

CHAPTER 50

COOLEYHIGHHARMONY

Boyz II Men arguably had the best first 3 album run in music history. *Cooleyhighharmony*, *Christmas Interpretations* and *II*. They sold a bazillion records, made some classic songs and set a new standard for performance and vocalists. Boyz II Men entered the industry with a veteran flare, and set their personal bar higher than any rookie act in R&B history. What couldn't they do? They could perform, they could deliver ballads and jams, but more important than anything, THEY COULD REALLY, REALLY SING. Boyz II Men have always had razor sharp vocals and the foundation of their entire careers were built on their debut album *Cooleyhighharmony*. Boyz II Men began recording their album in September of 1990 and wrapped in late November of the same year. On April 30, 1991 they released their debut album *Cooleyhighharmony*.

"Motownphilly" was the first single off the album. It was written by Michael Bivins, Shawn Stockman, Nathan Morris and Dallas Austin, who produced the song as well. It was the early 90's and although New Jack Swing was starting to die down a little, it was still an appreciated sound. It's a song that describes Boyz II Men's journey into the industry and it talks about their connection to their hometown of Philadelphia. It's up-tempo and full of horns and excitement. It's the kind of song that HBCU marching bands love to play. The song title itself is the group saying that they're bringing the classic Motown sound of songwriting and singing to the Philadelphia soul sound. It's quite a boast, but frankly that's exactly what they did. "Motownphilly" was a hit for the group, and the song peaked at 3 on the Billboard Hot 100 and got all the way up to 1 on the R&B charts.

"It's So Hard to Say Goodbye to Yesterday" was the second single off the album. It was released on August 20 1991. "It's So Hard to Say Goodbye" was originally done by G.C. Cameron. He was a member of The Spinners before the group left Motown, but he stayed with Motown to become a solo artist. The song was used for the film that the album title references, *Cooley High*. It was written by Freddie Perren and Christine Yarian. Although the original had production on the song, Boyz II Men's version is a cappella. It was an important move by them, because they needed to really show what they could do vocally. What better way to show off your voices than by a cappella? Boyz II Men took a song that was already melancholic and made it even more emotional. "It's So Hard to Say Goodbye" was one of the songs that Boyz II Men used to practice in the bathroom of their high school. On their first tour Boyz II Men opened for MC Hammer, and their manager was murdered in Chicago. They dedicated this song to him at every performance after that. The song did very well, and Boyz II Men proved that they could really deliver a song. The song peaked at 2 on the Billboard Hot 100 and 1 on the R&B charts.

"Please Don't Go" was the 4th single off the debut. It was written by group member Nathan and produced by Dallas Austin. With it being the first song on the album, it kind of sets the tone for what's to come. There will be no bubblegum, pop infused, kiddie songs on this album. They were dealing with raw emotion. I'm a Shawn Stockman fan and a huge one at that. I'd still like proof that he's even human, but I've been able to enjoy the music in the interim. As a sidebar, Shawn has an incredibly smooth EP called *Shawn*. Check it out. Shawn sings the lead on this song, as only he could. Surgically. "Please Don't Go" was put out after "Uhh Ahh" and served as their first single of 1992. Almost a full year after the album had been released. "Please Don't Go" peaked at 49 on the Billboard Hot 100 and got all the way up to 8 on the R&B charts.

"Little Things" is one of my favorite songs on the album. It's a mid-tempo song. It was written by Troy Taylor and produced by Troy and his partner Charles Farrar. It's about the value of the little things you can do to keep your relationship alive and healthy. The act of spending more time together instead of exchanging Rolex watches. The second verse speaks more to doing your best to keep your love happy. Shawn sings the lead on the entire song. The production comes off pretty layered with the use of keyboards and acoustic piano. Troy Taylor played every instrument on the song except for the drums. The drums were played by Dallas Austin. Good to know that he was putting those *Drumline* skills to use still.

Boyz II Men shot out of the cannon to success. *Cooleyhighharmony* was a meteor. The album sold over 9 million copies and won a Grammy award for Best R&B Performance by a Duo or Group with vocal. 30 years, 30 million albums, and 1 less member later, and they're still performing. Still recording, and have one of the largest most loyal fanbases ever.

FUN FACT: Boyz II Men headlined/hosted a cruise that took its guest from Miami to Nassau. They performed and hung out with the guests and staff on the cruise. It was called the Love Cruise.

1) What is your favorite song on the album?
   Answer:

2) Who is your favorite member in the group?
   Answer:

3) What is your favorite a cappella song by Boyz II Men?
   Answer:

4) What is your favorite Boyz II Men video?
   Answer:

www.ingramcontent.com/pod-product-compliance
Lightning Source LLC
Chambersburg PA
CBHW081146270326
41930CB00014B/3052